The End of War

Bill Freeman

Algonquin Educational Productions
2011

ISBN: paper book: 978-0-9878129-0-2 electronic book: 978-0-9878129-1-9

Design: Accurance, Inc.

Cover illustration: Francisco Goya, "The Third of May, 1808," Museo del Prado, Madrid

Algonquin Educational Productions
3 Seneca Avenue
Toronto, Ontario, Canada
M5J 2A1

Library and Archives Canada Cataloguing in Publication
Freeman, Bill, 1938-
The end of war / Bill Freeman.

Includes bibliographical references.
Issued also in electronic format.
ISBN 978-0-9878129-0-2

1. War. 2. War--Causes. 3. Peace. I. Title.
JZ6385.F74 2011 303.6'6 C2011-907457-5

TABLE OF CONTENTS

AUTHOR'S NOTE

All books are the result of a struggle between the author and the subject, and my journey on the issue of war is instructive because it tells much about the intellectual roots of this book. Like many others, I was involved in the peace movement as a young man, but dreams of world peace always seemed utopian to me. Above all I wanted to be a realist. That is why I studied sociology and later drifted to my true academic home, history, which told of empires, wars, class conflict and exploitation. It did not lead to optimism or utopian fantasies.

But although I was trained as an academic, I never ended up in the university. Above all I have been a writer and political activist, drawn to fight issues because I was impatient for change. In time I became an author of historical fiction for young people, describing the real hardships of the people in my country's past. I also worked on documentary film projects. Always the backdrop of my work was Canada. I am deeply immersed in the life and history of my country, and as I look at this manuscript, now that it is finished, I can spot its uniquely Canadian point of view.

Because of our connection to the British Empire, Canada was involved in both the First and Second World Wars, and they left a deep impression on the Canadian people. My father and his friends were in the military for six long years in the Second World War. One of my earliest memories as a young boy was being taken to the railway station to say goodbye to my father, dressed in his naval uniform, leaving the family to go to war. My grandfather's generation fought in the trenches of the Western Front from the beginning to the end of that tragic conflict. Like a lot of families that lived through these experiences, there was never much talk of war when children were present, but I know for our parents war was a constant threat.

It was the Cold War that threatened my generation. I can remember reading newspapers that followed the progress of the Canadian forces in the Korean War. For a long time war always seemed an imminent possibility, and the threat of nuclear war an ever-present nightmare. But though war was a constant danger, Canada never had conscription during the Cold War. As a result, Canadians are perhaps less militaristic than people of any other western country. I never served in the military (and I am thankful for that).

This is part of my legacy as a Canadian. Another part is the role my country played in international affairs. Canada is a middle power. Not by choice, but by virtue of our relatively small population. We live next to the United States and share much of its history and values. While Canadians have always had a critical view of the U.S. and its foreign policy, at the same time we admire the strength and energy of the American people.

If there is one thing that Canadians of my generation believe, it is that with effort and good will war can be avoided. Our governments reflected that point of view. It was a Canadian Prime Minister, Lester Pearson, who played a major role in resolving the Suez Crisis of 1956, and in the process virtually singlehandedly created the program of United Nations peacekeeping. For a long time Canada had contingents in virtually every U.N. peacekeeping mission. We have also accepted more than our share of refugees fleeing war, and recently Canada played a vital role in developing and promoting a new U.N. policy called Responsibility to Protect – R2P.

More recently Canada has been involved in a different type of war, Afghanistan, and Canadian troops suffered significant casualties in that mission. A nephew of mine and my wife's nephew both served in that difficult conflict, and their involvement brought home to me how my own personal history and the history of my family has been intimately connected to war even though I have never been on the battlefield.

For all of these reasons I jumped at the chance to write a book about Canadians during the First World War, when I was approached by a publisher. *Far From Home: Canadians in the First World War*[1] came out of a documentary film by the same name, produced by Richard Neilson, who co-wrote the book with me. It was a project that drew me into the world of war and the horrible consequences of that conflict. Young Canadian men went off to that war filled with excitement in the belief that this would be a wonderful adventure. Those who returned were disillusioned and in many cases shattered in body and spirit. The First World War is the beginning of the long nightmare of wars in our recent history that only now is drawing to a close.

This is the background of this book. It is informed by knowledge of history and sociology, but it should also be seen as part of a uniquely Canadian search for peace. Above all it is a plea that we heed our history and make every effort to create a world without war.

Finally, I am indebted to a number of people who helped in the creation of this book. My editor, Jean Paton, did more than clean up the errors in the text. She pointed out where ideas needed to be sharpened and clarified and I am indebted to her attention of detail. Bob Gibson steered me through the unfamiliar waters of eBook publishing and print-on-demand and helped to turn the experience into an appreciation of the new electronic publishing technology that is changing the way that books are created. Baye Hunter has helped me set up my blog/website, www.endofwar.info, which I hope will become a fundamental part of this project by stimulating discussions about war and the possibility of peace. And a special thanks to my partner, Paulette Pelletier-Kelly, whose patience and belief in the importance of the project helped me get through the difficult times that a book of this scope inevitably creates.

Bill Freeman
Toronto, 2011

INTRODUCTION

We live in the shadow of the twentieth century, the most war ravaged period in human history. Altogether, 160 million people died in that century's wars. The first years of the twenty-first century have not been much better. There have been recent or continuing wars in Iraq, Afghanistan, Sri Lanka, Colombia, Somalia, Libya, Sudan and Congo, and limited wars in several other countries in sub-Saharan Africa. A number of countries are perilously close to war, including Syria, Bahrain, Iran, Yemen and Israel-Palestine. Even worse, we now have fashioned weapons of mass destruction with the ability to end the human race, if not life as we know it on the planet.

The deaths of military combatants are only a small part of the costs of wars. It is estimated that four times as many people are injured than are killed in modern warfare, and civilian deaths outnumber battlefield deaths. There have been a number of occasions when there were mass genocides of civilian populations. The six million deaths of the Jews in Nazi Germany are the best known, but in that same conflict many Roma, homosexuals and Communists were sent to the gas chambers. In Rwanda in 1994 the ethnic majority Hutu killed an estimated 800,000, mainly from the minority Tutsi community, and in the ethnic and religious strife that swept over the former Yugoslavia after the break up of that country in the 1990s, thousands were murdered. It is estimated that in 2003 there were 33 million people displaced by war, 29 million of whom were displaced within their own country. Women and children make up over seventy per cent of all refugees.[1]

Women and children have always been the victims of war. Although more men than women die on the battlefield, children under the age of five are by far the most vulnerable to war-induced malnutrition and disease.[2] Women suffer from sexual violence; rape is a weapon of war. More than 20,000 and possibly 80,000 women were raped by Japanese troops in Nanking in 1937. Russian soldiers raped thousands of German women in the last stages of the Second World War, and today rape and sexual enslavement are used as weapons of war in the eastern Congo and Sudan.[3]

The psychological costs from the trauma of war are impossible to estimate. Young, physically and emotionally fit men, with the best training that modern armies can provide, often return from the battlefield suffering from a variety of ailments that have been called battle fatigue or shell shock in the past. The survivors of the concentration camps in the Second World War were crushed in body and spirit. Rape victims of Africa are filled with fear, panic and despair. Today victims of war are said to suffer from "post-traumatic shock syndrome," a psychiatric condition that describes a variety of symptoms such as excessive nervousness, anxiety, irrational fears, recurring nightmares and psychosomatic illnesses.

The effects of war do not stop at transgressions to individuals. Marauding armies, bombing, rocket and missile strikes cause widespread destruction. Factories are targeted, transportation facilities wiped out, housing left in ruins and farms abandoned. Hunger and famine are linked with war, and many conflicts of the past have resulted in the deaths of more people from starvation than combat. And none of this calculates the costs of maintaining armies and weapons systems which divert funds away from programs such as education, health care and building infrastructure that might bring benefits to the entire population.

Then what justifies the optimistic title of this book, *The End of War*? The end, or even the decrease, of war does not coincide with the facts or with the political thinking of our day, that holds that war will always be with us. Those on the right believe that there are threats of violence everywhere. War and civil conflict will always be with us because the poor covet the wealth of the rich. Those on the left see war as a symptom of the conflict inherent within capitalism and imperialism. This book argues that both of these perspectives are wrong, because they ignore the historical, political and social developments of the last two hundred years and particularly the developments since the end of the Cold War.

Every war is different. Each has its own historical context that shapes events, and the outcome is determined by things such as economic development, demography, technology, the availability of weapons and many other factors. Some wars are regional conflicts while the two "World Wars" of the Twentieth century ranged over every corner of the globe. Every war must be assessed independently, but they can be grouped in general categories.

Wars of empires have had the greatest impact on our history and have affected people in every country. They have led to the domination and exploitation of billions of people, have ended established regimes, led to the transformations of local cultures and languages; economic systems have been destroyed and foreign traditions and practices have been imposed. Imperialism has long been a major cause of wars, but things are changing. Empires are finally coming to an end because social, political and economic changes brought by modernity have transformed the world to such an extent that imperial domination is no longer a viable strategy for even the most powerful nation. Soon we will live in a post-imperial world where all nations will have responsibilities to maintain the peace.

Civil wars can be brutal conflicts, uprooting communities and resulting in death and destruction on a massive scale. Other regional wars pit ethnic or religious groups against each other and some have resulted in genocide. Still others are motivated by abject poverty that leads to the plunder of raw materials, food and valuables. Again there is reason to be optimistic. The extent and number of these types of wars have been much reduced in recent years. They are affecting limited groups of people, and the numbers killed have dropped significantly. Solving or facing these problems, not imposing solutions with the barrel of a gun, is the way forward.

What is creating these changes in the practice of war is the emergence of a new global economic and political system that is building interdependence between nations and people. This new system has only taken hold in the last twenty years, since the end of the Cold War. The movement is still in an embryonic stage, but already it has led to unprecedented economic and political changes in the so-called developing world that are fundamentally changing the world's geo-politics. Economic development and democracy and political participation build a sense of optimism and confidence in people that leads to more social stability and peace. War, degradation, hardship and poverty go together; peace, prosperity and the opportunity for community and individual development are at the opposite pole. The gradual reduction of poverty and the rise of more democratic practices around the world are slowly leading to the end of war.

But if we are to go that final step to end war, we have to do more – much more. International organizations, particularly the United Nations, must be reformed root and branch so that they become democratic institutions accountable to the people. Only then will we have the full power and influence to provide intervention in time of need, and social and economic programs that can address the underlying causes of war. Reforming international institutions is one part of the task, but even more important, people in every society and nation must develop and nurture attitudes and practices of toleration, mutual trust and respect of others. Much has been accomplished since the end of the Cold War two decades ago. If we can take these final steps, we can achieve the dream and reap the benefits of a world of peace.

This is what this book is all about. It looks at broad historical, social, political and economic forces to try to understand the direction of world geo-politics and the role that war plays in our world. The book even goes beyond this into territory that no historian would venture. The last chapter builds on this understanding of the present to make concrete suggestions of how we can create a world without war.

We need to fundamentally change how we view our world. The pessimism of the past has led to international inertia; there is much to be optimistic about. It is possible to live in a world without war, but it will not happen simply by wishing it. Peace will require the efforts and good will of people from all parts of the globe. This book is a small offering towards building a new consensus, so that we can realize the long-held dream of beating swords into ploughshares. It is time to dedicate ourselves to that goal.

Part I: War and Empire

INTRODUCTION

Many have speculated about the causes of war. Some have located them in supernatural forces. The Ancient Greek myths say humans are the playthings of the gods and wars are the expressions of the gods' moods or temperament. Roman generals spoke of their destiny – something godlike and beyond their control. In Medieval times there was the belief that war and its outcome were the result of the alignment of stars. Even today armies are sent into battle with prayers in the hopes that the supernatural can be persuaded to intervene on their side in the war.

A more modern explanation is to find the causes of war in man's own violent nature. Dostoyevsky pointed to inherent barbarity that resides within us all. "In every man a beast lies hidden – the beast of rage – the beast of lustful heat at the screams of the tortured victim – the beast of lawlessness."[1] No less a figure than Sigmund Freud saw the origin of war in the "death instinct," a part of the libido. He wrote, "It is clearly not easy for men to give up the satisfaction of this inclination to aggression."[2] Michael Ledeen, a leading American neo-conservative, recently said, "We are a warlike people, and we love war."[3]

These psychological explanations of war suggest that aggression is somehow in our genes; it is built into the very marrow of our being, and we will never lose the impulse for war and violence. But this is a very unsatisfactory explanation. There have been long periods of peace in the world, and today wars continue but they affect a limited number of people. War can unleash incredible cruelty; sadists and psychopaths exist in all societies, but that does not mean to say that war is caused by violence inherent in the human race.[4]

The only comprehensive explanation of war is that it is rooted in the historical and social conditions of societies. This approach assumes that every war is different because the conditions change over time. For that reason the explanation for wars varies depending on particular historical and social conditions. This does not deny that individuals are important, but the level of analysis is focused on the society as a whole.

There are many complex factors that create the social conditions for war. Religion has played an important role in wars in many parts of the world. Ethnic and racial divisions can lead to antagonisms between people that can escalate into conflict. Ideological differences were the chief cause of the Cold War and played an important role in the American Civil war and the many wars of liberation in the twentieth century. Recently, poverty has been cited as the most important factor of all.

These social and economic divisions are important contributing causes of wars, but there is another type that has been far more destructive than any other: imperial wars. Since the beginning of recorded history empires have used war as a tactic to gain economic and political domination over other people. There have been many empires in the past and they continue to this day, albeit in a different form, but all of them use war or the threat of war to impose their will and subjugate people.

If we are to understand the possibility for peace, then we have to understand the wars of empires and the struggles for liberation that have shaped the human experience. That is where Part I of this book begins.

CHAPTER 1: EMPIRES OF THE PAST

> They have plundered the world, stripping naked the
> land in their hunger, they loot even the ocean: they are
> driven by greed, if their enemy be rich; by ambition, if
> poor; neither the wealth of the east nor the west can
> satisfy them: they are the only people who behold
> wealth and indigence with equal passion to dominate.
> They ravage, they slaughter, they seize by false
> pretenses, and all of this they hail as the construction of
> empire. And when in their wake nothing remains but a
> desert, they call that peace.[1]

The Roman historian Tacitus quoted these words of a British
chieftain who resisted the Roman invasion of the British Isles two
thousand years ago.

In the long history of empires there is one consistent feature. All
empires use war and the threat of war to dominate and exploit others.
The British chieftain quoted by Tacitus understood this when he spoke
of ambition, greed and plunder. It was true in ancient times when the
first empires emerged, and it continues to be true today.

The Early Empires

No one knows when the first empire was formed, but it is believed
that there were empires in Africa long before there were written
records. When the Spanish arrived in the New World they found
powerful empires of the Aztecs and Incas that stretched over large
areas, and archaeologists are discovering evidence of other empires in
South America long before that.

The Egyptian Empire, formed 5500 years ago, was the first
imperial power that we know much about. The Egyptians conquered
and ruled territory that stretched from Sudan in the south to Syria in
the north. The empire contributed to the incredible wealth accumulated
by the pharaohs and contributed to the erection of pyramids, temples

and tombs that still stand today. This empire was destroyed by the Persian Empire, which in turn was defeated by Alexander the Great, a figure long mythologized by imperialists in both the ancient and modern world. All of these empires were created by war and defended by the strongest military force of the day.

Europeans view the Roman Empire as the imperial power that brought "civilization" to the territory that bordered the Mediterranean Sea.[2] The empire was formed by a series of wars that extended the boundaries of the empire and made millions subject to Roman rule. The Romans plundered the wealth of those they conquered, trade increased within the empire and the Patricians, the Roman aristocracy, grew incredibly wealthy.

The Roman legions were the source of Rome's power. In the time of the Republic (509 BC-27 BC) Rome had a conscripted army, but with the Empire (27 BC-476 AD) Rome developed a permanent, standing army. Roman military strategy emphasized the function of the army as a whole rather than individual bravery. The legion operated as a unit under the direction of the general, and these highly focused and disciplined efforts helped the Romans to overwhelm their less organized opponents. Soldiers enlisted for twenty years. At the end of their military careers they were often given land in the conquered territories. This helped to Romanize the empire and bring political stability. In time the generals came to control the Roman state, and many became emperors and powerful political figures.

The Roman legions defended the empire against attacks from the so-called "barbarians," enemies that lived outside the empire. They mounted campaigns to conquer new territory and imposed Roman laws and peace on the vast regions they ruled. *Pax Romana* it was called – the Roman peace. When there were no wars the legions built roads, aqueducts, and other public facilities. Roman culture and the Latin language spread through the empire. Trade and commerce flourished and literacy and education was promoted.

The Chinese Empire lasted even longer than the Roman. Before the empire was established, China was divided into hundreds of small states governed by local warlords. Some were as small as a fort and others as large as a city with surrounding territory. Wars were common between these mini-states as one leader or another tried to extend his rule over the surrounding area. The year 221 BC is accepted as the time when China became unified into an empire. Qin, the first Emperor, used his army to subdue a large area of the Han Chinese homeland. Over the centuries the empire gradually expanded until it came to control an area about the size of China today. The empire lasted until 1911 when the republic was formed, a period of over 2100 years.

In some ways the Chinese Empire is unique. Like all empires, it was created by military force and the original objectives of its rulers were domination and exploitation, but once conquest was complete that changed. A state bureaucracy was formed that administered the extensive territory. Writing became the basis of communication of government and literacy spread. Trade expanded and a system of laws encouraging trade was enforced. Banditry was suppressed, the power of local warlords was broken, and the Great Wall was built to protect the Empire from northern invaders. Like *Pax Romana* in the Roman Empire, the central government enforced peace within the territory that they controlled, but while the Roman Empire always had different provinces and ultimately collapsed, the Chinese Empire remained unified during its long history. People who were conquered were included into the empire. In time they came to see themselves as citizens of the empire and the emperor as their leader.[3] In this way China became a unified country. A country governed by law is very different from an empire ruled by military force.

The Mongol Empire of the thirteenth century is often disregarded because it lasted for less than 100 years, but in terms of land mass it was the largest empire the world has ever known. At its height the Mongols ruled a territory that stretched from Manchuria and Korea in the east to Poland, Hungary and the Ukraine in the west. It included parts of China, Afghanistan, much of the Middle East, Pakistan and parts of India.

The basis of the empire was the unification of the Mongol-Turkic tribes of Central Asia. These people were, and still are, semi-nomadic herdsmen who use horses to tend their flocks of sheep and other domestic animals. Once organized into a disciplined army they became mounted cavalry that had great mobility and speed. These horsemen were lightly armed, in comparison to the heavily armed European Medieval knights of the same period. They used lances and were famed as archers who could release arrows on horseback with deadly accuracy. They became expert at mounting attacks on fortified cities.

Mongol warfare could be brutal. The army would annihilate entire cities that refused to surrender to them, but if the population submitted they were treated leniently. Once a region was conquered the Mongols imposed a peace on the territory and brought the code of law called the *Yassa*. European travelers in the Mongol Empire at the time were struck by the degree of order in the kingdom. According to legends a naked woman could ride the length of the empire without being molested, or a man could walk with a bowl of gold without being robbed.

Commerce expanded within the Mongol empire. Merchants were given special documentation allowing them to trade throughout the realm. Reading and writing was encouraged and a postal system established. The teachers, lawyers and artists, were exempted from paying taxes. The famed Silk Road from the Eastern Mediterranean to China was established during this time. Marco Polo and other Europeans traveled safely along this route bringing exotic goods back to Europe from the Far East. These movements of people within the Mongol Empire greatly expanded the knowledge and understanding of the people of the world. The empire collapsed because of internal power struggles within the ruling elite, but the Mongols had a major impact on the people they ruled.

During the Middle Ages in Europe many empires were formed and collapsed. Some, like the Holy Roman Empire, lasted for centuries. Others continued well into the modern era, like the Austro-Hungarian Empire, the Russian Empire, the Ottoman Empire and the British Empire. Every empire has its own unique history and each is different from the others, yet they all share common features. War was the means of dominating territory and people and imposing imperial rule. The empires used their military power to establish political control, enforce peace and the rule of law. This helped them to economically exploit the dominated peoples.

Colonial Empires

Colonialism, or the Age of Exploration, as some like to call it, was an era of European economic expansion leading to world domination. It is a 500 year period of history beginning about 1450, when the Portuguese began sailing south along the West Coast of Africa, to about 1950 when it was clear to anyone who chose to look that European domination was at an end, because they could no longer prevail in war and their economic and political leadership was finished.

The early empires all conquered territory that was contiguous with their home territory. The territories of the colonial empires, on the other hand, were far removed geographically from the imperial centre, or "mother country." European colonialism was dependent on three key elements: gunpowder and superior weapons, the development of ocean-going ships, and the rise of strong, centralized state governments which directed, funded and ultimately benefited from the expansion. All of these elements emerged at about the same time in Europe, in the middle of the Fifteenth Century.

These colonial empires share the characteristics of earlier empires. War was the tactic or means of domination. That led to political control and systematic economic exploitation of the colonies by the imperial power. In the early days of colonialism plunder was the main economic motive, but as time went on trade became the chief form of exploitation. This form of economic system is called "mercantile capitalism." Colonies were the exclusive economic preserve of the colonial power, which decreed how and who would reap the economic rewards. Laws instituted by the colonial power restricted trade to merchants and ships from the "mother" country. In the early Spanish and French Empires trade was controlled by the king who gave monopolies to his favourites. The British gave monopolies to their major trading companies such as the Hudson Bay Company and the East India Company which exploited the colony for their own benefit and the benefit of the monarch. The British passed the Navigation Acts that forced the colonies to trade exclusively with Britain. The result was increased wealth of the European colonial powers and the expansion of their empires around the world.

The Spanish Empire

The Portuguese were the first to venture far out on the seas from Europe in the late fifteenth century. They established colonies in Africa, India, Brazil and as far away as East Timor, and their colonies became bases for trading. But it was the Spanish who established the first truly global empire. For a few years after Columbus' first voyage in 1492 the American colonies were a drain on the royal treasury, but that soon changed. Between 1519 and 1521 Hernan Cortes and his small band of conquistadors conquered the Aztec of Mexico; soon gold and silver were flowing to the treasury of Spain. Francisco Pizarro mounted an expedition against the Incas of Peru in 1531. By 1546 the silver and gold mines of the Americas were sending unimagined wealth back to Spain.[4]

The Spanish settlements soon spread from Mexico to Chile, across the islands of the West Indies and the mainland bordering the Caribbean. Spaniards ventured to Florida and California, and Spanish merchant ships sailed around Africa to India. In 1565 an expedition was sent to the Philippines, and by 1571 this vast island territory was incorporated into the Spanish Empire.

The growth of the Spanish Empire led to expanded global trade. Spanish galleons brought gold and silver across the Atlantic to Spain. From Manila in the Philippines the Spanish traded to China, India and ports all over the Far East. Silks, spices and other precious goods were bought using Spanish gold and silver. The goods were taken to Manila and then shipped across the Pacific to Acapulco on Mexico's west coast. From there they were taken overland to ports on the east coast and transhipped to Spain.

The Spanish quickly squandered their new wealth on European wars, ships, military armaments and luxury goods, but this new wealth transformed Europe. The flood of gold and silver led to a rise in prices, prosperity spread in Europe, cities grew in size, some families gained enormous wealth, and banking and commercial trading companies sprang up across Europe and in the Far East.

But this commercial empire was not without problems. The mines in the Americas that were the source of this new wealth were worked by native labour under terrible conditions. A large number of indigenous people were worked to death and millions died from diseases that were introduced by the Europeans. The native population fell precipitously. In the Caribbean large haciendas were formed for agriculture. Slaves were brought from Africa to work these large holdings.

This is an estimate of the impact of the European conquest of the Americas by Charles C. Mann, the author of *1491: New Revelations of the America Before Columbus.*

> [Before 1492, the Americas were] "a thriving, stunningly diverse place, a tumult of languages, trade and culture, a region where tens of millions of people loved and hated and worshiped as people do elsewhere. Much of this world vanished after Columbus, swept away by disease and subjugation. So thorough was the erasure that within a few generations neither conqueror nor conquered knew the world had existed."[5]

The unified kingdom of Spain was the most powerful military force in Europe during the 16th and early 17th centuries, but France and England were on the rise with their own empires. While the rest of Europe went through a period of economic expansion in the late seventeenth century, Spain was in decline. By 1713 Spain had lost all of its European possessions and became a vassal state of France. During the Napoleonic wars the Spanish Empire dissolved. And yet despite the decline of the Spanish Empire, the influence of Spain lives on in its former colonies. Spanish culture has merged with indigenous culture in much of South and Central America. Roman Catholicism is the religion of most of these people and the Spanish language is spoken by more people in the world than any other except Chinese.[6]

In the early stages of colonialism there were a number of wars where the Europeans crushed the local leadership and established their rule. Cortes invaded the powerful Aztec Empire of present-day Mexico in 1519 with 400 infantry soldiers and over a two-year campaign completely destroyed their empire. An even more striking example was the Spanish conquest of the Inca Empire. In 1532 Francisco Pizarro defeated an Inca army of 80,000 with 106 foot soldiers, 62 horsemen, muskets and cannon in the Battle of Cajamarca.[7] The Europeans were able to dominate these lands so completely by the use of firepower but also because the indigenous people were weakened by disease introduced by the Europeans.[8] War was the method of domination and military force continued as the way that the colonies were controlled.

But colonialism also led to a number of disastrous European wars. Spain used the power and new wealth gained from their colonies to become involved in wars in Italy and the religious wars of the Reformation. For eighty years the Spanish fought to put down a rebellion in Holland in the Dutch War of Independence (1568-1648). The War of the Spanish Succession (1701-1714) was fought among several major European countries. The Seven Years War (1756-1763) pitted the two major European powers, Britain and France. It was a global war fought in North America and India, but the chief battlegrounds were in Europe. Colonialism was a root cause of all of these wars as one colonial empire or another struggled to gain dominance over the others.

The French Empire

The French colonial empire was never as extensive as the Spanish or British. By the seventeenth century France had become the most populous and powerful country of Western Europe. The country was unified around an absolute monarch, had a large army and an expanding system of overseas colonies in India, the West Indies and New France (Canada). Not only was France powerful militarily, but it was the foremost commercial country of Europe, with Paris the leading city. French traders imported and exported goods and presided over a large and growing internal market. Bankers loaned money to commercial enterprises and funded kingdoms and principalities across Europe. These were the *nouveau riche* of France – the new wealth. However, the political power of France centered on the king and the aristocracy, the *ancien regime*, as they were called. Their wealth came from land and the exploitation of the peasantry.

In the eighteenth century France became involved in a succession of disastrous wars against the British and other continental powers. The Seven Years War was particularly ruinous for the French. By the end of that war they had lost New France to the British, they were driven out of India by the British East India Company and they lost many of their colonies in the Caribbean. It seemed their empire was at an end.

France was still prosperous and with inspired leadership the country could have avoided calamity, but the royalty and aristocracy were simply not up for the task. In 1789 famine and political turmoil in France erupted into full-fledged violent revolution inspired by the ideals of the enlightenment. The monarchy was overthrown, feudal privileges of the aristocracy and the Catholic clergy were abolished, and the guillotine was kept busy in a "reign of terror" eliminating members of the *ancien regime*.

Another consequence of the French Revolution was war with the other major powers of Europe. War and turmoil was to become a constant from 1792 to 1815. At first it was the revolutionary government of France that waged war against the other large powers of Europe: Austria, Prussia and Britain. Then, like Rome centuries before, it was a general, Napoleon Bonaparte, who rose to power. On November 9, 1799, Napoleon staged a coup which led to his dictatorship, and on May 18, 1804 he crowned himself Emperor of France.

Napoleon's vision of empire was to conquer other countries militarily and make them dependent on France. This was not to be a colonial empire. Rather it would be established by military power, and it would make France the undisputed commercial and political center of Europe, stretching from the North Sea to the Ural Mountains and from the Mediterranean to the Arctic. In time, no doubt, he believed he would be emperor of the world.

Napoleon built the *Grande Armée,* the most powerful army of its day. This was to be his instrument of imperial domination. He waged war across Europe from Italy to Austria, Spain to Prussia, winning victory after victory. By 1805 the only major European powers that remained outside his empire were Britain and Russia. Napoleon massed his army on the English Channel and prepared to invade, but defeat at the Battle of Trafalgar on October 21, 1805, resulted in the destruction of the French and Spanish fleets. Napoleon abandoned his plans to invade Britain and concentrated all of his military efforts to extend the French Empire within continental Europe.

Ultimately he failed. The disastrous invasion of Russia in 1812 shattered the *Grande Armée* and it was finally defeated at the Battle of Waterloo in 1815. Napoleon's empire was at an end. France had lost virtually all of its colonies. The vast territory of Louisiana had been sold to the Americans in 1803, and an even more devastating economic loss came in 1804 with the independence of Haiti.

It took time for France to recover its power and prestige, but in the 1830s the French created a new colonial empire by invading Algeria. By the late nineteenth century France had established control over French Indochina, with colonies in Vietnam, Laos and Cambodia. Later they gained extensive colonies in sub-Saharan Africa. It took the upheavals of the First and Second World Wars, and the wars of liberation that followed, before the dreams of a French colonial empire were finally ended.

The British Empire

The largest and most successful of the colonial empires was the British.[9] Like all empires before and since, this empire was created by military power and in this case it was the power of the British navy.[10] In the sixteenth century seamen from Devon and Cornwall ventured out in ships to fish on the Grand Banks off Newfoundland, and trade with merchants in European ports. By the 1560s English ships were trading in Africa and the Americas. Frances Drake sailed for the

Spanish Main in 1570 and for the next five years he plundered towns and stole gold and silver from the Spanish almost with impunity. When he returned to England, rather than being thrown into jail, Queen Elizabeth knighted him and treated him as a hero. The Spanish were outraged that the English were sponsoring pirates that preyed on their galleons and stole their gold. They were determined to crush this nation which honoured pirates and killers. In 1588 the Spanish King Philip II raised an armada of 130 ships, filled them with thousands of fighting men, and the fleet set sail for England, determined to teach this upstart nation a lesson.

The defeat of the Spanish Armada changed the course of history. In the decades after the Armada the British merchant fleet grew in numbers and strength until they dominated the seas in every corner of the globe. It was trade that was important to the British, and the most important trade during the seventeenth and eighteenth centuries was the slave trade. British merchants sailed to West Africa where they traded European goods with local leaders for slaves. They transported the slaves in their ships across to the West Indies, Brazil and parts of North America and then they brought goods back to Britain. It was very lucrative. This was not organized by government; it was independent merchants who controlled every aspect of this trade.

The settlements of the early British colonies in North America were organized in a similar way. For a fee, British merchant ships took settlers looking for religious freedom or economic opportunities to America. They would return with the holds of their ships filled with various goods, from agricultural products to furs. Gradually the settlements in North America grew and in time local government, based on English practices, was established. The American colonialists viewed themselves as Englishmen. They had their own ships and they traded across the Atlantic and further afield. Gradually through the seventeenth and eighteenth centuries a mercantile economic system emerged that was motivated and driven by trade and profit and supported and protected by the power of the British navy.

What transformed the British Empire was a series of wars in the mid and late 18th and early 19th centuries. After the Seven Years War (1756 to 1763) the British held New France[11] and many of the French islands in the Caribbean. But most important, the British now controlled all of India. The loss of the American Thirteen Colonies was a serious setback, but this was more than compensated by the exploitation of India, "the jewel in the crown of the British Empire." After the defeat of Napoleon in 1815, Britain was the leading political and economic superpower in the world. For the next 100 years the British navy ruled the seas: *Pax Britannia* – the British Peace.[12]

At the height of their power the British moved away from the system of mercantile monopolies that had been the foundation of their empire and advocated a system of free trade. In the 1840s the British repealed the corn-laws that restricted or taxed trade and announced to the world that unfettered free trade in goods for all nations would be their policy. This was a revolutionary proposal that appeared neutral on the surface but was based on self-interest. Britain was the leading economic power of the day, producing low cost industrial goods and delivering them inexpensively almost anywhere on the globe with its huge fleet of merchant ships. Even more important, Britain was the financial capital of the world and the British pound sterling was the world's international currency. The British made investments around the globe; they built and financed railways in scores of countries, and provided financing for projects in every corner of the globe. London became the intellectual center of the world, producing the leading artists, writers, scientists and engineers.[13]

This was a new kind of empire, with colonies around the globe protected by the military power of the British navy and army. British merchants, industrialists and financiers had great advantages but the empire was open to all who wanted to trade. The old mercantile empire that gave a protected monopoly to its own merchants was dead. The new empire was based on free trade in the knowledge that British entrepreneurs could still dominate.

The Age of Imperialism

The Age of Imperialism is said to stretch from 1850 to the beginning of the First World War in 1914. During this period Britain was the dominant Imperial power, with France a major competitor and

Germany and Italy joining in the exploitation. The United States was bent on westward expansion, Russia looked to exploit its vast territories in the east and coveted lands of the Ottoman Empire to the south around the Black Sea, the Netherlands had colonies in The Dutch East Indies (Indonesia) and Germany was beginning to emerge as a major power. This was colonialism at its height. In 1800, Europeans occupied or controlled 35% of the land surface of the world; by 1878 this had risen to 67% and by 1914 to over 84% of the world's land use.[14]

Europeans and Americans shared a set of values and beliefs that justified their imperial ambitions. Nationalism was a powerful force in the late nineteenth and early twentieth centuries and empires and colonial possessions were seen as a mark of a nation's greatness. Racism was accepted as part of the natural order of things. Europeans assumed that they were superior because they were educated white people, while those of other races and cultures were thought to be uncivilized and even savages. Indigenous peoples were felt be little more than children who welcomed colonial domination because of the benefits that it would bring. Rudyard Kipling, the British poet and novelist, explained it as the "white man's burden" to educate and uplift the uncivilized people of the world, a racist notion disguised in a humanitarian form. Even Christian churches were in favour of imperialism because it gave their missionaries access to the heathen.

Above all, militarism was at the basis of the ideology of the Age of Imperialism. Governments invested huge sums in their armies and navies. Soldiers were outfitted in resplendent uniforms and paraded through the streets of European capitals on every possible occasion. War was seen as a great adventure and noble calling that tested the manhood of the young and benefited civilization by weeding out the weak. This article glorifying the benefits of war and exploitation was published in the *New York Times* on March 26, 1909.

> In the perspective of history war must be admitted to have been a necessity, even a beneficial instrument in working out human destiny. It has built up nations; it has awakened and established the consciousness of race

and kinship. By war the living and advancing nations have reclaimed great and rich areas of the earth's surface from the impoverished ownership of the inert and dying nations. Without war this world would not be what it is now.

The Age of Imperialism saw the extension of European empires in the Far East, but the greatest expansion was in Africa. Before 1850 the French had a colony in Algeria and the British were in South Africa, the opposite end of the continent. There had long been trading along the coastline but no Europeans went into the interior. Africa was still the "dark continent," mysterious and unknown. As explorers penetrated up the rivers, into the rainforests and savannah grasslands, Europeans became excited about the prospects of exploiting the wealth of this vast continent.

The "scramble for Africa," as it came to be called, began in earnest in the 1880s. In 1884-85 the European nations met at the Berlin Conference and carved up Africa for themselves. It was agreed that any nation could claim any part of Africa as long as it could demonstrate that it controlled the area. With the discovery of diamonds in Kimberley, South Africa in 1870 and vast gold deposits in the Transvaal in 1886 the European desire for African colonies to exploit became overwhelming. By 1914 all of Africa was claimed with the exception of Ethiopia and Liberia. European settlers took vast areas of the most fertile land for themselves as if it was their natural right, and established farms with the labour of native people. Gold, diamonds, palm oil, cocoa, rubber, copper, peanuts and many other products flowed to Europe, and European-manufactured goods flowed to Africa. The profits were immense.

Throughout the Age of Imperialism war was used by the European colonial powers with impunity as a method of domination and control. The record of the major British wars in the period is a good example, but all of the other empires used the same brutal direct tactics to seize what they wanted.

In the Far East Britain fought the Opium Wars (1839-41 and 1856-60) to force the Chinese government to open their markets to opium, a product that was banned in Britain. The Chinese forces were defeated, the wars resulted in granting special trading rights to British merchants and Hong Kong became a part of the empire. The Chinese felt deeply humiliated by these wars. This was the beginning of intense anti-European feelings that led to the Boxer Rebellion in 1900 and contributed to the rise of communism in the 1940s.

In India the British fought a number of insurrections. The most serious was the Indian Mutiny of 1857 when Indian troops in the British Army rebelled and took over large regions of the north until they were put down by force. Three separate invasions of Afghanistan were launched from India by the British (1839-42, 1878-80 and 1919). These wars were part of a competition with the Russians for influence in Central Asia, called "the great game." Each of these invasions resulted in defeat and disaster for Britain.

There were several British wars in Africa, fought to establish and hold colonies. The Anglo-Zulu War (1879) in South Africa is the most famous because a British unit was decisively defeated by the Zulus in the Battle of Isandlwana, but soon the war went badly for the Zulu. Indigenous African people carrying spears were no match for Europeans armed with high powered rifles. Two wars were fought against the Boers (1880-81 and 1899-1902) in South Africa. Again the British Army prevailed but not before they were widely criticized for holding Boer families in concentration camps.

The Crimean War (1853-56) was different from the colonial wars. Britain, France and the Ottoman Empire were on one side and Russia on the other. The Russians had ambitions to encroach on the Ottomans and take over their possessions in Palestine and around the Black Sea. The British and French allied with the Ottomans because they wanted to stop the expansion of the Russian Empire and curtail its power. The casualties of this war left over a million dead. It was part of a chess game all the Imperial powers played to try and keep competing empires weak and promote their own interests.

What is striking about all of these wars in the Age of Imperialism was their naked aggression. There was no attempt to disguise the fact that war was the means to gain wealth and political objectives for the imperialists. The sovereignty of other countries, the political beliefs and economic interest of indigenous people, were simply ignored. To the Imperialists only their interests mattered. The lives and well being of ordinary soldiers in a European army were also of no consequence. If men were lost securing a colony it was worth the sacrifice for the glory of the empire. Soldiers were the cannon fodder of empires. These attitudes of superiority and elitism among the political and military leaders of the European colonial powers led in no small part to the calamity of the First World War.

German Dreams of Empire

By the middle of the nineteenth century, Germany, led by Prussia, was beginning to emerge as a major industrial and military power. Many Germans felt deeply frustrated that the lack of political unity had denied them the benefits of empire and they were determined to do something about it. The only way they could do that was through war.

Until the beginning of the nineteenth century Germany was made up of scores of small principalities each jealous of its own territory, customs and privileges. Prussia, in the north, was a powerful state that had grown in size and wealth because of its military strength. Austria in the south was another large German speaking state, but most German speaking people lived in small principalities. Following the defeat of Napoleon in 1815, thirty-nine states in the north came together into a loose political federation called the German Confederation dominated by Prussia. The confederation was a political and military alliance as well as a tariff union. The area rapidly began to industrialize.

There were deep political divisions within the German Confederation. Liberals, located mainly in the cities, agitated for greater individual freedoms, the extension of democratic institutions and support for the industrial working class. The largest and most successful political group was the Social-Democrats. Opposing them were the *Junkers*, conservatives who were in control of the military. They were anti-liberal, with little connection to the new industrial society that was emerging in Germany, and they feared the rising power of the urban working class.

The political conflict between these two groups came to a head several times but the most serious was in the 1848 rebellions that swept across Europe. After this struggle for political rights, middle class property owners received more political power and individual rights, but the state came down harshly against the leaders of the democratic movement. Many fled as political refugees and settled in the United States and Britain, the leading liberal democratic countries at that time.[15]

Leadership of the German Confederation was vested in the Prussian monarchy. The Kaisers were conservative and closely allied to the *Junkers*, although when it was politically expedient they would support the liberals.[16] Kaiser Wilhelm I came to the throne in 1861, and inherited this conflict. In 1862 he appointed Otto von Bismarck to the office of Prime Minister of Prussia. Bismarck was to achieve the dreams of German unification and the creation of the German Empire.

Prussia had military conscription. The country had a small standing army and a large reserve force that was trained and ready to be mobilized. Prussian soldiers were well disciplined and armed with the most up to date equipment. The artillery used by the Prussians, produced in Krupp steel foundries, was breech loaded and could fire accurate rounds in rapid succession.

After his appointment Bismarck engineered a series of wars. In 1863 he found an excuse to attack Denmark. Prussia was allied with Austria in this war. After the defeat of Denmark, the alliance fell apart and led to war in 1866 between the two German speaking countries. To the surprise of Europeans, Prussia decisively defeated Austria, one of the largest and strongest military powers in Central Europe.

These wars upset the balance of power of Europe, and now Prussia, with the support of the German Confederacy, had emerged as a leading power of continental Europe. The French Emperor, Napoleon III, was concerned. Despite its defeat in the Napoleonic Wars, France was still considered the dominant military power of Europe. It had the largest population at the time of any western or central European country, with 36.9 million people. Prussia was smaller with a population of 20 million.[17]

Bismarck was undeterred. In July 1870, after a series of diplomatic exchanges and escalating demands, a suitable pretext was engineered and Prussia declared war against France. Prussia rapidly mobilized and brought together the military forces of other German principalities. In a few weeks these forces occupied much of north eastern France. Then, in a series of battles over the next five months, the Prussians defeated the French. Napoleon III was captured and abdicated. France was in chaos, the government collapsed and the Third Republic was formed. The Paris Commune, an uprising of French workers, briefly seized the city and was put down by the French army.

The prestige of Prussia was enhanced with the defeat of the French. In January 1871 the German states, with the exception of Austria, proclaimed their union under the leadership of the Prussian king and called the nation the German Empire. Berlin became the capital, and two French territories, Alsace and Lorraine, were ceded to Germany. The German Empire had emerged as the leading industrial power with the most professional and powerful military force in Europe. Tensions in Europe increased. The armies of Germany and France doubled in size between 1870 and 1914. Bellicose statements by leaders of both countries became commonplace. Economic competition intensified as Germany increasingly took over the markets of France and Britain and emerged as the wealthiest country in Europe, second only to the United States in the world.

During the 1870s Britain had a policy of "splendid isolation" from the problems of Europe, but by the 1880s this had changed and Britain, like the French, eyed Germany nervously. A competition emerged between Britain and Germany for mastery of the seas, as both countries entered into a frantic race to build bigger and better gunned naval ships. Ship after ship rolled out of the dockyards as German battleships were matched with the British Dreadnaught. The British maintained their naval superiority over the Germans with twice the number of ships and firepower, but at great cost.

A series of alliances between the different European powers were negotiated as countries tried to gain strategic advantage over others. At first Germany formed a number of alliances, but after Kaiser Wilhelm I dismissed Bismarck in 1890 the country became increasingly isolationist. Germany's major allies were the Austro-Hungarian and Ottoman Empires. France and Britain became allies in 1904 in the *"Entente Cordiale."* When they were joined by Russia in 1907, the allies were called the *"Triple Entente."*

Europe was now divided into two military camps; it took only a single spark to set the continent afire. That spark came on June 28, 1914 with the assassination of Crown Prince Franz Ferdinand, Archduke of Austria, and his wife Sophie, in Sarajevo.

The First World War

The First World War was a direct result of the competition and rivalry between the imperial powers. It began as a competition to determine which empire would lead the world and reap the economic benefits, but it became a grim struggle to the finish that would end empires and create a world that was much more unstable and vulnerable than ever before.

It started with a blaze of patriotic feelings as men rushed to get into the battlefield. The war would be "over by Christmas," was the common belief on both sides, and men did not want to miss this chance of a lifetime for adventure.[18] The German army that took to the field in 1914 has been described as the most brilliant ever sent into battle.[19] This army of conscripts and professional soldiers had a tradition of victory, and morale was high. In France the call went out, patriotic speeches were made by politicians in town squares and men rushed to get into uniform. The French believed that their military tradition had instilled them with *"élan vital,"* a type of mystical fighting spirit that made the French fighting man more than a match for the German. Across Britain and the British Empire the drums of war were sounding. In Scotland the pipe bands marched and men flocked to the flag. In England the educated elite of Oxford and Cambridge became officers and factory and agricultural workers enlisted as private soldiers. Indian regiments prepared to go to the aid of Britain, and in Canada the initial target of 30,000 recruits for the army was oversubscribed.[20] The world has never seen such an enthusiastic rush to war.

The Germans had to fight the Russians on their Eastern Front and the combined forces of the French and British on the Western Front. They believed it would take the Russians longer to mobilize, so their plan was to defeat the French and British first and then turn on the Russians. As the war opened in August 1914 the French attacked Germany in an attempt to strike into the German industrial heartland in the Ruhr Valley and cripple their war machine. French infantry stormed well-fortified German positions and were mowed down by machine gun fire, achieving nothing. The Germans invaded France from Belgium in the north and drove back the French and British forces. It was then that things began to go wrong for the Germans.

The Russians had mobilized quickly and attacked Germany, occupying much of Prussia. Believing the French and British were close to defeat, the Germans withdrew some of their forces from the Western Front to send them to the east to defend against the attacking Russian army. This weakening of their forces was a decisive mistake. Gaps appeared in the German lines and the French and British attacked, putting the Germans on the defensive. By September 15th the German advance had stalled and their line was stabilizing. The Germans began to dig trenches and establish defensive positions. The war of attrition had begun.

The Western Front developed into a stalemate by the end of 1914. The Germans established a defensive line from the English Channel to the Swiss border. As much as possible they selected higher ground and built deep, well-fortified trenches. The British forces, in the western part of the line and the French in the east dug trenches opposite the German lines but they were not as well fortified. To the allied generals their position was only temporary until they broke through the German lines and achieved victory.

In past wars, armies were mobile. Infantry and cavalry were moved about to gain tactical advantage over enemy forces. In order to win, an army needed a good offence, but in this war technology gave defence the advantage. Machine guns were big, heavy weapons, not easily moved, but they could lay down a withering line of fire that made their positions virtually impregnable to attack by infantry crossing open ground. The other major weapon that gave advantage to the defender was artillery. More soldiers were killed in the First World War by artillery than by any other means.[21] Artillery fire could devastate soldiers attacking across open ground. The main reason armies dug trenches was as a defence against artillery fire, and yet even a deep trench would not protect against a direct hit.

On the Eastern Front the Russians initially had success against the Austrian army. Hindenburg, the newly appointed German general, led the counterattack and destroyed most of the Russian army. By the summer of 1915 the Russian army was essentially finished as a fighting force.

And so the stage was set that changed the vision of war as a great adventure that glorified empire, to the ultimate horror of the human experience. Men lived in the squalor of the trenches for weeks at a time. They witnessed the death of their comrades and suffered with the constant fear that their bodies might be shattered by bursting artillery shells or ripped apart by machine gun fire. The greatest tragedy of the war was that the generals, particularly the allied generals, never understood that the machine gun and artillery had changed the nature of modern warfare. French generals kept throwing troops at the German lines in the belief that *élan vital* would lead to victory, only to see their men mowed down and their bodies left to rot in no-man's-land.

The British generals were little better. British and Australian troops attacked the Turks at Gallipoli and all that was gained were appalling casualties. In the Battle of the Somme in the summer of 1916 the British along with battalions from the Empire were shattered. On the opening day they suffered 57,470 casualties, the bloodiest day in the history of the British Army. Altogether 623,907 allied soldiers were killed or wounded in this battle. This was the cost to win a few yards of ground that were soon lost again to the enemy. The only real victory for the allies was in the Middle East against the Ottoman Empire and that was more to do with an uprising of Arabs than European troops.

As the war dragged on conditions in the trenches worsened and casualties on both sides continued to climb. In 1917 a new commander-in-chief of the French army, General Robert Nivelle, planned fresh attacks on the German lines. He confidently predicted

25

that the French would achieve a breakthrough within 48 hours which would end the war. The battle turned into carnage for the French troops. Well-protected German machine guns cut down the attackers in a murderous crossfire. After a week the German lines held and 100,000 French soldiers had been killed or wounded, but still Nivelle insisted on continuing the attack.

A group of French soldiers, who were in the rear resting, refused to go back to the front. "Down with war!" they shouted. The officers tried to impose discipline. Several soldiers were court-martialled. Five were shot. But the mutiny spread. "We're not marching!" other soldiers shouted defiantly, and refused to move. Thousands were now involved and the mutiny was spreading. The men insisted that they were willing to defend their positions but they would not attack.

Past mutinies had been put down with swift, harsh discipline, but the French officers realized that the men had been pushed to their limit and if they were to impose discipline they ran the risk of armed rebellion. Almost the entire French Army was refusing to fight. In the end few of those involved in the mutiny were ever punished. General Nivelle was dismissed and the new commander-in-chief, General Henri-Philippe Petain, suspended all large scale attacks.[22]

In Russia, at the very same time, there was a similar revolt against war that would have far greater consequences. Almost from the beginning the war had been a catastrophe for the Russians. Conscription was enacted and millions of peasants and workers were inducted into the army, given a little training and then thrown into combat against a better trained, better led and better supplied German army. The result was devastating. By the end of 1914, only four months into the war, nearly 400,000 Russian soldiers had been killed and another million wounded. Then it got worse.

Social conditions in Russia were bad before the war. The country was rapidly industrializing but it was still controlled by an aristocratic government led by Tsar Nicholas II who had little contact with or understanding of the people. Workers in the cities lived in vast slums, and the peasants in the countryside suffered a meagre existence. With the war conditions worsened. Food distribution broke down. Starvation became a serious problem; prices rose; and anger intensified against the rich who had the ability to protect themselves against hardships.

By mid-1915 Russian soldiers were being sent to the front lines without proper uniforms, sometimes without shoes. Many were sent into battle without weapons or ammunition, with orders to pick up guns from the enemy or fallen comrades. By the end of October 1916 it is estimated Russia had lost between 1.6 and 1.8 million men in the war. An additional two million were prisoners and one million were missing, for a total of five million casualties. Mutinies began to occur. Officers were shot by their soldiers. Whole companies and then regiments deserted or refused to fight. By February 1917 bread riots and strikes shut down Russian cities. Civil authority broke down and the government was totally unable to deal with problems. Finally, on March 2, 1917, the Tsar abdicated.

The liberal government that came to power made one fatal mistake. It continued the war against Germany. Conditions deteriorated even more, and on November 7, 1917[23] the Communists, under the leadership of Vladimir Lenin, gained power on a slogan of "peace, land and bread." Lenin knew that if his government was to survive they would have to get out of the war no matter what the cost. On March 3, 1918 they signed the Treaty of Brest-Litovsk that gained peace with Germany but ceded vast territories to the central powers.

In the experience of trench warfare and the political struggles of 1917 a new kind of pacifism emerged. Intellectuals joined by political activists and trade unionists became pacifists, and the anti-war movement spread. Political protests occurred across France and the English-speaking world. There was resistance to the draft; men chose prison over going to war. People were learning that they had the power to protest decisions that led to the deaths of thousands.

With Russia out of the war the advantage appeared to shift to Germany and its allies but other developments worked against them. American popular opinion had supported the allies from the beginning of the war. After American merchant ships were sunk by German submarines, President Woodrow Wilson declared war against Germany on April 6, 1917. This brought vast new resources and fresh manpower to the allied side, but the Americans soon learned that they had to use conscription rather than volunteers to fill their army quota. Even in the United States, isolated from the hardships of the conflict, the dreams of war as a great adventure had vanished and men had to be coerced into the army.

As the war wore on there was experimentation with new types of offensive weapons. Aircraft were used for observation by both sides early in the war. By 1917 planes were used to bomb enemy positions and machine gun enemy lines. Soon there were major battles in the sky. Air warfare did not have a great impact on the outcome of the war – but it foreshadowed the future.

The tank was also developed in the First World War into an effective offensive weapon used to break the deadlock of trench warfare. By 1917 the British were using tanks to cross no-man's-land and directly attack machine gun emplacements to break through enemy lines. Their advantage was mobility and the protection provided by their heavy steel armament, but they were vulnerable to attack by artillery.

It was not tanks or aircraft that led to the final outcome of the war. By 1918 both sides were nearing exhaustion. After the Germans settled with the Russians they concentrated their forces on the Western Front. In March 1918 the Germans launched their attack. All across the Western Front they broke through the allied defences and made unprecedented gains. In some places they advanced 60 kilometres (40 miles). Panic set in among the allies. A German victory seemed imminent; the German Kaiser Wilhelm II declared a holiday.

But the German attack stalled. Their troops were exhausted and had outrun their supply lines. The allies counterattacked and drove the Germans back, giving the allies their first major gains in the war, with the bulk of the American troops just beginning to arrive. On August 8, 1918 the allies began the "Hundred Days Offensive," the final drive that won the war. The allied pressure did not let up until Armistice Day, November 11, 1918.[24]

The First World War had been motivated by dreams of empire and enhanced military and economic power. Instead it led to the destruction of four empires, the German, Russian, Austro-Hungarian and Ottoman Empires, and it was the beginning of the end of the

French and British Empires. The war changed the world more than any other event in modern times. The belief in the glories of empire had vanished. War was understood as an unspeakable horror. The moment was ripe for turning away from the imperialism of the past. But instead, decisions made by political leaders led to an even greater calamity.

Aftermath of War

Everyone looked for someone to blame for this war that had resulted in 8.5 million killed and over 21 million wounded. For those on the winning side the most convenient scapegoat was Germany. But this was hardly realistic. All of the Imperial powers had played a role in creating the calamity. The desire for revenge and retribution came to dominate the 1919 negotiations for the Treaty of Versailles. The French wanted to permanently weaken Germany and be compensated for the losses that they had suffered in the war. The Americans promoted the idea of nationhood for people and the development of international institutions through the League of Nations. The result was a redrawing of the map of Europe which satisfied no one and created a host of new grievances. The treaty not only stripped Germany of its overseas possessions, it required Germany to pay war reparations, which impoverished the country. It was hoped that the treaty would lead to peace and yet it became a major contributing cause of the next World War.[25]

In the months after the war political turmoil swept many countries in Europe. Civil war broke out in Russia as the new Soviet regime struggled to establish its authority over the country. Germany faced continual political and social upheaval. France and Britain lurched into what seemed like permanent economic crisis as they were forced to sell off foreign assets to pay the debts created in the war.

Only the United States had made gains. America now was the economic powerhouse of the developed world. The United States had suffered relatively small losses in the war and had benefited enormously economically. The U.S. was poised to play a major leadership role in world affairs, and yet at this crucial moment the country retreated into isolationism, despite the urgings of President Woodrow Wilson. The United States did not even ratify the League of Nations, Wilson's own proposal, and the first attempt at world government languished and ultimately failed.

The First World War seemed to change everything and yet no one could adjust to the new reality. Pessimism was everywhere: in politics, art and science. Even our understanding of the individual changed with the adoption of Freudianism in the 1920s. The concept of the unconscious – that deep, dark well of raw emotion and unbridled feelings that live within every individual – was an idea that struck a chord among those who had lived through the nightmare of the war. The very notion of what it meant to be a human had changed from a rational, reasoning person to an individual governed by unconscious, irrational forces.

Art and literature changed as the intellectual climate was transformed. The flowery poetry with its romantic allusions that was common before the war disappeared, and in its place was a pared-down realism that cut to the core with plain and often brutal language. Themes of alienation and the search for meaning in a world without values became the subject of novels. Visual artists explored distorted images and by the late 1920s some artists had abandoned representational art altogether as their images strived to express the dark forces and urges of the unconscious.[26]

Germany faced the gravest crisis. Returning soldiers flooded into the cities. Many were wounded physically and scarred psychologically. People were exhausted from the war effort. Food production and distribution had broken down. There were bread riots. Unemployment was high. Mobs of people roamed the streets looking for work and food. The treaty requirement that Germany pay reparations was impossible. The country had no money so the state began to print money to pay the bills. This led to hyper inflation by 1922 and the German mark became almost worthless, wiping out the savings of the middle class and ruining the economy. By 1923 it appeared that the worst of the political instability was over and the economic recovery of Germany was underway, but by then the Nazi Party led by Adolf Hitler was on the rise. Hitler used the economic hardships that came with the 1930s depression to seize power in 1933, and Germany's experiment with the Weimar Republic was over.

Designs for World Domination

The causes of the Second World War are diverse and complicated, but like so many wars of the past, the root cause was empire. The single most important contributing factor was the imperial ambition of Japan and Germany. The lessons of the First World War about the limits of empire, and the destruction and hardships that war caused to nations and individuals, were ignored, as the leaders of Japan and Germany dreamed of economic ascendancy and world domination by naked military aggression.

Not unlike the imperialists before the First World War, the Nazis were racists, but they were more explicit in their belief of the superiority of the Aryan, or German race. Germans, in their view, were at the top of the racial hierarchy followed by Slavic people and other "mongrels." At the bottom were Jews and Gypsies (or Roma). Homosexuals, leftists, the disabled and Communists were also collected down near the bottom. Hitler mythologized the German state and believed that Germans should hold their first loyalty to the state itself. To the Nazis the state was the "embodiment of the collective will." This notion was promoted and circulated with various myths and outright lies that glorified the state and the German people.

The fascists rejected liberal democracy, even though Hitler used the democratic process to come to power. They promoted corporatism where all economic activities were to be devoted to the promotion of the goals of the state. Capitalism and particularly *laissez faire* capitalism was rejected, but the greatest enemy of the fascists was Communism. The hatred of Communism in general and the Soviet Union in particular was a near obsession.

Militarism and imperialism were central to their ideology. The Nazis believed that great nations grow out of military power. Their objective initially was to use their military might to incorporate all of the Germanic people into the German state. Once the war was underway they became intent on world domination, in the belief that the German people were superior and deserved to dominate. The Nazis were determined to build an empire that would rule the world. Hitler spoke of it as a "Thousand Year Reich," the Nazi dream of empire and world domination.

Imperial Japan had its own plans for domination. Japan was the leading industrial power in the Far East by the 1880s, and like the European imperialists, built a powerful military to support the dreams of economic domination. The Japanese used their military power to take over Korea in the 1890s, and after their victory over the Chinese in the Sino-Japanese War (1894-95) they were ceded Formosa and parts of Manchuria. In 1910 Korea was annexed. Imperial Japan was developing an empire not unlike the European colonial empires. Militarism was on the rise. "Enrich the country. Strengthen the Army," became the slogan.

Japan had become the leading industrial nation of the Far East, exporting manufactured products across the region and even beyond, but it had a significant problem. The Japanese Islands are heavily populated, but the country's agricultural production is limited, and it lacks the raw materials needed for industrial production like coal, iron ore and rubber. It was believed that, if Japan was to expand and prosper, the country would have to have access to raw materials. The imperialism practiced and promoted by the Europeans was to use military power to dominate and exploit others and the Japanese set a similar course to dominate the Far East through military expansion. By the 1930s their political beliefs had become similar to the fascist ideals held in Germany. They were strongly anti-communist, xenophobic and racist. The state was idealized; service to the emperor was held as the greatest purpose of all individuals.

In 1936 Germany and Japan entered into the Anti-Comintern Pact with the supposed intent of stopping Soviet aggression; in fact it was a military alliance between two fascist powers. Later Italy joined and it came to be called the Tripartite Pact. What bound them together was that all three countries were anti-communist, racist and bent on developing and extending their empires through military power. Finally in 1937 the Japanese used yet another minor political incident to invade the Chinese mainland, and the Second Sino-Japanese War had begun, leading to the Second World War.

The Second World War

The Second World War was a world wide conflict that ultimately involved over seventy countries. It resulted in the deaths of at least 62 million people, making it the deadliest conflict in human history, and at least four times that number were injured or displaced. For more than half a decade the war raged over vast regions of the globe causing death, terror, hunger, displacement and severe economic hardships. This momentous event reshaped the world's political landscape, and it is no exaggeration to say that even yet we live in the post Second World War era.

There were two major theatres of the war: Europe and the Far East. The Japanese invaded China and occupied the coastal regions and up the Yangtze River valley. In July 1941 they launched an attack on French Indochina, controlled by the Vichy French. Then on December 7, 1941, Japanese warplanes launched a surprise attack on the American naval base at Pearl Harbor. Within a few hours their armies moved against Thailand, the Philippines and British colonies in Malaya and Hong Kong. The United States immediately declared war against Japan, and a few days later Germany and Italy declared war against the United States.

In Europe the war began on September 1, 1939 when Germany invaded Poland, and the Soviet Union invaded from the east and occupied the eastern part of Poland. This was part of a plan carefully crafted by Hitler to take the Soviet Union out of the war. After the fall of Poland, Europe settled into a period called the Phony War as all of the countries armed at a furious pace. The French and the British massed their armies in northern France and waited for the attack. On May 10, 1940 the war resumed when the Germans launched their *blitzkrieg* tank attack into France. The British Expeditionary Force, along with a number of French and other allies, fell back to the town of Dunkirk on the British Channel, and in one of the most remarkable events of the war the British were able to evacuate 338,000 British and allied troops from the beaches of Dunkirk. The Germans continued their invasion south into France. Paris was occupied on June 14 and France capitulated on June 25. The first phase of the war in Europe was over.

Britain and its commonwealth allies were now fighting the Germans alone. Hitler planned to invade the British Isles, but the British held naval supremacy in the English Channel. If the Germans controlled the air, their aircraft could attack British ships, control the channel and launch an invasion. The struggle for air supremacy called the Battle of Britain began on July 9, 1940 and went on to May of 1941.[27] The Royal Air Force ultimately was able to prevail because of the superiority of British aircraft and their use of radar to warn of attack. By early 1941 it was clear to Hitler and the German high command that it would be impossible to invade the British Isles and they changed tactics. Preparations were made in secret, and on June 22, 1941 the Germans invaded the Soviet Union in what was to be the decisive campaign of the war.

From 1941 to the end of hostilities in 1945 the war was truly a global conflict fought in several countries in difficult protracted campaigns. In the midst of the struggle Hitler launched the "final solution," the extermination of the Jews, Roma, homosexuals, handicapped, Communists and anyone else that was deemed an enemy of the state. The sheer colossal size of the conflict was difficult to imagine even by the people involved in it. Every campaign in the war was vital to the effort, but two were particularly important to the ultimate outcome: the struggle between the Germans and the Soviet Union in Eastern Europe and the American-Japanese War in the Pacific.

The German invasion of the Soviet Union in June 1941completely surprised the Red Army. The German military was larger, better equipped and better led than the Soviets and they smashed through the defences with a *blitzkrieg* attack. As the Red Army retreated, many were killed or captured by the Germans, but the remaining forces continued to attack the Germans and casualties mounted on both sides. The Eastern Front became the biggest theatre of war in human history with some of the largest and most brutal battles. Atrocities on both sides reached a ferocious level of cruelty and disregard for human life. Both sides suffered from exhaustion, starvation and the bitter cold of the Russian winters. The climax of the campaign occurred in the Battle of Stalingrad that lasted from August 1942 to February 1943. In the bitter fighting it is estimated that between 1.7 and 2 million Soviet and Axis soldiers were killed, wounded or captured, but the German army was stopped, and by the fall of 1943 the massive Red Army was rolling westward, pushing the Germans back in a series of fierce battles. The Germans were exhausted and overextended while the Soviet forces were still gaining strength. In the meantime, on June 6, 1944 the allies landed in Normandy and began advancing towards Germany from the west, liberating France, Belgium and the Netherlands as they went. By January 1945 the Red Army entered Warsaw and entered Berlin by April 25th. Finally, on May 7, 1945 the Germans signed an unconditional surrender. The war in Europe was over.

After Pearl Harbor the Japanese won victory after victory as they invaded and occupied a score of countries in the Far East. In the meantime their war in China, which occupied the majority of their troops, was becoming a stalemate. The Japanese could control the cities and railroads but not the vast Chinese countryside. They turned increasingly to a campaign of terror, but that only made the Chinese more determined to be rid of the invader.

The Americans were not prepared for war but almost overnight the country's entire industrial production became dedicated to armament production. Planes, tanks, ships and every other imaginable weapon rolled off assembly lines. Conscription swelled the ranks of the military. It took only a matter of months before the U.S. had the largest and best equipped military in the Pacific.

The decisive engagement in the war was the Battle of Midway on June 7, 1942. During this naval battle the Americans destroyed four Japanese aircraft carriers and a heavy cruiser while losing only two ships. Though Midway was the turning point for the war, the Japanese continued to fight with ferocity, and it was some months before the Americans finally won naval and air superiority. After the battles of Iwo Jima and Okinawa the Americans knew that they would face stiff resistance if they were to invade Japan and they settled on a bombing campaign and naval blockade. The strategic bombing was devastating. In one night alone, March 9-10, 1945, over 100,000 people were killed in a firebombing raid on Tokyo. Finally on August 6 an atomic bomb was dropped on the City of Hiroshima and on August 9 another atomic bomb annihilated the City of Nagasaki. On August 15, 1945 Japan surrendered unconditionally.

The Second World War again proved the importance of technology in war. The most important weapon in the land war was the tank. *Blitzkrieg* attacks gave offence the advantage and again armies became mobile. The war in the Pacific and the Battle of the North Atlantic showed the importance of sea power. After the Battle of Midway the American ships overwhelmed the Japanese navy and their defeat was certain. But the most important development was airpower. Allied bombing raids into Germany harmed industrial production and crippled cities. Fighter aircraft could harass supply lines and attack enemy positions during battles. In the Pacific fighters sank ships, and the final fate of the Japanese Empire was sealed with the atomic bombs delivered by high flying aircraft.

Imperialism and War

The Second World War was finally over. The monumental struggle had changed everything. The German, Italian and Japanese Empires had completely collapsed. Britain and France were finished as major world powers. In the years after the war they faced financial crises and the end of their colonial empires. Europe and much of Asia lay in ruins. Millions of people had died in the conflict and those who survived were exhausted. In 1945 only two powers of any consequence remained: the Soviet Union and the United States.

The Second World War is usually understood as a struggle against fascism but it must also be seen as a consequence of the long tradition of European imperialism. Both Germany and Japan were bent on using military power to create empires that would politically subjugate and economically exploit other people. Imperial ambitions were finally revealed as a bankrupt practice and ideology built on the arrogant belief that military power justified the destruction of countries and the death and ruination of millions of innocent people.

At the end of the Second World War a new optimism dawned. Fascism, racism, naked aggression and empires seeking world domination had been defeated. It seemed in that heady moment of victory in the summer of 1945, that the age of imperialism was over and a new age had finally dawned. But the Cold War would soon demonstrate that the forces of imperialism were not so easily defeated and war in different forms would continue.

CHAPTER 2: ATTEMPTS TO CREATE A MULTILATERAL WORLD

In 1795, not long after the American and French Revolutions, Immanuel Kant wrote, "Perpetual Peace: A Philosophical Sketch,"[1] in which he proposed a "league of nations" to stop war and promote peace. Over the past two hundred years there have been major efforts to establish international institutions and conventions to find ways to use negotiation and compromise to resolve differences between nations. Citizen peace movements have grown and then faded, but until now efforts to stop war have been a failure.

The Congress System

Treaties between nations were the first widely used instruments of international relations in Europe. Typically, at the conclusion of a war, diplomats from the warring sides would meet and draw up conditions to settle the conflict. These treaties would reflect the new power relations that had emerged from the war, and they would bring a resolution to the issues between the warring parties. The terms of the treaty would resolve issues such as the transfer of territory from the loser to the winner, the repatriation of prisoners, and the amount and form of reparations.

Up until the middle of the eighteenth century this arrangement worked well enough but then problems emerged with the system. The treaties were limited to the countries that were signatory to the agreement even though the causes of the war may have involved others, and they reflected the power relations at the conclusion of the war. Often the treaties created more problems than they solved because one side or the other felt the settlement was unfair or unjust. Leaders were tempted to believe that maybe in the next war their military would win victories on the battlefield and be able to negotiate better terms in the next treaty. The system did nothing to stop wars, and in some instances may even have contributed to the next war.

Societies were changing. Before the eighteenth century only aristocrats were involved in the affairs of state, but as Europe modernized the rising merchant and industrial classes became concerned because wars seriously disrupted their businesses and everyone had to pay for them through taxes. Members of the growing working class in cities and agricultural workers were often forced into the military against their will. They became the "cannon fodder" who paid the ultimate price for war either on the battlefield or as a result of economic hardships.

As the Napoleonic Wars drew to a close, members of the diplomatic community met in Vienna to reshape Europe. Nine days before the Battle of Waterloo, on June 8, 1815, an agreement called the Congress of Vienna was signed that settled the major issues that had led to war. From the outset there were criticisms of the Congress. It reconfirmed the old aristocratic order that had been shaken during the French Revolution and ignored the rising demands for civil liberties and democratic rights. Despite this the Congress of Vienna today is viewed as one of the most successful peace treaties ever negotiated.

The Congress treated France in a non-punitive way even though the Napoleonic Wars had disrupted much of Europe for over ten years. France was allowed to keep its military but its power was balanced with the military power of other nations; Britain was given the right to rule the waves, free access of all nations to the seas was guaranteed, and there were a number of adjustments to the boundaries of European nations. But its greatest success was that the Congress of Vienna introduced what was called the "Congress System" or "Concert of Europe."

Periodically over the years between 1815 and 1914 the major powers of Europe met to resolve problems that threatened peace. Although they had only informal power, these countries acted as a type of world government to ensure peace. At the same time the Congress System promoted international law and the resolution of disputes through international courts. This ultimately led to a Permanent Court of Arbitration, established in 1900. The first Geneva Conventions were also agreed to in this period, establishing rules for the treatment of prisoners of war as well as provisions for the sick and wounded during war.

Remarkably, despite the criticisms of the Congress of Vienna, it contributed to one hundred years of peace. There were no major European wars from 1815 to 1914. Prosperity, wealth and a new sense of security grew in the wake of the Congress, and this led to optimism and a belief in progress that characterized the nineteenth century. But the success of the Congress System was limited. Nothing was done to stop the arms race that emerged at the end of the nineteenth century, and nothing could stop the inexorable march towards war in the days after the assassination of the Austrian Crown Prince in 1914.

The League of Nations

The First World War made many political leaders of the day realize that they needed a permanent international body to actively promote peace and disarmament. The British Foreign Secretary, Sir Edward Grey, is credited with the idea of the League of Nations, but it was the American president, Woodrow Wilson, who used his political influence to get the proposal adopted. Wilson came to the 1919 Paris Peace Conference, called to draw up the treaty to end the First World War, with the League as the centerpiece of his fourteen point peace plan. The League of Nations was adopted and established as part of the Treaty of Versailles when it was signed on June 28, 1919. It was the first attempt to set up a permanent international organization to stop war, promote disarmament and settle disputes through negotiation.

From the beginning the League was handicapped. The American President, who was a Democrat, had used his influence to establish the international organization, but when he took the agreement back home the Republicans in the Senate voted against the proposal, and it was not ratified. For the next twenty years the United States, the wealthiest and most populous developed country, retreated into isolationism and had little to do with international affairs. The League came to be seen as controlled by Britain and France, the major European powers that had won the war. Other countries soon made it clear that they did not intend to be restricted by the decisions of the League.

In the first years of its operation the League had some successes. Former German and Ottoman colonies and possessions were administered under League mandates by Britain, France and other countries. International bodies concerned with specific issues like health, labour standards and control of the illegal drug trade were established under the auspices of the League.[2] The headquarters of the League was established in Geneva and the Council met regularly to discuss issues. By 1934 it had grown to 58 members, the largest it ever achieved.

But while there were some successes, the problems were even greater. It was widely believed that the arms race prior to the First World War was one of the major reasons for the war, and if war were to be avoided in the future then the arms race had to stop. The League solution was called "collective security." All countries were to guarantee the security of all other countries; this would provide the confidence to allow countries to disarm. This was fine in theory, but collective security required political leaders to believe that other countries would come to their country's defense if they were attacked. This was hard to accept in the unstable world of the 1920s and 30s. The League invested considerable political capital in the disarmament issue and achieved little more than political acrimony, which damaged its prestige.

By the 1930s the economic crisis of the depression led to a number of international incidents that the League could not solve. In 1931 the Japanese invaded and occupied a part of Manchuria. When the League passed resolutions condemning the invasion, Japan withdrew from the League rather than withdrawing from Manchuria. An even more flagrant act of aggression was the Italian invasion of Abyssinia (Ethiopia) in 1935. The international press covered the invasion closely. There were allegations that the Italians had poisoned water supplies, killed unarmed people and used chemical weapons, artillery and machine guns against poorly armed Abyssinian forces. The League condemned the aggression, Italy withdrew from the League and no one came to the aid of the Abyssinians.

The failure to stop the Italian invasion of Abyssinia was the effective end of the League of Nations. In 1933 Hitler and the Nazi

Party gained power in Germany, and the rearmament of Europe began in earnest. When the German military reoccupied the Rhineland in March 1936, a clear violation of the Treaty of Versailles, the League made little protest. The Spanish Civil War started shortly afterwards and the League made feeble attempts to stop the international support that was given to the two sides, but that failed and the League's voice virtually disappeared in the build up to the Second World War. It limped along until 1946 when it disbanded and merged with the United Nations.

There were many reasons for the failure of the League. The refusal of the United States to join and actively participate crippled its efforts. The League was closely identified with the Treaty of Versailles, which was, by the 1920s, felt to be a failure; by association, the League was seen as a failure. The focus on disarmament proved to be fruitless. But the real problem was that the League could not enforce its decisions. It had to rely on the great powers, which had no interest in engaging in military operations to enforce League resolutions if they had to risk the lives of their military and pay the cost themselves. Soon it was clear that the League was a powerless shell. It was not auspicious for those who dreamed of a world of peace. The first major international effort to end war had ended in failure.

Roosevelt's New International Order

The U.S. policy of isolationism seems almost quixotic today, but at the time it made a great deal of sense. American society has deep European roots, but the United States is an ocean away from Europe. The U.S. was the most prosperous country in the world at the time, with its huge internal market, but it was not a major world trader. Why should they become involved in what seemed to be interminable European wars? But the U.S. policy of isolationism came to a sudden and abrupt end with the Japanese attack on Pearl Harbor on December 7, 1941. The Americans became fully engaged in the Second World War and played a major role in the defeat of both Germany and Japan.

It was the American President, Franklin Delano Roosevelt, who led the United States during the war. Unlike most Americans, he was an internationalist as well as a strong supporter of democracy and democratic institutions. Roosevelt understood that the conditions of the war had created an opportunity where a democratic, multilateral world might finally be created, and he used all of his considerable influence to try and construct that world.

In August 1941, before the United States had entered the Second World War, Roosevelt met with British Prime Minister Winston Churchill at Argentia, a Newfoundland outpost. At the end of their meeting they issued a joint declaration called the Atlantic Charter which set out the principles that they believed should guide or shape international relations after the war.

The influence of Roosevelt and his brand of liberal ideas can clearly be seen in the charter. It proposed in general terms a system of world government that would arbitrate disputes and promote and protect peace. A key term of the Charter was the rejection of any territorial changes as a result of war. The principles outlined a world of free trade, open markets and freedom of the seas, which they believed would improve labour and living standards around the world. The Charter also set out a democratic world order and the abandonment of force by nations. Churchill[3] and Stalin, who later signed the Atlantic Charter, were not keen on abandoning the use of force. Stalin even opposed free and open markets. Only Roosevelt was idealistic enough to insist on trying to build a new international order that would establish peace among nations. He stood in the liberal American tradition of Woodrow Wilson who was instrumental in establishing the League of Nations. Roosevelt had lived through that experience and was determined that this time a form of world government supported by international institutions would be successful.[4]

This is the wording of the last clause of the Atlantic Charter that links the abandonment of the use of war, the establishment of international institutions and disarmament.

> [We] believe that all of the nations of the world, for realistic as well as spiritual reasons, must come to the abandonment of the use of force. Since no future peace can be maintained if land, sea or air armaments

continue to be employed by nations which threaten, or may threaten, aggression outside of their frontiers, [we] believe, pending the establishment of a wider and permanent system of general security, that the disarmament of such nations is essential. [We] will likewise aid and encourage all other practicable measures which will lighten for peace-loving peoples the crushing burden of armaments.

It was the Atlantic Charter that shaped the efforts to create a new international order towards the end of the Second World War.

As part of the effort to establish international institutions, in July 1944 representatives of 45 allied countries met at Bretton Woods, New Hampshire to make recommendations on the management of the world economic system. It was widely believed that the major underlying cause of the Second World War was the economic chaos and hardships that came after World War I in Europe and the worldwide depression in the 1930s. Roosevelt had moved the United States away from *laissez faire* economic policies to more government control and a regulated economy. The belief was that if the world was to avoid economic chaos, promote economic development and high employment levels, governments had to play a leading role in establishing an economic environment that would create growth, stability and high employment. There was also a consensus that trade should be liberalized by reducing tariffs and other protectionist measures. Out of Bretton Woods came a group of new international organizations that continue to play an important role in stabilizing currencies and promoting and facilitating international trade. They include the World Bank, the General Agreement on Tariffs and Trade (later the World Trade Organization, WTO) and the International Monetary Fund (IMF).[5]

But the most important organization established in this period was the United Nations. Again it was the Americans and the American President who promoted the UN and led to its establishment. In January 1942, at the height of the Second World War, twenty-six allied governments signed the "Declaration by United Nations" in which they pledged to uphold the Atlantic Charter and fight the war until the Axis Powers were defeated. In April 1945 several nations and non-governmental organizations met in San Francisco to discuss the establishment of the UN, and on June 26, 1945, just weeks before the end of the war, the Charter of the United Nations was signed by fifty nations.[6]

The stated aims of the United Nations were to prevent war, safeguard human rights and provide a mechanism for international law. One of its earliest and greatest accomplishments was the Universal Declaration of Human Rights in 1948, which guaranteed human rights for all people. The establishment of the U.N. was a great achievement, but its structure remains its greatest problem. It vests the power with nation states, not democratically elected individuals, and a veto was granted to five powers that had played a leading role in winning the Second World War: the United States, Great Britain, France, the Soviet Union and China. Those countries still have a veto, despite the major geopolitical changes in the world since that time. In spite of this the U.N. has been in the forefront of the struggle for the peaceful resolution of international conflicts since it was formed.

The Nuremburg Trials, held after the end of the Second World War, also set legal precedents on the conduct of war. These were a series of trials of the most prominent members of Nazi Germany to determine whether they were guilty of crimes against humanity. The trials were controversial at the time, and are still debated in legal circles. From a legal point of view the difficulty was that the victorious nations were holding the leaders of Germany, a defeated nation, accountable for actions that were not illegal in Germany at the time the crimes were committed. The counter argument that prevailed was that there are broader principles of humanity, such as safeguarding the lives of others, and that all politicians and citizens must respect regardless of the laws in force at the time.

The trials found many of the Nazi leaders guilty and some were executed. These trials had a great influence on the development of international criminal law. On the conduct of war, the most important decision was that the Nuremburg Trials ruling that aggression – the invasion of one state by another – is the greatest crime. As the chief

U.S. Prosecutor Robert Jackson said at the time, "we should remember that we're handing these Nazi war criminals a poisoned chalice. If we ever sip from it, we must be subject to the same principles or else the whole thing is a farce."[7]

Roosevelt died before the United Nations came into existence, but it is his most important legacy. To FDR and the people around him the United Nations was a means to prevent war and stop the arms race. Within weeks of its formal signing, however, atomic bombs were dropped on the Japanese cities of Hiroshima and Nagasaki, forever changing the course of world affairs. The U.S. President who ordered the dropping of the atomic bombs was President Harry Truman, Roosevelt's successor.

The Truman Doctrine

Most people who had lived through the dreadful days of the Second World War, when armies marched across territories, cities were destroyed and millions killed, wanted nothing more to do with war. If ever there was a time when populations were anti-war it was Europe and East Asia in 1945.

Europe was devastated and its people exhausted. Germany was in ruins. Millions of people had perished in the war in military combat, concentration camps and bombing raids; cities had been turned into rubble. It is estimated that Europe had at least eight million refugees at the end of the conflict. The Soviet Union emerged from the struggle as a clear victor with a modern army that had done more to defeat the Nazis than any other nation, but at a terrible cost. Twenty million Russians had been killed in the war, thousands of cities in the European part of the country had been destroyed, factories had been bombed and scores of bridges and roads were impassable.

In the Far East, Japan too lay in ruins, its cities and factories bombed, millions of people killed and many on the verge of starvation. China had been wracked by war for almost ten years, and after the conflict with the Japanese came to an end, the civil war between the Communists, led by Mao Zedong, and the Nationalists, led by Chiang Kai-shek, resumed with new fury. Indochina, Philippines, Indonesia,

Malaya and other countries in the Far East had been devastated by the war and their citizens faced starvation and utter destitution.

At the end of the Second World War the United States was the preeminent military and economic power. The U.S. almost single-handedly defeated the Japanese. Three hundred thousand Americans had been killed in the war, a relatively small number compared to the casualties of other countries. By the end of the war, eight million men and women were in the American armed forces. With the exception of the attack on Pearl Harbor, there had been no fighting on U.S. soil. The country's cities were not damaged and factories were running at full production. Fully 50% of all industrial goods produced in the world in 1945 were manufactured in American factories. The United States had a very strong balance of payments, and the U.S. dollar was the only international currency accepted around the world.

The situation in Central Europe was particularly critical after the war. At the Potsdam Conference in August 1945 the allies divided Germany into four military occupied zones. The German lands east of the Oder River[8] were transferred to Poland. About 15 million people of German origin lived in these lands before the war and orders were issued that they must leave their homes and relocate west of the Oder River. Millions of people fled or were evacuated and thousands starved or froze to death traveling in unheated railroad cars in the dead of winter.

The entire area was on the verge of collapse. Hundreds of thousands of former German soldiers were interred in prison camps.[9] The economy had virtually come to a stop and the means of exchange was barter and cigarettes. Starvation was widespread and German political leadership had ceased to exist. The allied armies provided the only source of order, but they were preoccupied with dismantling their armies and returning to a peacetime way of life.

The Americans were at the height of their prestige after the war but so were the Communist Party and the Soviet Union. The victories of the Red Army were the turning point in the war in Europe. Many people had become convinced of communist ideology, which believed that the root cause of this devastating war was the capitalist system.

After the war the Communist Party gained many supporters in Western Europe; it became a leading political party in both Italy and France.

But the political situation in the Soviet Union was complicated. Joseph Stalin, the Soviet leader, was a dictator who imposed his rule with a ruthless reliance on secret police, political prisons called the gulag and the elimination of so-called enemies of the state. The Soviet leaders had long had imperial ambitions; with the conclusion of the Second World War, communism was imposed on the occupied countries of Eastern Europe with the power of the red army. In effect the Soviet Union was using its military to force communism on conquered people, just as the empires of the past had imposed their rule and culture on others with the power of the military.

By 1946 the leaders of the west were beginning to feel that the Soviet Union had become a potential threat, bent on world domination. Winston Churchill, the British Prime Minister during the Second World War, was one of the first to raise the alarm. On March 4, 1946 he gave a speech in Fulton, Missouri, with President Harry Truman at his side, in which he described an "iron curtain" that had descended on Europe.

> From Stettin in the Baltic to Trieste in the Adriatic an "iron curtain" has descended across the Continent. Behind that line lie all the capitals of the ancient states of Central and Eastern Europe. Warsaw, Berlin, Prague, Vienna, Budapest, Belgrade, Bucharest and Sofia; all these famous cities and the populations around them lie in what I must call the Soviet sphere, and all are subject, in one form or another, not only to Soviet influence but to a very high and in some cases increasing measure of control from Moscow.[10]

Britain had been devastated by the Second World War. The country was close to bankruptcy from the debt it had incurred during the war. Cities had been bombed, and people were exhausted from their efforts. The Labour government of Clement Attlee did not have the resources or desire to maintain the British Empire. Independence was granted to India, Burma, Sri Lanka and Pakistan[11] and the British Mandate in Palestine was terminated.[12] Britain was finished as a world power and Winston Churchill and Clement Attlee knew it.

Today this speech is remembered for its prediction of the Cold War, but the real intent of the speech for Churchill was a call to Americans to become the world leader. This is the opening paragraph of that same speech.

> The United States stands at this time at the pinnacle of world power. It is a solemn moment for the American democracy. For with this primacy in power is also joined an awe-inspiring accountability to the future. As you look around you, you must feel not only the sense of duty done, but also you must feel anxiety lest you fall below the level of achievement. Opportunity is here now, clear and shining for both our countries. To reject it or ignore it or fritter it away will bring upon us all the long reproaches of the aftertime.

Military power was essential for peace, in Churchill's opinion. Later in the speech he was even more explicit. "From what I have seen of our Russian friends and allies during the war, I am convinced that there is nothing they admire so much as strength, and there is nothing for which they have less respect than for weakness, especially military weakness." The British navy had imposed *Pax Britannia* from 1815 to 1914. The Roman legions had imposed *Pax Romana* for 500 years. Now it was the American's turn to impose *Pax Americana* through the power of their military. This was Churchill's message. It did not take long before events pushed the United States into this new role.

A civil war had broken out in Greece between Communist insurgents and the national government. By 1947 it looked as if Greece was about to be taken over by the Communists. Britain had long been a close ally of Greece, but it did not have the resources to help. The British government went to the Americans and told them that unless they helped, Greece would become a communist state. It was this crisis that led to a reversal of American foreign policy.

On March 12, 1947 President Harry Truman addressed Congress in a speech that outlined what has come to be called "The Truman Doctrine." In this speech he said that without American help Greece would inevitably fall to communism, with grave consequences for the entire region. These "totalitarian regimes intimidated and coerced free peoples," and represented a threat to peace and the national security of the United States. In his words, it was: "The policy of the United States to support free peoples who are resisting attempted subjugation by armed minorities or by outside pressures." As part of this new policy, the United States gave grants of $300 million to Greece and $100 million to Turkey, a close neighbor.[13]

The Truman Doctrine is the beginning of the Cold War. Prior to this time American politics were drifting towards isolationism, and the Soviet Union was treated as an ally. The Doctrine was a clear statement that the United States would resist communism. Truman's rhetoric reflects the sharp new ideological division. The United States, in his words, had become the leader of the "free peoples" while the Soviet Union was a "totalitarian power." The lines were drawn between what Truman called the "free world" and communist dictatorships.

Other policies and programs quickly flowed from the Truman Doctrine. The Marshall Plan was designed to create a strong economic and political foundation in Europe so that the people could resist communism. Named after the U.S. Secretary of State, George Marshall, the plan was developed by Americans and Europeans in July 1947. Economic assistance was offered to all European countries but it was rejected by the Soviet Union and its allies.[14] In total some $13 billion of U.S. economic and technical assistance was given to Western European countries, a considerable amount of money at the time.

The impact of this assistance was dramatic. The next two decades saw an economic resurgence of Europe with unprecedented growth rates. Once again Europe became strong economically. The Marshall Plan was not the only contributor to this growth, but it was an important step in the rebuilding of Europe. Soon Europeans were beginning to discuss greater economic integration, which in time evolved into the European Union.[15]

Not only the Americans were alarmed at the growing threat of the Soviets and their allies; Western Europeans were even more concerned. They were close witnesses to the imposition of Soviet power over Eastern Europe and the continuing military presence of the Red Army. Already a giant fence with observation towers was being built along the "iron curtain" demarcation line. In June 1948 the Soviets restricted access to the western held sectors of Berlin, forcing the Americans and their allies to mount an airlift of food and supplies.

In 1948 a number of European nations signed the Treaty of Brussels which created a military alliance between Britain, France, Belgium and Luxembourg. This led in the next year to the extension of the military alliance that included the countries that signed the Brussels treaty and the United States, Canada, Portugal, Italy, Norway, Denmark and Iceland. The new alliance was called NATO, the North Atlantic Treaty Organization.

Before the decade was over two additional events occurred that sharpened the conflict. In 1949 the Soviet Union detonated its first nuclear device. And in the same year the communists gained power in China. On October 1, 1949 Mao Zedong proclaimed the People's Republic of China and named Peking its capital. Chiang Kai-shek led 600,000 nationalist troops and two million refugees from the mainland to the Island of Taiwan.

Roosevelt had seized the opportunity to put in place the institutions which would be the foundations of a multilateral world where all nations would play an equal role in ensuring a world of peace and prosperity. Already, less than two years after his death, the opportunity had slipped away. The world had become polarized into east and west led by two superpowers, the Soviet Union and the United States. Multilateralism had faded very quickly in the face of the real politic of the Cold War.

CHAPTER 3: THE AMERICAN EMPIRE

Many Americans are deeply offended when the term "American Empire" is used. After all, the United States was forged in a revolution against the most powerful colonial empire of its day. Democratic ideology and practices are deeply ingrained in the belief system of the American people, and freedom and independence are more than slogans. Americans fight for their rights in their communities, their institutions and even in their personal relationships. But the reality is that the U.S. has long acted as an imperial power, and all Americans have benefited from it.

The Roots of the American Empire

When the United States was first formed its people were strongly opposed to European colonialism. In 1823 the U.S. proclaimed the Monroe Doctrine which stated that European powers were not to interfere in the affairs of the independent countries of the Americas. This was a principled stand in opposition to imperialism and colonialism, which was at its height in Europe at the time, but there were other policies of the young country that were not so enlightened.

As American people pushed west across the North American continent in the eighteenth and nineteenth centuries they became involved in a number of Indian Wars which pushed native people onto reserves and took their land. The Mexican-American Wars began first in Texas in 1837 and finally concluded in the invasion of Mexico in 1848. This resulted in the "Mexican Concession" that gained a total of 12% of U.S. territory. The Spanish American War in 1898 gained the United States territories that included Puerto Rico, Philippines and Guam. In almost twenty occasions in the first thirty years of the Twentieth Century the United States sent troops into Caribbean and Central American countries. All of these wars and interventions have the clear markings of imperialism, the use of military force to dominate and exploit other people, and they were justified by the ideology of "manifest destiny," an affirmation of the superiority of the American people.

In 1976 Edward N. Luttwak published an influential book about the Roman Empire in which he distinguished between "territorial" and "hegemonic" empires. Territorial empires, he said, occupy territories with their armies. They throw out the old rulers and directly rule the territory. In hegemonic empires the internal affairs of the countries remain in the hands of the original rulers but they become vassals, taking their orders from the imperial power.[1] Of the two empires that were established after the Second World War, one was a territorial empire and the other a hegemonic empire.

In the concluding days of the war the Red Army of the Soviet Union occupied a number of Eastern European countries. The Soviets removed the fascist leadership the Nazis had put in place and installed communist leaders. An economic and political alliance was established called the Warsaw Pact, but it was dominated by the Soviet Union. In 1956 the Red Army put down a rebellion in Hungary and again in 1968 they suppressed another uprising in Czechoslovakia. Although there was some local control, the Soviet Empire has all of the characteristics of a territorial empire.

After the Second World War the Americans created a hegemonic empire. Local leadership controls the internal affairs of countries within America's "sphere of influence," but on international issues these countries follow American leadership. Within the American Empire countries are independent and sovereign, with their own forms of government and policies, but for decades the American leadership of the empire was unquestioned. It was Washington that provided the most significant military force of the empire, and Washington set the political and economic policies that countries within the empire accepted, whether those policies suited their needs or not.

Economically, the Americans established an international trading system within their empire, where tariffs and other restrictions on trade were gradually reduced and the U.S. dollar was the preferred currency of exchange. The IMF and the World Bank monitored and supervised this system, providing aid when countries got into difficulties, while the WTO set the rules for trade. These organizations were independent but dominated by the United States through the support of the powerful U.S. dollar. This economic system benefited all of the countries involved, but the chief benefits went to the United States.

The policies and actions that supported this hegemonic empire were followed by successive Democratic and Republican administrations after the Truman Doctrine was announced, and it received widespread bipartisan support by the American people. It was the Cold War and the need for defence that provided the original *raison d'être* for the American Empire. Today the empire is challenged on a number of fronts, but it remains the most powerful military and economic force in the world.

The American Military

The source of power of every empire is the power of the military. The American grand military strategy goes back to Pearl Harbor and the early days of the Second World War when the decision was made that the United States must have the strongest military force on the globe. After the war there was a brief period when the U.S. cut back on its military, but with the onset of the Cold War the United States embarked on a policy of constant military preparedness. In time this permanent war economy changed the very nature of the United States, its political, economic and social institutions and the role it plays in world affairs.

Until the Second World War the American military was an inefficient, rather clumsy instrument. Americans traditionally distrusted the military not only because it had to be supported by high taxes but because there was a fear that the military could be used against the people. In the First World War and the early days of the Second, Europeans were contemptuous of the poor quality of the American officers and the lack of discipline of the troops. But by the end of the Second World War the Americans had created a military with a strong officer corps, an understanding of the importance of discipline, training and good armaments and an appreciation of the sacrifices and hardships necessary for victory on the battlefield.

After the war there were many men and women who decided to make a career in the military. They had a vested interest in maintaining a high level of military spending because their careers – particularly the careers of the officers – depended on it. The Cold War provided the justification. The American military now had a clear mandate. They were to prepare for war against communism. Once the Korean War began in 1950 there was no need to invent a justification for the military build-up. Politicians could point to Communist aggression and the need to be prepared to confront it wherever and whenever it appeared.

But was the Soviet Union a real military threat? Now, some sixty years after the confrontation between east and west was forming, we still do not know.[2] Certainly the CIA, the American military and politicians in the United States and the Western Alliance constantly overstated the threat of the Soviets in order to justify high levels of military spending and the need to deploy new weapons.[3] In turn, the political rhetoric in the west, and the rapid growth in the size and power of the American military and weapons systems, generated fear among the Soviet leadership, leading to an increase in their military spending. A classic arms race had broken out. Fear led to an increase in armaments on one side, which in turn led to fear and an increase in armaments on the other side, which led to an increase on the other, and so it goes. But was this military build up necessary? Tim Weiner, in his book on the history of the CIA, relates this story:

> The man who eventually took control of the Soviet Union after [Stalin's] death, Nikita Khrushchev, recalled that Stalin "trembled" and "quivered" at the prospect of a global combat with America. "He was afraid of war," Khrushchev said. "Stalin never did anything to provoke a war with the United States. He knew his weakness."[4]

Perhaps the opportunity for peace between the Soviet Union and the United States existed as long ago as the late 1940s. We just don't know. What we do know is that a political competition and an arms race had emerged that would last for almost fifty years.[5]

American Military Strategy

By the end of the Korean War it was apparent that the U.S. had two different types of military strategies with two separate and distinct weapons systems. The conventional system was an extension of the capability of the army, navy and air force that had developed during the Second World War. The second strategy was one of all-out nuclear war.

In the Cold War the United States, the Soviet Union and their allies on both sides spent a large proportion of their military budgets on conventional armaments. It is estimated that during the Cold War the Americans spent $8 trillion on armaments, most of that on conventional weapons. There were huge expenditures in aircraft, ships, and various land based weapon systems. The lethal power carried by a well equipped combat soldier increased several times in the years after the Second World War.

Over the course of the Cold War the Americans developed a highly mobile army. In the Vietnam War helicopters became the preferred way for the military to move their troops about during combat. Over the years artillery played a less important role than it had in either the First or Second World Wars, replaced by lighter weapons carried by the infantry, mobile units of tanks and other armoured vehicles and a reliance on air power. The tactics in recent years have emphasized an even faster and more mobile force with precision bombing as the key to its offensive force.

In the nineteenth century the British had shown that command of the sea was vital for a world power, and as their ability to control the seas ended in the Second World War, this role was taken over by the Americans. During the Pacific campaign of the Second World War it was American sea power that led to victory. Only in the last days of the war, with the bombing campaign of Japanese cities, did air power come to play a major role in the campaign. In the Cold War the Americans continued their command of the seas by building fast ships

56

that carried an array of the most sophisticated technological equipment and both conventional and nuclear weapons. At the center of the navy battle group is the aircraft carrier, supported by battleships, cruisers and destroyers. Today the navy has eleven naval battle groups with eleven nuclear-powered aircraft carriers. Perhaps the most formidable vessels in the fleet are the nuclear submarines armed with nuclear missiles that can stay submerged for months at a time. The U.S. navy can launch attacks on coastal regions with various assault and amphibious vessels, and strike virtually anywhere in the globe with aircraft, rockets and guided missiles.

The Second World War demonstrated the importance of air power. Until 1947 the Air Force was part of the American Army. Even to this day the army operates a fleet of helicopters and other aircraft to support ground troops. The aircraft that operate out of aircraft carriers are part of the navy. The U.S. Air Force has a full range of the most sophisticated aircraft from fighter jets and long range strategic bombers to unmanned reconnaissance aircraft and cruise missiles. Today they operate a fleet of drone aircraft that can bomb enemy positions. These drones are flown by pilots half a world away, able to control the drones by watching images on monitors.

The second military strategy of the U.S. was the nuclear strike force. The United States was the first country to develop nuclear weapons and is the only country to use them in times of war. It was assumed that the Americans would hold the monopoly on these weapons for a long time because of the cost and sophistication of developing nuclear warheads, but in 1949 the Soviets surprised the Western Allies by detonating their first nuclear weapon. This sparked a frantic race for nuclear superiority. President Truman ordered a crash program, and in 1952 the Americans detonated their first hydrogen bomb. One year later the Soviets set off their own hydrogen bomb and in 1961 they exploded the so called Tsar bomb, the largest bomb ever detonated. Stockpiles of weapons were produced at a furious pace. By 1966 the United States had 32,000 nuclear warheads. Today that number has been reduced to 5,736 active nuclear warheads as a result of modernization of the weapons systems and disarmament agreements with the Soviets, but U.S. nuclear weapons are the most advanced and have the ability to obliterate the world several times over.

At first the Americans planned to deliver nuclear weapons with long range bombers. The problem was that the slow bombers could be shot down by enemy fighter aircraft. They also could not carry enough fuel to get deep into the Soviet Union and back again to the home bases. The answer was rocket technology, Inter Continental Ballistic Missiles (ICBMs), launched either from land based platforms, ships or nuclear submarines. These missiles could strike anywhere in the world.[6]

The fear of nuclear war had a very unsettling effect on people around the world. War has always led to feelings of powerlessness and alienation as armies killed and devastated territories and countries, but the possibility of nuclear Armageddon seemed truly horrific. In an instant, because of decisions made by a small number of remote political and military leaders, millions of people could be killed – or the entire human race exterminated. It was recognized that there is virtually no defence against incoming nuclear missiles.[7] The United States and the Soviet Union had embarked on the policy appropriately named MAD – Mutual Assured Destruction. MAD suggested that neither side could afford to unleash nuclear weapons because such an attack would lead to the destruction of both the attacker and the defender.[8]

Adapting the Military Strategy

There was some resistance to the militarization of both sides during the Cold War, particularly by people outside the United States. Speeches were given at the United Nations by leaders of non-aligned nations decrying the arms race and its enormous waste of resources and talent. Critics pointed to the period prior to the First World War as an example of how an arms race could lead to war. By the late 1950s opposition to the arms race and nuclear weapons in Britain grew into a huge peace movement called the "Campaign for Nuclear Disarmament" (CND). Many prominent academics, scientists and intellectuals of the day were involved in CND; the philosopher

Bertrand Russell is still identified as the leader of the movement although he was its head for only a short period of time.

Despite its broad support, the CND was hampered by its policy that all nuclear powers, and Britain in particular, should unilaterally dismantle their nuclear weapons regardless of the policies of other countries. At the height of the Cold War, when both the United States and the Soviet Union bristled with thousands of warheads and ICBMs, this was seen by most people and political leaders to be simply unrealistic.

During the 1950s, the Eisenhower administration relied on nuclear weapons as the first line of defence. By 1960 that view was challenged and President Kennedy and the presidents who followed began a massive rearmament program of conventional weapons based on the assumption that the wars of the future would be fought by armies on the ground. Since that time much of U.S. military spending has gone into the three armed services and the development and stockpiling of conventional weapons.

Another major development for the American military was the elimination of conscription in 1973. The anti-war protests of the Vietnam War were led by young men who were about to be conscripted into the army. That is why the anti-war movement was centered on American university campuses. As the war drew to a close, President Nixon announced the end of the draft. This was a very popular political move, but popularity was not the reason for Nixon's decision.

Military strategists had come to realize that a modern army did not need a huge number of military personnel. With the reliance on airpower, and the improved weapons carried by each soldier in the field, the United States could deliver a devastating concentration of fire power with a limited number of military personnel. Rather than numbers, what was necessary was to have a mobile, well armed and highly trained military force that could work in a coordinated way. Good communication, extensive training and a high level of morale and discipline: these were the necessary elements of a modern military. That was only possible in a full time army made up of volunteers.

At the end of the Second World War the United States built a number of military bases in occupied countries or close allies. The biggest of these bases were in Germany and Okinawa, Japan. These huge military establishments were used as staging bases close to places where attack was expected. Over the course of the Cold War the number of military bases expanded until they were located in every continent except Antarctica.

At the end of the Cold War it was expected that some of these overseas bases would close, but just the opposite happened. The National Security Report of 1990 said that overseas bases were needed to "project power into areas where we have no permanent presence."[9] The report points to the Middle East as a trouble spot that needed particular attention because it is a major source of oil. Since then the Americans have extended their overseas operations and today have over 730 permanent bases located in every part of the world and manned by about one million military personnel.

Chalmers Johnson describes these bases as garrisons or outposts of the American Empire. His book *Blowback* details how the American military and the servicemen who live on the bases have caused huge problems that have reflected very badly on the prestige of the United States, but these bases remain the key to the American strategy of imperial domination, and military leaders have no plans to close them.[10]

The Americans have built the strongest military force the world has ever seen. From the beginning of the Cold War to the present, they have used it to protect and expand their empire and challenge their enemies. They have done this in Korea (1950-53), Vietnam (1956-75), Grenada (1983), Panama (1989), Kuwait-Iraq (1991), Somalia (1992-94), Bosnia (1994-95), Haiti (1994), Kosovo (1999), Afghanistan (2001-present), and Iraq (2003-present).[11] At one time the Chinese taunted the Americans, calling them a "paper tiger," but that has never been the case. The Americans have always been prepared to use their military muscle to gain their political objectives.

The Military-Industrial Complex

On January 17, 1961 President Dwight D. Eisenhower made his farewell address to the nation. In that speech he warned against the growing power of the "military-industrial complex."[12] He pointed out that for the first time in America there was a confluence of interests between the military, which required armaments, industry, which wanted profits and needed money to research, design and manufacture the armaments, and the government, which would be paying for the armaments and the full costs of the military. Eisenhower warned that the concentrated power of these interests threatened the very democratic way of life of the United States.

Sociologists point out that this interlocking set of interests is reflected in the "circulation of elites." Top military personnel often take senior positions in companies that produce military hardware or provide services for the military after they retire.[13] In that way they bring insider knowledge and influence to the companies that employ them. The same is true of the political elite. For example, Dick Cheney was a Republican political aide in Washington early in his career, then a member of the House of Representatives, part of the White House staff under Nixon and Secretary of Defense under George H. W. Bush. In the Clinton years when the Republicans were out of office he became the Chairman and CEO of Halliburton Energy Services, a company that often worked under contract to the Defense Department. During his tenure he dramatically increased the company's government contracts and profitability. He then became U.S. Vice President under George W. Bush.[14] There are many other examples of individuals who moved between government, the military and the private sector at high levels.

In recent years the term military-industrial complex has fallen into disuse but the military continues to have a huge influence on the American economy and political system. Large geographical regions of the United States such as Southern California and Washington State are reliant on defence production. In some areas as much as 15% of the workforce is employed in defence industries and military related jobs.[15] With the economic multiplier effect, at least 50% of the economies of some regions of the United States are directly dependent on military spending. This has had a profound impact on the American political process. Congressional budget debates focus on defence appropriation as the politicians fight to maintain high levels of defence spending in their districts where jobs and the economic well being of their constituents depend on it. Deals are made and votes are brokered by members of Congress – "I'll vote for your appropriation if you vote for mine" – and all of this is justified under the broad concern of maintaining defence against foreign threats and building a strong military. For the politicians, however, spending on the military has more to do with getting them re-elected than meeting a military threat.

Military spending in the United States has become a vast program to redistribute money through the American economy. The government taxes the whole population and then spends the money on the military and armaments. This re-circulates wealth and helps the economy. Other developed countries redistribute wealth by spending tax revenue on social services, education and Medicare. Since the Second World War American politicians have "primed the pump" of the economy with military spending, and as a consequence the United States has developed a permanent war economy that is difficult to end or even challenge.

This is how Paul Koistinen, who has written on the militarization of the United States, explains the impact of military spending on American politics and society:

> Once military spending began to escalate rapidly from 1950 onwards, the nation simply lacked the policies, the institutional structures, the traditions and the experience for controlling its war machine. The voice of the armed services would grow in the formulation of foreign policy. The military's influence would become pervasive throughout society and various industries, whole communities and entire regions would become economically dependent upon military spending for their prosperity, even their existence. Once that occurred, America would become a warfare state.[16]

In 2011 the official Pentagon budget is projected to be $708 billion. When other defence-related costs are added in it is estimated that the true defence costs to the American taxpayers will be close to $1 trillion. This is more than the entire rest of the world spends on defence. Recently Robert Gates, Secretary of Defense in the Obama administration, called for a closer partnership with the companies in the armament industries. He pledged "to work with the White House to secure steady growth in the Pentagon's budgets over time."[17]

The permanent war economy has militarized and fundamentally reshaped the United States since the Second World War. The defence establishment is now at the absolute heart of the economy, politics and the American way of life.

The Economic Empire

Some Americans claim that their role as leader of the Western Alliance costs them money and this is proof that they are a benevolent power not an empire. There is a grain of truth in this. When American military expenses are added to other foreign costs they total over 40% of the U.S. federal budget, but this is hardly the whole story.[18] Since the end of the Second World War the economic well being of large American companies and thus the health of the American economy has been dependent on the international economic system, and that economic system is supported and sustained by American political and military power.

A new economic world order emerged after the Second World War, just as the Americans were assuming leadership. Prior to the war the economic policy of the United States, followed by administration after administration, was to isolate and protect the U.S. market by keeping out imports with high tariffs and other taxes against imports. The tariff on most goods in this period was about 40%, and in some instances even higher.

After the First World War most developed countries tried to recover from the economic devastation of the war by protecting their markets with high tariffs. Even Britain, which had advocated free trade in the nineteenth century, became protectionist. Smaller countries often conspired to keep the value of their currencies low to encourage exports and discourage imports. The sum total of the effect of these protectionist policies was to discourage international trade.[19] By the time of the Second World War a consensus had emerged that these restrictions on international trade had played an important role in causing the Great Depression of the 1930s which was a chief contributing cause of the war. Roosevelt, Churchill and other leaders wanted to encourage trade in the hopes that this would lead to co-operation between nations, increase prosperity and lessen the chance of war.

It was at the Bretton Woods Conference of 1944 where the foundation of the new economic system was put in place. After the war protectionism was reduced and this stimulated trade. The U.S. tariffs, for example, have been lowered from about 40% in 1945 to about 4% today and similar reductions have occurred in other countries. Between 1948 and 2006 international trade in merchandise expanded from $124 billion to $12 trillion a year.[20] GATT (General Agreement on Tariffs and Trade) was so successful that in 1994 the World Trade Organization (WTO) was set up with the official status of an international organization. Today the WTO has 153 member states. It focuses on international agreements in the areas of trade in goods, intellectual property, telecommunications, banking and investment, transportation, education, health and the environment.

Financial markets have also become truly international. The stocks of large companies are often listed on stock markets around the world. Americans can buy shares in Korean companies; South Americans can buy European government bonds and Russian steel producers can purchase steel companies in the United States and Canada. Individuals and companies can even speculate on foreign currencies. There are still some restrictions on the flow of money, and some countries have regulations on foreign ownership of their companies, but financial markets are much freer than at any time in our history and for that reason when there is a shock to the system, like the U.S. sub-prime mortgage crisis of 2007-08 and the stock market crash in 2008, it affects the entire world.

One problem with the Bretton Woods agreement was the use of the gold standard. With the American expansion abroad and particularly the costs of the Vietnam War, the United States found it difficult to maintain the gold standard and in 1971 President Richard Nixon took the U.S. off the gold standard. Since that time the international currency has been the U.S. dollar and countries hold their reserves in U.S. dollars. They do this to pay for imports but the real reason is to have dollars in reserve when there is a run on their currency.

This "dollar hegemony," as it is called,[21] has been of tremendous advantage to the United States because the reserves of U.S. dollars held by other countries, have kept the dollar high. This overvalues the American economy and makes imports inexpensive for Americans. It also makes it much more affordable for U.S. owned and financed corporations to expand abroad. As an added bonus it has meant that the U.S. military can operate in foreign countries with less cost. This is how one expert explained it:

> World trade is now a game in which the US produces dollars and the rest of the world produces things that dollars can buy. The world's interlinked economies no longer trade to capture a comparative advantage; they compete in exports to capture needed dollars to service dollar-denominated foreign debts and to accumulate dollar reserves to sustain the exchange value of their domestic currencies.... This creates a built-in support for a strong dollar that in turn forces the world's central banks to acquire and hold more dollar reserves, making it stronger.[22]

An economic system of low tariffs, increased international trade, free financial markets and relatively stable currencies linked to the U.S. dollar became the basis of the international economic system after the Second World War. In recent years these economic changes along with the revolution in telecommunications, mass media, the Internet, an increase in travel and migration and other social changes have changed the world in such a profound way that a new name has been given to it, globalization. [23]

Multi-national corporations have been the chief beneficiaries of globalization. Today it is estimated that there are more than 60,000 multi-national corporations operating in two or more countries. The multi-nationals are headquartered around the world and their ownership is widely dispersed. They produce about 25% of the global economic output; the top 100 multi-nationals control 16% of the world's productive assets. The multi-nationals employ more than 86 million people, 19 million of them in the developing world. All of these jobs tend to pay more than others in the same country. These companies hold the key to the edifice of the international economic system, and the stock market is the portal through which we evaluate the success and failures of individual companies.

The continued wealth of the United States, Europe and other countries in the developed world is dependent on the success of multi-national corporations, and supporting these corporations and the international system of trade is the core concern of the American Empire. Just as the British, in the heyday of their empire, designed laws and regulations so that their merchants and industrialists could reap the benefits of their colonies, and used the British Navy to ensure the freedom of the seas, so the Americans use their power to ensure that a framework of international laws and treaties are in place to allow the multi-nationals to continue to exploit their markets and use their military to protect and enhance their economic interests. This is how *New York Times* political columnist Thomas L. Friedman expresses it.

> The hidden hand of the market will never work without a hidden fist – McDonald's cannot flourish without McDonnell Douglas, the builder of the F-15. And the hidden fist that keeps the world safe for Silicon Valley's technologies is called the United States Army, Air Force, Navy and Marine Corps. [24]

Another way that the Americans have used their power to promote their economic policies abroad has been through the International

Monetary Fund and the World Bank. These institutions have been set up to assist developing and underdeveloped countries in times of need, such as a run on their currencies or loans of last resort. Both the IMF and the World Bank are controlled by the Americans and the price they extract for providing assistance is that the countries must follow U.S. demands, such as reducing government expenditures, balancing their budgets and opening their markets for trade.

An example of how the American Empire operates is to be found in the crisis in the Middle East. The United States, Japan and their closest allies in Europe must import oil to fuel their cars and trucks and to run their industries. At one time the U.S. produced all of the oil it consumed. By 1972 the U.S. was importing 28% of the oil it consumed, today it imports 55% and by 2025 it will import 70%. In 2005 the United States imported 3.7 billion barrels a year; Europe imported 2.8 billion barrels, and Japan 1.9 billion barrels.

The high standard of living in the United States is dependent on cheap oil and gas for the transport of goods, the production of electricity and the mobility of the population. Eighty-eight percent of the U.S. workforce travels to work by car,[25] much higher than any other country in the world. The majority of Americans live in low density communities or small towns and suburbs and people in these communities are car dependent. In Europe there has been a realization that they must move away from oil dependency, and the Europeans are building extensive systems of public transit, high speed trains and experimenting with alternative types of energy. This may change with Barack Obama's leadership, but until now there is little investment such as this in the United States.

The only source of oil that can meet this ravenous demand is the Middle East. But Middle Eastern countries have been politically unstable in recent years because of the rise of Muslim fundamentalism and political agitation against conservative regimes. The invasion of Iraq in 2003, a country with the second largest oil reserves in the world, was explained as an effort to eliminate the Iraqi program of weapons of mass destruction and to bring peace, stability and democracy to the region. Cutting away the political rhetoric, the real reason the Americans invaded Iraq was to bring stability to the region so that the multi-nationals could gain access to the oil reserves.

Until the end of the Cold War some countries were able to stay outside the international economic system, but that is no longer possible. Developing countries need private investment and trade to improve the living standards of their people and today there is no alternative but to participate in the international economic system. Even China, a country that in theory still is communist, is a member of the WTO. Cuba, the only country that continues in its opposition, has paid a heavy economic price for its independence.

Globalization now affects everyone from the presidents of the largest multi-nationals to the workers on the plant floor, and from poor farmers who grow coffee beans in Central America to Indian information technology workers. The growth of the multi-nationals has shifted wealth away from small enterprises to the large corporations with the financial resources and marketing power to deliver products on a world scale. In the process the large corporations have grown wealthy because they can dominate the market and set prices at a profitable level. Small companies and individuals are forced to work in areas that have a much higher risk of failure and are not as well compensated. Globalization and the liberalization of trade have done much to improve living standards around the world, but the primary beneficiaries have been the multi-national corporations.

The Political Empire

Some believe that the Americans had a grand plan to establish global domination after the end of the Second World War, but there is little evidence to support that view. After the declaration of the Truman Doctrine they assumed leadership in a rather clumsy way, but the American political system quickly adapted to this new challenge.

The United States had a decentralized form of government including state governments, the House of Representatives, the Senate and the President competing for power and influence, but that has changed. The crisis of the Second World War led to the strengthening of Washington, and many administrative functions were centralized and put under the control of the President. Not only is the President responsible for establishing foreign policy, he is also the "Commander in Chief" of the military. In his hands is concentrated more political and military power than any emperor of the past.

This concentration of power in one person gives a great advantage to the American imperial project. The European Union and its president, by contrast, has little influence on world affairs because most of the important international decisions in Europe are made by member states, not the EU. The General Secretary of the United Nations is handicapped by the conflicting and uncoordinated interest of the members of the Security Council. An American President, on the other hand, can make a decision on a military issue and action can be initiated immediately.

The power of the President is also strengthened because elected politicians regularly give the President's foreign policy almost universal, non-partisan support. The Gulf of Tonkin Resolution, which President Lyndon Johnson used to expand the Vietnam War, was passed by the U.S. Senate with only two opposing votes. The resolution to authorize the invasion of Iraq in 2002 was passed in the Senate by a vote of 77 to 23 and in the House of Representatives with only three dissenting votes, despite the fact that the invasion was widely opposed by American allies and was a violation of international law because it did not have the support of the U.N. Security Council.

This concentration of power is supported by the secret nature of decision-making in foreign affairs. The President directs the activities of the CIA, and approves every major initiative, but the activities of the intelligence agency are never revealed. Secret briefings are available to the President at any time. The United States is a huge country with a population of over 300 million people, yet the number of people actively interested and involved in international issues is very small. Foreign policy has become the preserve of the experts and the political elite, isolated from the people. This stops ordinary citizens from participating in foreign issues, and because there is no effective civilian oversight the President gains added power.

The American leadership of the western nations was made much easier by the situation in Western Europe and the Far East. After the

Second World War the Europeans witnessed first hand the division between the communist and non-communist worlds. Many were frightened of the possibility of Soviet invasion and occupation, but they had no appetite for war because they were exhausted by the struggles of the Second World War. They were only too happy to rely on the deterrence of the American military. A similar situation existed in the Far East. The Korean War illustrated that some communist countries were willing to use force to dominate others; only the Americans had the military power and political determination to resist.

As the undisputed leader of the Western Alliance, the Americans deepened and strengthened their relationships with their allies. NATO was formed in 1949 and the Southeast Asia Treaty Organization (SEATO) in 1954. These were to be the primary alliances against communist expansion. SEATO was always a weak alliance and with the political divisions that arose during the Vietnam War it became weaker. Finally in 1977 it was disbanded. Both Japan and West Germany were outside these alliances because they were not allowed to rearm after the Second World War, but they were still close political allies of the United States and provided important military bases for the Americans.

Even with the broad consensus that communism must be confronted, opposition to the policies of the United States grew during the Cold War. Once the Cold War was over it became more difficult to maintain political support for American foreign policy. The Soviet Union was "defeated" in the American understanding of the struggle, and the policy objective of opposing communism was finished. If the Americans were to continue with their political dominance, they had to adopt a new set of foreign policy objectives. In time these objectives came to be defined as supporting the "strategic interests" of the United States that were vital to the functioning of the western alliance.

Only one overarching strategic interest could meet that goal and unify the alliance: oil. Access to oil is absolutely vital to all the developed countries, but particularly the United States, and that has been the prime motivating factor in determining American foreign policy since the end of the Cold War. The United States government claims it is fighting a "War on Terror" but in fact these wars are motivated more by the need for access to oil than the effort to hunt down a group of terrorists centered in the remote tribal areas of Pakistan.

The Media

During the twentieth century governments came to realize the importance of propaganda in keeping public support for their policies. Maintaining support for war is perhaps their greatest challenge. Early in the First World War the British mobilized their population by claiming that the Germans had slaughtered Belgian women and children, even cutting off the arms of babies. These claims were wild exaggerations, but that did not seem to matter. Public support for the British war effort soared. During the Second World War propaganda became a major component of the war effort. The Nazis pushed propaganda to the ultimate by simply telling outright lies in order to maintain public support.

The Americans have been involved in propaganda for at least as long as the Europeans. Popular support for the Spanish-American War in the United States was created by the sensational reporting of the Hearst Newspaper chain. During the First World War the American news coverage of the sinking of the *Lusitania* by a German submarine contributed more than any other event to the American entry into the war. The American government hardly needed to use propaganda in the Second World War. The United States had been attacked by the Japanese and the Germans declared war against the U.S., but once the war was underway the Americans produced dozens of films supporting the war effort and gave front line access to reporters. Roosevelt was a master in the use of radio with his fireside chats. He spoke of the "four freedoms" that he said Americans were fighting for. Journalists reporting from the front gave a sense of the hardships and sacrifices of those "fighting for freedom," and that boosted support for the war.

With the onset of the Cold War the government's message became much more complicated, but with the media's help the American public soon came to accept the claim that communists were fanatics and the Soviet Union and the People's Republic of China were bent on

71

world domination. During the Korean War the North Koreans and Chinese were "gooks," "reds" and "commies." There were radio programs with such titles as "I was a Communist for the FBI," and films such as "Red Nightmare: the Commies are Coming." The media talked about the possibility of a sneak Soviet nuclear attack. In the 1950s the "Red Scare," the fear of communists infiltrating American institutions, was widespread.[26]

Most news outlets and reporters brag of their independence, but it is difficult to get stories about complicated issues in countries remote from the United States. In many instances journalists had to depend on government sources for information, leaving the media very susceptible to manipulation.[27] It was difficult to verify claims, and rarely did reporters have the resources to investigate. They accepted government statements at face value and reported them as fact in their news outlets.

The Vietnam War began to change this co-operative arrangement between the media and the government. In August 1964 President Johnson claimed that two North Vietnamese warships had attacked American destroyers in the Gulf of Tonkin. This incident persuaded Congress to pass a resolution giving Johnson legal justification to escalate the war. Later it was found out that the incident had been provoked by the Americans and that Johnson had used it to manipulate the U.S. Congress into giving him *carte blanche* in the war. Stories came out in the press that indicated that the American government was willing to distort the truth to manipulate the political process.

But it was not the Gulf of Tonkin incident that turned Americans against the war. The daily television diet of news from Vietnam brought the war "into the living rooms of the nation." The reporting was as accurate as could be expected under wartime conditions, and told from the point of view of the American troops, but the stories underlined the inconclusive nature of the war and led millions of people to understand that the war could not be won and the sacrifices of "American boys" were pointless. Every time there was a prediction by an American general or politician that there was "light at the end of the tunnel,"[28] it seemed that there was another attack by the Viet Cong leaving scores of dead. Gradually Americans came to understand that they could not win the war.

In the attempt to find blame for the defeat, Americans pointed their fingers at things such as the counter culture but at the top of the list was the media. It was said that the war coverage had undermined the determination of the American people, which led to widespread protests and the loss of support for the war. This "blaming the messenger" was hardly fair but that did not matter. The media was to blame, in the eyes of many, and some were determined to correct the problem.

Almost immediately after the end of the Vietnam War there was a dramatic example of the power of the press; this time that power was not exaggerated. In the Watergate Scandal Bob Woodward and Carl Bernstein revealed that a minor burglary at the Democratic National Committee headquarters on June 17, 1972 reached into the highest levels of the administration. In time reporters were able to show that the Nixon administration was involved in a host of "dirty tricks" that included campaign fraud, sabotage, illegal break-ins, improper tax audits, laundered money and illegal wire tapping. Ultimately the story so discredited Richard Nixon that he was forced to resign. This was unprecedented in American history.

These events made it very clear that the media was not just another business. It had the power to shape public attitudes, influence public policy and affect political events. By the mid 1970s various conservative groups in the United States had come to the conclusion that the power of the media had to be curtailed. Right-wing watchdog groups were set up to harass journalists, editors and publishers and promote conservative causes. These groups include the American Legal Foundation, the Media Institute, the Center for Media and Public Affairs and Accuracy in Media (AIM).

The owners of media outlets began to assert their control. In most instances they were large corporations who had the same interests as the multinationals and the political elites that govern the country. In time more conservative newspaper publishers and editors were put in place. Investigative journalism almost disappeared from the pages of newspapers and on television. Crusading reporters were shuffled off the scene or not given time to do the research for their stories. Right wing commentators were given space on newspaper op-ed pages. Television news turned into a form of entertainment. Celebrity culture – the focus on media stars and the rich and famous – replaced the hard hitting journalism that sought the story behind the news. All of this was justified by saying that these are the stories the people wanted, but the role of the independent voice of the media that demanded accountability and understanding was largely ignored.

Gradually by the 1980s the American media was defanged by these efforts. President Ronald Reagan, the "great communicator" as he was called, made the American public feel good about the country while the American Empire continued to operate in every corner of the globe. In time the American press became a shadow of its former self. This finally climaxed in the greatest failure of the American media in our age – the run up to the Iraq War, when the American media, including the most respected news outlets in the country like the *New York Times* and the *Washington Post*, accepted untruthful statements of political leaders at face value and gave credence to statements that were simply lies. This led to the acceptance of the claim that the Saddam Iraq regime had weapons of mass destruction; after the invasion that was shown to be untrue. Even the actual coverage of the war was done by reporters who were "embedded" in American combat units, hardly a practice that allows for hard hitting, objective reporting during wartime.

Later there was much soul searching by members of the media that they had done so little to challenge the claims of the administration. On May 28, 2004 the *New York Times,* the most influential newspaper in the United States, published an apology in which they criticized the quality of their reporting.

> In some cases, information that was controversial then, and seems questionable now, was insufficiently qualified or allowed to stand unchallenged. Looking back, we wish we had been more aggressive in re-examining the claims as new evidence emerged or failed to emerge.[29]

But the failure of the *New York Times* pales in comparison to news outlets like Fox Television. The commentators at Fox were cheerleaders for the Iraq War and uncritically repeated the claims of Washington neo-conservatives. Those who disagreed with their point of view were accused of being unpatriotic and belittled by political commentators. Fox had become little more than a propaganda unit calling for war, like the Hearst newspapers in the Spanish American War. Much of the American media had lost its objectivity and uncritically supported the government.

Political, Economic and Military Elements of Empire

Like every empire that has gone before, the American Empire uses its military strength to achieve its political and economic objectives. Because the United States is a democracy, with an open political system, the assumption of most Americans is that their government operates in the best interests of everyone. They are often dismayed that large numbers of people outside the U.S. oppose their government's policies and actions because they assume that America's interests are everyone's interests.

The reality is that many people outside the United States have a clear understanding of American foreign policy because they see at close hand the activities of such agencies as the CIA and the American military. They understand that U.S. foreign policy is dictated by American self-interest; it is never benign and rarely humanitarian. The history of the American Empire in action clearly illustrates this point.

75

CHAPTER 4: THE EMPIRE IN ACTION

If you have a hammer in your hand, goes a popular American saying, everything looks like a nail. If you have a superb military, then why not use it as a hammer to gain your political objectives? That is the *modus operandi* of empires. The United States has often used this approach since assuming world leadership after the Second World War. In fact they have had different types of hammers and they have used them in a variety of ways. Sometimes this has been to their advantage, but often it has been to the detriment of their political objectives and their prestige abroad.

Containment

In the years after the end of World War II, the political landscape of the globe polarized. In the east the Soviet Union and its East European allies along with China established communist economies and systems and government. In the west the United States emerged as the leader of independent and semi-independent, capitalist countries in Western Europe and the developing world. A number of countries tried to stay out of this super-power conflict by establishing the Non-Aligned Movement in 1955.[1] This movement was led by India and included countries in the developing world, but inevitably most countries were drawn towards one side or the other of the Cold War. The prospect for peace seemed dismal. With the Truman Doctrine a line had been drawn in the sand. Aggression would not be committed against communist countries, but if any nation in the so called "free world" was attacked by communists they would be defended by the Americans and their allies. This policy came to be called "Containment."

The long drawn out Cold War had begun. Much of the conflict was expressed in ideological terms by propaganda machines on both sides of the divide. The communists claimed that the capitalist societies were dominated by a ruling class of capitalists bent on exploitation of workers, women and minorities, while the Americans hurled insults at

76

the communists, calling them undemocratic, totalitarian, state-dominated societies where citizens had no civil rights. There was truth in both of these accusations, but they were often distorted beyond recognition for political purposes and with tragic results. In the United States Senator Joseph McCarthy hunted former communists and "fellow travelers" resulting in the persecution of many and the imprisonment of some. In the Soviet Union a similar form of fear and paranoia resulted in many dissidents and innocents losing their lives or spending years in the Soviet gulag.

But the Cold War was much more than an ideological struggle. It led to a number of hot wars that tested the determination of both sides of the conflict. These wars were a test of will, created and shaped by the policy of containment.

Korea, Cuba and Vietnam

War and threats of war dominated the political life of this period. In June of 1950 the Cold War suddenly turned hot when North Korea invaded South Korea in an attempt to unify the country by force. It soon turned into a confrontation between communism and the so-called "free world." Korea was the first test of the policy of containment.

When the invasion occurred the Soviet Union was boycotting the United Nations. The Americans seized this opportunity and a U.N. resolution was passed sanctioning military force against the invaders. The U.N. military effort was led by the Americans but many allies joined the effort including the British, French, Canadians and Australians. In the initial invasion the North Koreans pushed the South Koreans to the very southern tip of the peninsula and they seemed about to be defeated. Once the U.N. forces joined in the war the North Koreans were overwhelmed and pushed back to the Korean/Chinese border. The Chinese, feeling threatened, joined with the North Koreans and, in some of the bloodiest fighting of the war, pushed the U.N. forces back to the 38th parallel, the original border between North and South.

Fighting in the Korean War was more like fighting in the Second World War than in any of the wars that have followed. Large, land based armies confronted each other and fought to gain or hold territory. The position of the front, the place where the two armies confronted each other, indicated the progress of the war. Air supremacy was key to victory on the battlefield. The North Koreans and Chinese had overwhelming superiority of manpower, but they were stopped by the bombing raids of Sabre jets, the latest American military aircraft. The war ended in a stalemate with the signing of an armistice agreement in July 1953, but not before there were more than 5 million casualties.[2]

To the Americans the Korean War was a major success of the policy of containment. There was real concern that the war would escalate into a conflict between the two superpowers, but that did not happen. The Americans had overwhelming nuclear superiority at this time, but the Soviet Union also had nuclear weapons. General MacArthur, the U.S. general in charge of the operation in the early stages of the war, wanted to use the American nuclear arsenal, but President Truman was opposed because of the fear that the resulting nuclear exchange would devastate the entire globe. The war was extremely destructive to the Korean people, but it remained limited to the Korean Peninsula. The strategy of a limited war had been born.

Perhaps the greatest threat to peace during the Cold War was the "Cuban Missile Crisis." In 1959 Fidel Castro led a revolution, overthrowing the Batista regime. The Americans were concerned that this was a communist regime and helped Cuban expatriates trained by the CIA to launch the Bay of Pigs invasion in April 1961. This attempted military takeover of the country was a disaster for the Americans. Castro, fearing more American attacks, made an alliance with the Soviet Union and Khrushchev secretly agreed to put missiles on Cuban soil that could strike into the United States.

In October 1962 the United States discovered the missile locations and demanded that they be dismantled. This sparked the fourteen days of intense negotiations, with fears that it could escalate into all-out war at any moment. The Cuban Missile Crisis finally ended when Nikita Khrushchev announced that the missiles would be removed. In those tense days it seemed very likely that the policy of containment was finished and the Cold War would suddenly become very hot, but again the Americans prevailed and they concluded that the policy had been a success.

While the Korean War was concluding another conflict in the Far East was also coming to an end, the First Indochina War. Vietnam had been a French colony, and when the Japanese occupied the country in the Second World War, many French stayed on as administrators. With the surrender of the Japanese, Ho Chi Minh, the Vietnamese nationalist leader, declared independence. The French, with the help of the Americans, reasserted their control and the Viet Minh, the followers of Ho Chi Minh, fled into the mountains and began an insurgency.

At first the insurgency was a guerrilla war of attrition against the French, but with the victory of the communists in China the Viet Minh received better weapons from the Chinese and the Soviet Union and the war intensified. The Americans saw the war in Vietnam as another attempt at communist expansion. They increased their support of the French until they were paying 80% of the French war effort. But it was to no avail. In May 1954 the French were defeated in the battle of Dien Bien Phu. The Geneva Accords signed later that year ended the conflict, the French left and Vietnam was partitioned. In the north a communist government was installed, led by Ho Chi Minh, and a U.S. backed regime took power in the south.

The new leader who took power in the south was a fiercely anti-communist Catholic, Ngo Dinh Diem. The Geneva Accord called for elections on the issue of reunification but Diem refused to hold them. President Eisenhower later justified this by saying that if there were elections 80% would have voted for Ho Chi Minh.[3] In response a low level insurgency in the south was begun by the Viet Cong in 1957.

The North Vietnamese and Viet Cong saw this new war as a struggle to reunite the country and rid Vietnam of foreign domination. In the view of Ho Chi Minh, this was a war of independence like many other nationalist struggles against colonialism that had gone on in the past, including the American War of Independence. The Americans saw it in Cold War terms. In their view the war was part of a communist attempt to gain world domination, and must be resisted and contained. If Vietnam fell to the communists, then Cambodia, Laos, and ultimately all of South East Asia would fall "like dominos."

Gradually the Americans were drawn into the war in support of the South Vietnamese. They sent military advisors in 1962, but the insurgency grew stronger and more American military personnel were sent to help. After the Gulf of Tonkin incident the American strength increased to 500,000 troops; soon they were playing the major combat role in the war.

The difficulty for the Americans was that the nature of war in Vietnam was different than any that they had fought before. The First and Second World Wars and Korea involved large armies on both sides who confronted each other with conventional tactics of attack and defence. The Vietnam War was fought by the Viet Cong, and the Viet Minh from the north who joined them using guerrilla warfare tactics. Guerrilla fighters merged with the people in the countryside and would attack only when they knew they had the advantage. The guerrillas were a mobile force that carried light weapons. They would hit the enemy in carefully planned ambushes and then merge into the countryside before their enemy could recover. Usually the guerrillas would avoid large scale conventional battles because they knew the Americans and South Vietnamese were much better equipped and could call in air strikes for support.

The Americans were at a huge disadvantage in this type of warfare. They did not know the countryside, the language of the people, their history or culture. American troops found it almost impossible to determine who was a friend or foe. Despite their huge advantage in weapons, patrolling troops or air strikes often killed innocent people. Soon the South Vietnamese people, particularly those living in the countryside, distrusted and feared the Americans even more than they feared the Viet Cong.

The Americans changed their tactics by aggressively combing the countryside in an attempt to flush out the guerrillas but usually the enemy eluded them. North Vietnam was bombed in the hopes of ruining the infrastructure of the country so they could not pursue the war, but the North Vietnamese moved their war production into the countryside and increased their war efforts. In the south the Americans bombed suspected enemy-held territory. Defoliants were used to strip the leaves off trees so Viet Cong and Viet Minh infiltrators could be spotted from the air, but the chemicals poisoned the countryside and destroyed the crops of South Vietnamese peasants. The Viet Cong were everywhere. A number of fortified hamlets, set up by the Americans to give protection to peasants, came to be controlled by the Viet Cong guerrillas that used them as places of supply and rest.

As the Americans and South Vietnamese army escalated the war, more and more of the South Vietnamese population became alienated. Many Americans knew their tactics were not working but did not know what to do about it. U S. President Lyndon Johnson spoke about the importance of winning the "hearts and minds" of the South Vietnamese people, but American military tactics only drove them into the camp of the Viet Cong. A war of attrition had emerged and the longer it lasted the greater the advantage of the Viet Cong.

In the early stages of the war American leaders like General Westmoreland said things were getting better and predicted victory, but to the American public just the opposite seemed to be happening, as casualties mounted. In 1968 the Viet Cong launched the Tet Offensive with a co-ordinated series of surprise attacks on over 100 cities and towns. The offensive went on for two months before it was beaten back. Again the American generals claimed victory and pointed to the heavy losses of the enemy, but now even the U.S. political leaders were beginning to understand that they were engaged in an unwinnable war. In the Tet Offensive the Viet Cong lost many of their best soldiers, but they were able to replace them with trained forces from the north and recruits from the south. Their morale remained high.

Opposition to the war mounted in the United States. There were enormous demonstrations against the war in Washington and virtually every city and university campus across the country. The United States had become polarized. The American people are very patriotic and wanted to support their government and the soldiers who were risking their lives for their country, but as the war went on many came to understand that it could never be won, while others were deeply disturbed about the moral issues of the war. No other war in American history has polarized the public like the Vietnam War.

Richard Nixon was elected president of the United States in 1968 on the promise that he would bring "peace with honor," but he achieved neither in Vietnam. Casualties increased and opposition to the war mounted. The nightly newscasts gave reports of the number of American dead and the "body count" of the enemy as if somehow this was an indication of how the war was progressing. All it did was serve as a daily grim reminder of the hopelessness of the war. By the early 1970s most Americans wanted out of the war no matter what the cost. Finally the Paris Peace Accords were signed in January 27, 1973 and the agony came to an end. In March 1975 the communists overran the south, Saigon fell and the war was finally over. Over 58,000 Americans had been killed in the Vietnam War and 150,000 wounded, but the casualties for the Vietnamese were much worse: over 250,000 South Vietnamese and 600,000 North Vietnamese were killed in the conflict.

In the United States the mythology has developed that the Americans could have won the Vietnam War except for the opposition at home. This is simply not true. The reality is that the Americans, with the most modern and best equipped army in the world, had been defeated in the field by a determined and well organized insurgency. That was the painful lesson learned in Vietnam.

Secret Wars of the CIA

While the United States fought hot wars in Korea and Vietnam, secret clandestine wars were being fought by Americans in other parts of the globe. The Central Intelligence Agency (CIA) conducted these wars. The CIA is a branch of the American government with thousands of employees and a budget of billions of dollars in direct appropriations and more money channelled indirectly through the State Department and the military. But for much of its history the CIA has been beyond the control of Congress or the American President. Their specific terms of reference are to operate only in countries outside the United States.

Almost every country has secret or semi-secret agencies that gather intelligence about their friends as well as their enemies and keep track of individuals or groups that might be plotting violence. Some do not like it, but most feel that intelligence-gathering is a legitimate role of government, designed to protect citizens and provide political leaders with the information they need to conduct the country's affairs and protect it from its enemies. But the CIA went well beyond the role of collecting information. It supported covert operations to subvert and overthrow unfriendly governments. All of this was done under the guise of stopping the spread of communism and protecting the "free world."[4]

The agency was involved in propaganda efforts in several ways, funnelling money to anti-communist magazines and newspapers, funding Voice of America radio programs which beamed propaganda into Eastern Europe, providing funds to right-wing political parties during elections, paying bribes to politicians, infiltrating student organizations and the peace movement abroad, funding right-wing trade unions, supplying weapons to groups opposed to communism, committing acts of sabotage or other types of violence, and supporting a long list of right-wing dictators who terrorized their own populations. The CIA for most of its history supported anti-democratic movements around the world as long as they were anti-communist. These operations conflicted with deeply held American values of democracy, freedom of expression and the self-determination of people.

Although they had money, power and influence, more often than not the CIA botched operations and created problems for the United States. Rarely did agents speak the language of the countries that they operated in, and often they were ignorant of the country's history, religion and culture.[5] They failed to understand that socialism to most people outside the United States meant little more than support for state intervention in the economy, or social democracy not communism. The sole criterion they used to judge groups and individuals was whether or not they were anti-communist. For much of its history the promotion of democratic and human rights was unimportant to the CIA even though they supposedly were on the front line in the defence of the "free world" and democracy. Their level of incompetence and poor judgment is staggering.

Not long after the start of the Cold War, the CIA recruited hundreds of Ukrainians in Western Europe who had been displaced from their homeland. The CIA trained these recruits in sabotage and parachuted them into Ukraine in the hopes that they would disrupt the economy and foment revolution, only to see every one of them arrested and either sent to the gulag or executed. Somehow it never occurred to the agency that a mole might be giving information about their operations to the Soviet KGB.[6] Similar operations met the same fate in North Korea and Communist China and again hundreds of agents met death by firing squad.

The complete lack of CIA agents in the Soviet Union and Communist China, their avowed enemies during the Cold War, was perhaps the greatest failure of the intelligence agency. Tim Weiner, in *Legacy of Ashes*, claims that in total the CIA only recruited three Soviet agents in the entire history of the Cold War and one they held illegally in prison for three years because they believed, incorrectly, that he was a double agent. Throughout the Cold War the CIA could not make any accurate estimate of the Soviet military strength, and had no idea of the Soviet leaders' thinking. They did not predict the Soviet invasions of Hungary in 1956, Czechoslovakia in 1968 or Afghanistan in 1979, and they were taken by complete surprise by the collapse of the Soviet Union in 1990. The only reliable information they received came from the intelligence agencies of their allies, the British and Israelis, and the use of satellites. At least with satellite pictures CIA agents could see tanks, aircraft and missiles and could count the number on the ground.

But as distressing as these failures of the CIA must have been to the American leadership, a much greater failure, with graver political consequences, was their covert operations in countries of the developing world. Here the Soviet Union competed with the United States for political influence. Both sides recognized that this was a vital battleground of the Cold War. The Soviets would support left wing groups that were either communist or were sympathetic to the communists, and the Americans supported right wing, anti-communist groups. The difficulty for the CIA was that they often could not tell the difference between political leaders who were anti-communist and those who only wanted to use American power and money to impose their rule on defenceless people. The list of bungled operations and doubtful political alliances is long.

After the end of the Second World War a series of wars of independence broke out against European colonial powers in countries like Indonesia, Vietnam, Malaya, Algeria and Kenya. Rather than speaking out against colonialism, the United States helped the European colonial powers by providing them with aid, armaments and support. This was done despite America's own historical struggle against Britain in the War of Independence. This alliance with colonial powers embittered many of the new leaders of the developing world and made them distrustful of the Americans.

In 1953 the CIA mounted a covert operation to destabilize the democratically elected Iranian government of Dr. Mohammad Mossadegh because he had nationalized the Anglo-Iranian Oil Company. The CIA felt this was a sign of communism and mounted an operation to overthrow the Iranian government which was run out of the American Embassy. The CIA supported Mohammad Reza Pahlavi, the former Shah. Soon there were riots and military support for the Shah, paid for by CIA money. In the coup Dr. Mossadegh was placed in jail, charged with treason and the Shah installed in power. At the time the CIA hailed this covert operation as a great success, but the Shah went on to institute a one-party state supported by the secret police that engaged in torture and atrocities that was hated by millions. The role the Americans played in the 1953 coup is still remembered by Iranians. It played an important part in the 1979 revolution and the vitriolic anti-American feelings that continue in Iran to this day.

The Cuban Revolution was perhaps the most dramatic of the CIA failures. When Castro seized power in 1958 the CIA hardly knew his politics. At first there was sympathy for the new regime, but that soon changed when businesses were nationalized and freedoms restricted. The CIA, following the directions of the American president,[7] organized a clandestine army made up of Cuban expatriates. The Bay of Pigs invasion (1961) was a disaster. All of the attackers were either

killed or captured, and Cuban leaders bragged about their victory over
the United States to the world. The Cuban missile crisis (1962) was
almost bungled because of the lack of reliable information about the
intentions of the Cuban or Soviet governments. [8] After the crisis, in
one of the lowest points in American foreign policy, the brother of the
president, Robert Kennedy, was involved in plots to murder Castro
with the help of the CIA.

In the 1960s the CIA participated in scores of covert operations
around the world in Vietnam, Laos, Thailand, Iran, Pakistan, Bolivia,
Colombia, the Dominican Republic, Ecuador, Guatemala, and
Venezuela. Vietnam and Southeast Asia absorbed their attention for
almost twenty years only to see their efforts end in failure. The CIA
backed a coup attempt against President Sukarno of Indonesia in 1958
only to end in failure.[9] Then in 1965 they backed a successful coup led
by Suharto, a brutal army general with little concern for human rights,
which led to the deaths of an estimated 500,000 people and the
imprisonment of one million.[10] To this day many Indonesians blame
the Americans for their treachery in this operation.

In South America, the so called backyard of the United States, the
Americans supported several military and civilian dictatorships from
1976 to the mid 1980s. The CIA and the U.S. military trained scores of
army and police officers at the School of the Americas at Fort
Benning, Georgia in the latest techniques of covert operations, counter
insurgency and interrogation. These officers were then sent back home
where they applied these techniques of torture and murder to terrorize
their own people. In every case the terror was directed against
agricultural labourers or poor people in cities in support of the political
elite made up of the wealthy landowning classes and industrialists.

The Americans supported right wing dictatorships in Argentina,
Chile, Uruguay, Bolivia, Brazil, Nicaragua, El Salvador, Ecuador and
Peru. In Argentina the military carried on what has come to be called
the "Dirty War." This was state sponsored terrorism carried out by the
military government of Jorge Rafael Videla. Up to 30,000 people
"disappeared" in this operation, most of them students, trade unionists
and other members of the opposition. In Chile the CIA actively
worked to overthrow the democratically elected government of

President Doctor Salvador Allende in 1973 and helped General Augusto Pinochet seize power. "Pinochet reigned with cruelty, murdering more than 3,200 people, jailing and torturing tens of thousands in the repression called the Caravan of Death."[11] Chile now officially recognizes that the total number of people killed, tortured or imprisoned for political reasons during the Pinochet regime totals 40,018 people.[12]

The CIA operated around the world, supporting an assortment of military dictators and right wing governments. These covert activities rarely became known or subject to the scrutiny of the American public at the time. One exception was in the early 1970s when the failure of the Vietnam War led to a wrenching reassessment of American foreign policy, and the activities of the CIA were put into the spotlight by Congress. In 1975 Henry Kissinger, then the U.S. Secretary of State in the Ford administration, wrote a report for the President which has since become public. The report details some of the illegal activities of the CIA. The conclusions go on to say that there were things much worse that he did not cover. Kissinger called many of the CIA operations "a horror book," clearly illegal and "raising profound moral questions."[13]

What Kissinger did not mention was the damage CIA operations did to American prestige abroad. Many people in the developing world knew about the illegal and immoral activities of the CIA. In fact it is likely they knew much more about the CIA and its activities in their country than citizens of the United States. American politicians did not like to talk about what the CIA was doing and a complicit press turned a blind eye. In much of the developing world the United States had become a country that was to be feared for its overwhelming power and distrusted because it backed undemocratic elites that imposed their rule by terror. To make this worse all of this was done in the name of freedom, democracy and anti-communism. This raised "profound questions" indeed and has led to anti-Americanism in many parts of the world.

But despite Kissinger's criticism, CIA operations continued. In the years Jimmy Carter was President the agency was directed to support human rights, a Carter priority. That initiative accomplished little because the people who supported human rights in the developing world were often the very same people that the CIA had seen as their enemies for years. Once Ronald Reagan became President the agency found itself on more solid ground, focusing once again on the Soviet Union, the "evil empire" as Reagan called it. Soon the CIA was involved in controversy with the Iran Contra scandal and their support for right wing militias in Central and South America.

Although American intelligence efforts and the operations of the CIA represent the greatest failure of American foreign policy in the post war period, that does not mean to say that the United States had no political influence. The Americans wielded great power everywhere in the non-communist world. This came in part because of their military strength and their bases strategically placed around the world. Financial aid and the sale of military hardware also were helpful. But most of the influence of America came from economic power. The United States had the ability to open its markets to goods from other countries; even more important, the investment decisions of American companies could help to lift a country out of poverty. Leaders of all countries were willing to sacrifice a great deal to gain economic advantages like that.

American Surrogate Wars

Not only did the United States become involved in clandestine and covert operations to support anti-communist groups, it also became involved in a number of surrogate wars – wars that were fought by others with the help of the United States. That help came in the form of weapons, logistical support, intelligence and money. In most cases these were regional or local wars fought between left wing and right wing factions within a country, although often it is difficult to determine whether different groups had any ideology at all. In many cases people had taken up arms simply to defend themselves against marauding armies bent on plunder. None the less, these wars killed and displaced hundreds of thousands, if not millions, of people.

One of the most destructive, and least talked about, set of wars took place in Southern Africa. The racist apartheid regime of South

Africa came to power in 1948. This created widespread opposition among the South African black majority. Opposition groups were declared illegal and driven underground. Opposition members fled to surrounding countries, and soon much of Southern Africa was involved in so called "bush wars." These wars were fought by local people, often divided along communist/anti-communist lines, but a better description is that these were wars of liberation. The South African apartheid regime supported the anti-communists with the help of the Americans, although the United States has never admitted any involvement with these conflicts.

These wars were devastating. The Angolan Civil War lasted from 1975 to 2002. Over 500,000 people were killed and millions were displaced. In Mozambique a war of liberation against the Portuguese colonial power began in 1961 and went on to 1974. The Portuguese left then, but the war changed into a struggle between left and right factions and continued until 1992. It is estimated that over one million died in this conflict, over 1.7 million people fled the country and millions more were displaced internally. Southern Rhodesia, today Zimbabwe, was also swept up in these conflicts, as the whites tried to hold onto power and the rebels sought to dislodge them. The war of liberation was led by Robert Mugabe and finally in 1980, after 30,000 casualties, the country gained independence. These wars caused unspeakable hardship to extremely poor people with few resources. They came to an end only when the white South African apartheid regime finally gave up power and the ANC government took over after elections in 1994.

In Central America, again the Americans supported right wing groups in civil wars and insurrections. The Salvadorian Civil War from 1980 to 1992 resulted in 75,000 people killed and thousands homeless. In Nicaragua the left wing Sandinista government took power in 1979 when the country was at the point of ruin. President Ronald Reagan authorized financial and logistical support for a right wing militia group called the Contras who terrorized the Nicaraguan people by engaging in sabotage and economic disruptions.

The largest and longest American involvement in Latin American wars has been in Colombia. A bloody conflict between left and right has gone on in that country since the 1940s and continues to this day. Making things more complex, in the 1970s powerful drug cartels emerged who grow, process and export cocaine and other drugs mainly to the United States. Today FARC, supposedly a Marxist group, carries on a guerrilla war from their power base in the mountains, but reports suggest their main activity is providing protection for the drug cartels. The Americans support the right wing government of Colombia in their campaign against FARC with weapons, money and logistics.

In the Far East the United States has given support to the Philippines in their long struggle against communist and Muslim insurgencies, and has given some support to Indonesia in the low-grade war in Areh, an area in the northernmost tip of the Island of Sumatra. During the Vietnam War American military support was given to anti-communist governments and groups in Laos, Cambodia and Thailand.

American support for Israel did not arise out of the Cold War. Support for Israel has more to do with U.S. domestic politics and American sympathy for Jewish aspirations for a homeland. Because of that political commitment the support of Israel has long been a vital interest of the United States. Since the formation of the State of Israel in 1948 the Americans have supplied the Israeli military with billions of dollars worth of military equipment. They have also helped the Israelis build their own armament industry and it is widely rumoured that they have provided logistical support in times of war. The Israelis now have a stockpile of nuclear weapons, though it is not known if the Americans helped them develop this capability.

The unwavering American support for Israel and the wars that Israel has fought with its neighbours have played an important role in the politics of the Middle East. A complex of factors contributed to the rise of nationalism, Islamic fundamentalism and political instability in the region. The turmoil in the Middle East has become the greatest concern of the American Empire since the end of the Cold War because of western dependence on Middle Eastern oil and the continuing support of the state of Israel.

The Islamic Revolution in Iran that led to the overthrow of the Shah in January 1979 led to the establishment of a fundamentalist Islamic state in that country. Iran's next door neighbour, Iraq, was led by Saddam Hussein. He saw the chaos in Iran as an opportunity to extend his influence over the region, and on September 22, 1980 Iraq invaded Iran. The Americans, in what is now seen as one of their greatest political blunders, chose to back the Iraqis in this war, giving them military hardware and operational intelligence.

This eight year war was devastating to the region. It was a conventional war featuring trench warfare, infantry attacks on machine gun positions, poison gas attacks and tank warfare. At the end of the war the two exhausted sides agreed to return to the original borders. The Iran/Iraq War has been one of the most costly in recent decades. Iraq is estimated to have had casualties estimated at between 250,000 and 500,000 and estimates of the Iranian losses range as high as 800,000 dead and hundreds of thousands more wounded. The economic losses on both sides were in the hundreds of billions of dollars.

As the Americans were drawn into surrogate wars in the Middle East, the Soviet Union became even more deeply involved in the region. Islamic fundamentalism was having a significant impact on this huge, complex country. The ideology of the Soviet Union was atheistic and secular, but in the southern part of the country 45 to 50 million people identified themselves as Muslims. They had long been restless with the authoritarian communist regime, and with the rise of radical Islam the Soviet leadership feared revolutionary fervour would sweep the southern republics.

Afghanistan was an especially difficult problem for the Soviets. The two countries are adjacent to each other and there has long been considerable trade and travel back and forth. In 1978 the Afghan communists launched a coup in which the ruling elite were killed. After seizing power, the communists instituted a campaign of radical land reforms. They insisted on the equality of women, a very sensitive issue in this conservative Muslim country. There was repression of religious groups in the countryside and summary executions. Soon Afghanistan was at the point of insurrection and anarchy. Factions within the communist leadership were battling each other. The Soviet leadership felt they could not stand by while Afghanistan slid into chaos and conservative Islamic groups took power. On December 24, 1979 over 100,000 Soviet troops invaded the country to re-establish order and support the communist regime.

The Soviet invasion of Afghanistan was a disaster. The Soviet Union was condemned by China as well as the entire non-communist world. It led to the end of *détente* and virtually all discussion between east and west stopped. The U.S. led a boycott of the 1980 Olympic Games in Moscow, which had been planned as a showcase of Soviet society. Worse yet were the results on the battlefield. The United States, Britain, Pakistan and Saudi Arabia armed the Afghan opposition called the Mujahedeen and launched yet another surrogate war. The Soviet army tried to fight a conventional war with tanks and heavy equipment but they were overwhelmed by the lightly armed and mobile Mujahedeen using guerrilla tactics. Like the American experience in Vietnam, the Soviets could win conventional battles but the Mujahedeen knew the people and the countryside. They attacked, using tactics of ambush and retreat. The Mujahedeen had the loyalty of the people, particularly those who lived in the countryside, while the Soviet army was made up of young, poorly trained recruits who had no familiarity with the language and customs of the people and no idea of how to fight an insurrection. Soon the struggle became a war of attrition and it was only a matter of time before the Mujahedeen prevailed.

The war was devastating for Afghanistan. There is no accurate data on the casualties but it is believed that well over one million Afghans died in the conflict and many more were wounded. Over 5.5 million people were displaced and became refugees as a result of the war. The official casualties of the Soviet Union were 13,833 killed and over 50,000 wounded. A society on the verge of becoming modern and independent had been destroyed.

Some would argue that these surrogate wars and particularly the war in Afghanistan played a major role in the collapse of the Soviet Union by containing communism. This alone, they say, justifies the American involvement. But does it? A more likely explanation for the collapse of the Soviet Union was economic problems. Communism could not deliver the goods for the people. The Soviet Empire was over-extended in Eastern Europe and did not have the resources to support the states within its orbit of influence. The war in Afghanistan underlined that weakness.

All of these surrogate wars were wars of empire, funded and motivated by the United States, the strongest imperial power in their world. These conflicts were a long way from the United States and barely registered on the political landscape at home, but they resulted in loss of life, the destruction of schools, homes and infrastructure. The Americans justified them with the claim that it was essential to halt the spread of communism, but other than Afghanistan, none of these wars had significance in the Cold War. They were local conflicts between different factions and groups. The United States used these wars to extend their influence in the world and had little interest in the deaths and hardships that they caused.

Wars of the Sole Superpower

Over the period of the Cold War American leaders justified their actions with the claim that they were involved in a life or death struggle with communism. With the collapse of the Soviet Union in December 1991[14] and the end of the Cold War, that rationale was finished. The United States had emerged from this struggle as the sole superpower and the world's last remaining empire.

Now there seemed to be no justification for the maintenance of the huge American military force. There was discussion, particularly in Europe, of a peace dividend. Countries could scale back their military spending and invest in social programs, but this was never seriously considered in the United States. America had reaped great economic and political benefits from its dominant position in the Cold War, and the power of the U.S. military supported that dominant position. They were not about to give this up. The massive military and arms industry also had a vested interest in maintaining a high level of military spending.

It was not long before the American justification for intervention abroad shifted. Now the Americans would not focus on containing communism; they would defend American vital interests. There are a number of American vital interests. These include the defence of allies, the promotion of free trade and globalization. Americans also intended to protect and promote the unregulated form of capitalism that had emerged during the Reagan presidency, but there was one vital interest that was more important than any of the others, and that was the protection of the world's oil supplies. This "vital interest" of the United States has spawned three wars, a number of terrorist attacks and other incidents since the end of the Cold War.

The Middle East has the world's major deposits of oil and this region has been in turmoil at least since the Second World War if not before. There are many reasons for this instability. Middle Eastern Muslim countries are deeply divided between Sunni and Shiite religious groups. Socialism and communism have been influential ideologies in all Middle Eastern countries, and nationalism has a special potency in the region. Oil has produced great wealth for a small number of families but little of the wealth has filtered down to the millions who live in poverty. The existence of the state of Israel and the plight of the Palestinian people is deeply resented across the Middle East. Added to this volatile mix is the continued existence of a number of authoritarian regimes, which suppress any dissident groups.

The British and Americans have long been involved in the politics of the Middle East and this adds to the instability of the region. In 1980 American President Jimmy Carter announced that Persian Gulf oil was "vital" to American national interests and that the U.S. would use "any means necessary, including military force" to gain access to it."[15] It was President Ronald Reagan who supplied Iraq with arms in the Iran/Iraq War and the reason was the same. Oil was an American vital interest and every effort would be made to secure access to this precious commodity. Iran was also seen as an enemy of the United States since the Iran hostage crisis that had extended from November 1979 to January 1981.

Soon the American vital interests of oil turned Iraq and Saddam Hussein from an ally of the United States to an enemy. In August 1990

Iraq invaded Kuwait, a tiny, oil rich, principality. Kuwait was led by a ruling group friendly to the west, but more important, the invasion was a threat to Saudi Arabia, a close ally of the Americans and the source of huge deposits of oil. The invasion was a clear violation of international law. The United Nations condemned it and authorized the use of force to remove the Iraqis from Kuwait. Economic sanctions were immediately placed against Iraq and the Americans began to organize a military force to expel the Iraqis. The coalition that was put together was made up of forces from 34 nations, with the Americans and British contributing the overwhelming numbers in the coalition.

It took some months to assemble the coalition and move the military force into position in Saudi Arabia and the Persian Gulf. The assault, called "Operation Desert Storm," began with air attacks on January 17, 1991 and within hours the coalition held air supremacy. Extensive use of computerized bombing attacks and missile air strikes were used by the Americans. Some call this the first computerized war. The ground attack began on February 24 with an armored assault. Two days later the Iraqis began to retreat out of Kuwait, setting fire to the oil wells as they left. The retreating column of vehicles was caught in the open on the Iraq-Kuwait highway. They were bombed and strafed so thoroughly it came to be called the "Highway of Death." Finally President George H. W. Bush declared a ceasefire 100 hours after the ground assault began and the war was over.

The Americans were ecstatic about the outcome of the war. "By God, we've kicked the Vietnam Syndrome," President Bush declared. Only 181 coalition members were killed by enemy fire in the war while thousands of Iraqis were killed. It was interpreted as a complete vindication of the American policy of vital interests and, more important, the war demonstrated to the world the superiority of the American military.

Saddam Hussein was blamed for the war, and as the Gulf War drew to a conclusion, there was discussion in American political circles that they should use their overwhelming military power to attack Bagdad and remove Saddam. The President rejected this course. In light of the subsequent invasion initiated by his son this decision remains controversial. The President recognized that a full invasion of

Iraq would be difficult, but a more important reason for not invading Iraq was that he believed that the war should not exceed the authorization given by the United Nations.[16] In this sense George H. W. Bush was an internationalist who believed in multilateralism. He spoke about a "new world order" that he believed would emerge from the end of the Cold War and promised a sharing of political powers with other nations.

But the conflict in Iraq continued for the next ten years. At the urging of the Americans, Shiites in southern Iraq rose in rebellion. The Saddam regime put the rebellion down with force and several rebels were executed. The United Nations imposed sanctions against Iraq. UN inspectors combed the country looking for weapons of mass destruction. No fly zones were imposed on the Iraqis. The economy of the country was in ruins, poverty soared and thousands of people died from lack of medical care and malnutrition, but Saddam Hussein seemed to have an ever stronger grip on power.

Other conflicts kept the politics of the Middle East at a boiling point in the 1990s. The Israeli army prevailed against Palestinians, humiliating them with a system of control and harassment and occupying land in the West Bank. Out of frustration, Palestinians responded with terrorist attacks using suicide bombers. Across the Middle East militant Islamic factions were turning to violence to deal with their mounting frustrations. Then, on September 11, 2001 a group of young Muslims mainly from Saudi Arabia struck at what they felt to be the very heart of U.S. power: the World Trade Center, a symbol of American capitalism, and the Pentagon, the symbol of American military power. A fourth aircraft in the planned attack that crashed into a farmer's field in Pennsylvania had targeted the White House or House of Representatives in Washington, symbols of American political power.

The terrorist attack of 9/11, a mere eight months after George W. Bush assumed office, was a shocking event for Americans. It provided the crisis that the newly elected neo-conservatives used to take American foreign policy in a radical new direction by launching the War on Terror. This new war was different from any war that Americans had ever fought. Wars are conflicts between nations or struggles between factions within a country. The War on Terror was a war against secret groups that used terror as a tactic to promote their political ends.

The justification for the War on Terror is found in what has come to be called the "Bush Doctrine." Its origins can be traced back to Ronald Reagan's militant anti-communism and the cold warriors of the 1950s, but the most recent antecedent was a document called "Defense Planning Guidance," written in the dying years of the presidency of George H. Bush by Paul Wolfowitz, and dated February 18, 1992.[17] That document argued that the United States should "prevent the re-emergence of a new rival." It should engage in pre-emptive war, attacking its enemies if it was judged they were dangerous, and should act unilaterally, even if U.S. allies were not supportive. In 1992 these policies were too radical to be accepted, but under George W. Bush they became the foundation of America's foreign policy.

The Bush Doctrine is found in a document called "The National Security Strategy of the United States of America." The strategy is framed in language that reflects humanitarian and democratic values.

> Our goals on the path to progress are clear: political and economic freedom, peaceful relations with other states, and respect for human dignity... America must stand firmly for the nonnegotiable demands of human dignity: the rule of law; limits on the absolute power of the state; free speech; freedom of worship; equal justice; respect for women; religious and ethnic tolerance; and respect for private property.[18]

But the document also made it clear that American interests would be achieved by war.

> We must be prepared to stop rogue states and their terrorist clients before they are able to threaten or use weapons of mass destruction...We must deter and defend against the threat before it is unleashed...To

> forestall or prevent such hostile acts by our adversaries,
> the United States will, if necessary, act pre-emptively.[19]

The Bush Doctrine is the assertion that the United States has the right to take pre-emptive military action against states that pose a threat to U.S. national security. Noam Chomsky has pointed out that this policy goes beyond pre-emptive war and is a policy of "preventive war." Pre-emptive war is a defence against a country or group intending to attack. Preventive war is the use of war "to eliminate an imagined or invented threat."[20] Preventive war is exactly what happened in both Afghanistan and Iraq.

After the Soviet withdrawal from Afghanistan in February 1989, the communist government was able to stay in power until April 1992, when Kabul came under the control of the Mujahedeen. After a protracted struggle an even more radical conservative Muslim group called the Taliban came to power in 1996. The Taliban imposed a harsh version of Sharia law. They also allowed the radical terrorist group al Qaeda and its leader Osama bin Laden to locate in Afghanistan and set up training camps. Many of the terrorists in the 9/11 attacks were trained in these camps.

After 9/11 President George W. Bush authorized bombing attacks on the al Qaeda camps and a number of other Afghan targets. Bush demanded the Taliban regime give up Osama bin Laden, and the government of Afghanistan offered to bring him to trial in an Islamic court. Later they offered to surrender him to a third country for trial but the president rejected both offers. The Americans were preparing for war.

In the north of Afghanistan a group called the Northern Alliance had been fighting a civil war against the Taliban. The Americans, along with the British, allied themselves with the Northern Alliance. In November 2001 the Americans intensified the bombing and the Alliance launched an attack with the help of the American and British Special Forces.

Within a matter of weeks the Taliban were overwhelmed when their initial retreat turned into a rout. Kabul, the capital, fell on November 13th, and the Taliban forces abandoned their control of the cities and fled into the mountains. Most made their way across the border and into the tribal areas of Pakistan. Osama bin Laden, it is thought, escaped in the chaos of a battle in the Tora Bora Mountains, and Mullah Omar, the leader of the Taliban, fled his headquarters in Kandahar on December 7th and disappeared. To all appearances the war was over and a new government was soon installed.

There is still some controversy around whether the initial attacks on Afghanistan by the Americans and British were legal. A nation is allowed to defend itself under Section 51 of the UN Charter. Al Qaeda had claimed responsibility for the 9/11 attacks, but the bombing in Afghanistan went well beyond an attack on the terrorist camps. On December 20th the Security Council passed a resolution "supporting international efforts to root out terrorism."[21]

The campaign in Afghanistan had ended in what seemed to be an easy victory and afterwards the Bush administration turned their attention to a much more difficult problem, the situation in Iraq. The Saddam Hussein regime was loathed in almost every quarter of the world. With the ever tightening economic sanctions the living conditions of the people had deteriorated alarmingly, but Saddam, his family and the top members of the Baath Party continued to live in luxury. Opponents of the regime were arrested and some summarily executed. President Bush described the Iraqi regime as part of the "axis of evil," and claimed regime change was essential. It became clear in 2002 that the United States was preparing to go to war.

The Bush Doctrine asserted that the U.S. had the right to take pre-emptive military action against nations that posed a threat to American security. There had long been the fear that the Saddam regime was developing weapons of mass destruction. After the Gulf War the United Nations carried out weapons inspections but found nothing. Senior members of the U.S. administration did not believe that and claimed that the Iraqis had continued their program. On September 18, 2002 the CIA briefed the President saying that the Iraqis had abandoned their program, but the president and his advisors did not accept this and continued their search. Joseph C. Wilson, a former ambassador, was sent to Africa to trace a rumour that the Iraqis were trying to acquire nuclear material. When he reported there was no truth to the claim, he and his wife were attacked by members of the Bush administration. A few days before the vote in the U.S. Senate authorizing the war, about 75 Senators, in a closed-door meeting, were told that Saddam Hussein had the means to attack the eastern seaboard of the United States with biological and chemical weapons by means of unmanned aircraft. This was completely false.

The misinformation was used in a systematic way to mislead the public. Top U.S. officials claimed there were links between the Iraq regime and al Qaeda but other than one questionable meeting that may have never happened, no links were ever found. Many Americans came to believe that Iraq had something to do with the 9/11 attack, and that misperception was never corrected.[22] The most significant moment of misinformation in this detailed campaign came when Colin Powell, the American Secretary of State, addressed the Security Council of the United Nations, where he repeated all of these claims and waved about a vial of anthrax as if this demonstrated the threat of Iraq.

Significantly, members of the Security Council rejected the American claims. Realizing that the French and Russians were prepared to use their veto to deny the resolution to justify the war, the Americans withdrew it. Widespread opposition to the war around the world had grown. It is estimated that 36 million people took part in over 3000 protests. Later Kofi Annan, the Secretary General of the United Nations, said, "I have indicated it [the Iraq War] was not in conformity with the U.N. Charter. From our point of view, from the charter point of view, it was illegal."[23]

On March 20, 2003 the invasion began. The invading force took Baghdad on April 9 and the Saddam regime fell. The Americans searched the country in an attempt to find weapons of mass destruction but no weapons were ever found. Under international law this was an act of aggression and clearly illegal.[24] The difficulty was that no other nation was strong enough to challenge the Americans, and so nothing was done. The American President and the administration set out to convince public opinion, the members of the United Nations and their own political leaders that Iraq posed a serious threat to their security.

Their complete failure to do that led to a crisis of leadership of the United States.

Superpower and International Agreements

The primary justification for the growth of American power was to confront the Soviets during the Cold War. In that era the U.S., with its colossal military, economic and political power, was the unchallenged leader of the Western Alliance, and American leadership was deemed essential on every level, from the Israeli/Palestinian confrontation to wars in Africa and the former Yugoslavia. The United States was the only country with the economic strength to shape issues such as international trade and monetary problems. Even on social issues like health, pollution and education, the U.S. voice dominated international discussions. Throughout the Cold War the United States was the unquestioned preeminent power in the world, but that has now changed.

The George W. Bush presidency led to disaster for the United States. The invasion of Iraq, an independent sovereign country, was carried out without the sanction of the United Nations and according to international law was an illegal war, justified on the flimsiest grounds that later proved to be a fabrication. Members of the international community and even many in the United States now understood that the U.S. was an empire, bent on achieving its goals by war with no regard to others. But Iraq is just the most glaring example of American unilateralism. During the Bush Presidency the United States withdrew from many international treaties and agreements that might limit its ability to wage war. This is a list of the most important international treaties or agreements from which the U.S has withdrawn:

- In December 2001, the U.S. officially withdrew from the 1972 Anti-Ballistic Missile Treaty.

- In 1972 the U.S., along with 143 other nations, signed the Biological and Toxic Weapons Convention, but in 2001 the U.S. refused to approve strengthening the convention to allow on-site inspections. At Geneva that year U.S. Undersecretary of State John Bolton stated that, "the Convention is dead."

- In July 2001, the U.S. was the only nation that refused to vote in favour of the U.N. Agreement to Curb the International flow of Illicit Small Arms.

- The Comprehensive Nuclear Test Ban Treaty was signed by Bill Clinton, the U.S. President, on September 24, 1996, which bans all nuclear testing, but it was never ratified by Congress. Under George W. Bush the Test Ban Treaty was rejected and preparations were made for the United States to test and build a new generation of nuclear weapons.

- The Bush administration refused to carry out the U.S. promise to work towards the elimination of nuclear weapons, made when it signed the Nuclear Non-Proliferation Treaty in 1968.

- In February 2001 the United States refused to join 123 other nations who pledged to ban the use and production of anti-personnel bombs and mines.

- The United States has repeatedly opposed the establishment of the International Criminal Court at The Hague to try political and military personnel charged with war crimes and crimes against humanity. A bill passed in the U.S. Senate denies the court jurisdiction over U.S. military personnel.

- In 1997 the U.S. was one of the few nations that refused to sign the Land Mine Treaty that bans the use of land mines. This treaty was negotiated and promoted by Canada, one of the closest allies of the United States.[25]

- In 2006 the U.N. voted for a new international arms trade treaty. One hundred and fifty-three U.N. countries voted in favour. The U.S. was the only country to vote against the treaty.

- On December 3rd 2008 ninety-three countries signed a landmark treaty banning cluster bombs. The United States, along with China and Russia, refused to sign.

This list only deals with military issues but there is an equally long list of international agreements dealing with social, environmental, racial and gender issues that have been rejected by the Bush administration.

- As of June 2007, 172 countries had ratified the Kyoto Protocol dealing with global warming and climate change – but not the United States. The Bush administration blocked the release of scientific information linking greenhouse gas emissions to climate change and the link between greenhouse gas emissions and the frequency and strength of hurricanes.

- In 2003 the Bush administration pledged $15 billion in the fight against HIV/AIDS in Africa, making it the largest contributor to the fight against the pandemic, but one-third of the money for prevention can only be used in abstinence programs. This has discouraged condom use. Many critics including Stephen Lewis, formerly Special U.N. Envoy for HIV/AIDS in Africa, claim that the use of condoms is the most effective way to prevent the spread of the virus and this program is harming the fight against the pandemic.

- In May 2001 the United States refused to meet with other nations to discuss putting controls on electronic surveillance of phone calls, faxes and e-mails.

- The U.S. has refused all invitations to participate in Organization for Economic Co-operation and Development talks on ways to crack down on offshore tax and money-laundering havens. It is estimated that world wide, $500 billion in tax revenue is diverted each year to avoid paying taxes. This is six times the amount the developing nations give in the form of aid to underdeveloped countries. Illegal tax shelters are sapping the ability of governments in the developing world to provide vital services.[26]

- In July 2001, the U.S. was the only nation among the G-8 to refuse to support the proposed International Plan for Cleaner Energy.

- The United States continues to enforce its illegal boycott of Cuba.

- In 1984, during the Reagan Administration, the United States withdrew from UNESCO, because this leading U.N. organization had been critical of media concentration. The U.S. still is not a member.[27]

Most of the democratic nations of the world support multi-lateral agreements that strengthen the interdependence of countries because they believe that such agreements will lead to co-operation, mutual trust, disarmament and the end of war. The United Nations is dedicated to these efforts. Under the leadership of George W. Bush, the United States rejected multilateralism. Under his leadership America became unilateralist, and inward looking, the lone cowboy state answerable to no one.

By arrogantly choosing to go it alone the Americans were following the path of most empires, but they were not up for the task of preeminent world leadership. Just as they reached the apex of power – their so-called "sole superpower" status – the United States became badly overextended and rapid decline set in. The American Empire faces an unprecedented crisis caused by failed military adventures and economic chaos as a consequence of neo-conservative policies. The end of empire is within sight.

Part II: The End of Empire

INTRODUCTION

We are living through the most fundamental political, economic and social changes in human history, and those changes are having an impact on all aspects of our lives, including international relations. For decades the Soviet leadership carried on with the same old forms of autocratic government and then, unexpectedly, the Soviet era was over. Soviet society had changed and people were no longer prepared to tolerate undemocratic government and miserable living conditions. New leaders, a new type of government and a new economic system were put in place and the Cold War came to a sudden and abrupt end.

As those events unfolded, international politics seemed poised for a transformation into a much more co-operative system of relationships. U.S. President George H. W. Bush spoke about the "new world order," suggesting that the end of the superpower confrontation would lead to a more multilateral world, and yet it did not happen. Presidents Bill Clinton and George W. Bush continued the same imperial policies that the United States had practiced during the Cold War.

But today we are finally on the brink of change. This is not because a new set of politicians like Barack Obama have come onto the world stage; they are simply giving expression to the new politics. The reason is that economic and social changes have made it impossible for empires to dominate other nations and people. A multilateral world is emerging not because empires are somehow immoral, but because in a modern world it is impossible for empires to impose their will by military force.

Part I of this book explored how empires have used war for their own political and economic advantage. Part II examines how the forces of modernity are changing the social, economic and military conditions and are leading to the end of empire and the end of war.

CHAPTER 5: MODERNITY AND DEMOCRACY

Empires of the past were created and defended by the military, but political power rested with the central authorities. The Romans ruled their provinces through governors directly responsible to the Emperor, backed by the power of the Roman legions. The British appointed governors to rule their colonies. After a period they set up legislative councils or parliaments of locally appointed or elected citizens who advised the governor, but the British continued to rule. All of the colonies were required to have strong economic and political ties to the "mother country."[1] The empire was held together by the British Navy and Army.

The United States developed an empire that allows much more local control than any imperial power of the past. Countries within the U.S. sphere of influence are sovereign states that make their own laws and policies. They are held together through military alliances, economic agreements, trade, investments, political ties and cultural and educational links that bind them into a loose federation. But within that federation the United States is first among equals. The U.S. provides the leadership, the finances and above all the military muscle to hold it all together. In return America has reaped the benefits; but can that system continue?

Authoritarian Rule

Prior to the industrial revolution virtually all states around the world were authoritarian and autocratic. Strong kings or local rulers enforced their will by force. For example, in France, prior to the revolution of 1789, the king was isolated from the people and lived a life of luxury at the court surrounded by aristocrats and other hangers-on who made up the governing elite of the country. France was the largest and wealthiest European country at the time and the center of the cultural life of the continent, if not the so called "civilized world," as the Europeans liked to express it. In the eighteenth century the French king led the country into a series of disastrous wars but it all seemed to make little difference to the king and his courtiers. Court life went on at a merry pace.

The wealth of the king and the aristocrats was based on land. They owned large estates which were farmed by peasants. But a new economy based on trading and manufacturing was emerging, and the wealth created by this new economy led to the rise of a new class of people the French called the *bourgeoisie,* who were shaking the foundations of France and Europe. The *bourgeoisie* were wealthy and powerful economically, but they had no political power because the king and the aristocrats monopolized all political decisions. The king and his friends had no interest in the new economy or the concerns of the *bourgeoisie.* For example, roads were in bad repair, bridges were washed out but the king did not see any need to repair them. But to the *bourgeoisie,* good roads were essential to get their goods to market. Taxes were put on trade goods to pay for the armies and armaments in wasted wars and still the roads were not repaired.

The grumblings of the *bourgeoisie* turned to political demands and then manifestos. When these were rejected, politics went underground; plots were hatched. The king responded with repression, imposed by the secret police, and then finally revolution broke out, a nasty, chaotic, bloody affair that resulted in the king and most of the aristocratic elite losing everything, including their heads. This was all because of an antiquated political system that monopolized political power in the king and could not respond to change.

The record of dictators in our own time is little better. Hitler, Mussolini, Franco, and the Japanese military all formed dictatorships that governed closed societies and tolerated no dissent. Stalin ran a police state held together by the elimination of his enemies and the imprisonment of millions. The wars that these dictators are responsible for were disastrous for whole continents of people. Ultimately they led to the end of their rule, the destruction of their own and scores of other countries.

Today it is not kings or aristocrats who hold a monopoly on political power in autocratic countries, often it is military leaders. The United States and other democratic countries have had military political leaders, but they were elected democratically and conformed to the country's democratic laws and traditions. Not so in many developing and underdeveloped countries. They rule in an autocratic way with the support of the military, the most powerful, disciplined and unified force in the country.

In Indonesia General Suharto came to power in 1965 with the help of the Americans through the CIA. Indonesia is a huge, sprawling, island nation of two hundred and thirty-five million people of varied ethnic and religious backgrounds. In his rise to power Suharto crushed the Indonesian Communist Party, killing party supporters and a variety of other people who opposed the military takeover. Over the next thirty years of Suharto's rule, another 300,000 were killed. Suharto also used his political power to accumulate wealth. It is estimated that up to $35 billion was taken out of the economy by his family and billions more by his close associates. Finally in 1998, after riots and street protests, Suharto was driven from power. Since then the Indonesian people have struggled to establish democracy and suppress the power of the military. All efforts to prosecute Suharto, his family and other members of his ruling elite have been abandoned.

Other developing countries have similar political histories. This is the evaluation of Pakistan's military rulers in 2008 by Marcus Gee, a Canadian journalist.

> Under army rule for more than half of its life as a nation, Pakistan has been through three wars and seen four civilian leaders overthrown by the army.... While the military spends billions on new weapons for its troops and golf courses for its officers, half of the population of 160 million is illiterate and a third does not have enough to eat. Active and retired military officers run everything from waterworks to universities, and military-run companies make products from cornflakes to cement. As a result, other institutions – parliament, the civil service – have eroded or fallen into irrelevance.[2]

Pakistan and Indonesia are not isolated examples. The history of South American military regimes in the 1960s, 70s and 80s are a litany of bungled social and economic programs and murders and torture of thousands of people. In Africa autocratic leaders called the "Big Men" came to power with the end of colonialism and independence. They used their political power to enrich themselves and their supporters and to crush opposition.[3] There were similar atrocities in the Middle East and Southeast Asia. All of these autocratic governments depend on support from a strong military and rely on a secret police who terrorize, imprison and sometimes murder dissidents. At the time of the Cold War, many such military regimes had the support of the United States; some continue to enjoy that support to this day.

Authoritarian regimes, whether they are led by kings, dictators, colonial governors or military rulers, are inherently unstable. They provide bad government not only because they depend on force, but because laws are imposed that satisfy the needs of the rulers and their followers but not the people. As a result, large sections of the population see the laws and regulations as unfair and illegitimate. This in turn results in political and social instability, and sometimes insurrection and civil war.

Modernity and Government

Milton Friedman and his fellow neo-liberals link the rise of democracy to capitalism.[4] In their view the two support each other because both advocate individual choice. Capitalism depends on the millions of choices that consumers and investors make every day, while the basic tenet of democracy is that the people choose their leaders in free elections. In an influential essay, Francis Fukuyama, a key conservative political thinker, predicted "the universalization of Western liberal democracy as the final form of government."[5] This is more ideology and opinion than analysis. History suggests that democracy is related to the rise of modernity, not capitalism.

The developed countries of today were not always prosperous societies. They became that way as a result of a process that historians call the industrial revolution. A more comprehensive and broader term is simply "modernity." Today the forces of modernity are changing societies in every region of the globe and are having an impact on every ethnic, racial, religious and social group in the world. We are in the midst of a truly fundamental social revolution that is transforming the lives of everyone on the planet; and that process has had, and will continue to have, an impact on the conduct of war.[6] Social scientists point out that the process is not inevitable and different societies have adapted in various ways, but almost all societies are becoming modernized. These changes affect every aspect of the social fabric of societies, including the political process.

Today the level of development of societies is described by three very general categories: "developed," "developing" and "underdeveloped" societies. Europe, North America and Japan are considered modern, industrial, developed societies. The developing world, countries like China, India, Russia, Brazil and others, are countries in rapid transition towards developed status. Much of sub-Saharan Africa and other parts of the so-called underdeveloped world are societies that have only recently begun this process. Of the six billion people in the world, about one billion live in the developed world, one billion live in the underdeveloped world and four billion live in the developing world.[7]

Social scientists point out that development in each society seems to be caused by unique and different circumstances.[8] One common thread is changes in the "mode of production." In pre-industrial Europe the production of food was on large estates or farms. Goods like cloth and iron tools were fabricated in villages by craftsmen. With the expansion of trade, the production of many goods became located in factories. Over time markets expanded, transportation improved, factories grew in size and cities became centers of production. The beginning of this process of modernity in Britain, the first country to become industrialized, was about the year 1750. Other European countries and the United States began the process about fifty years later.

These economic changes caused a number of profound social changes. One of the most fundamental: the growth in population. In 1750 it is estimated that there were 791 million people in the world.

By the year 2000, only 250 years later, there were close to 6 billion,[9] an increase of seven and half times. Traditional societies had high birth rates, but also high death rates, keeping the population relatively stable. As societies began to develop improvements in nutrition, sanitation and medical care, there was a drop in death rates. Infant mortality rates plummeted. More people lived into adulthood and had children of their own, resulting in rapid population growth. Today, in the developed world, population growth has slowed. Birth control practices have led to a drop in the birth rate, and now, in virtually every developed country, births and deaths are about in balance and the population is stable. In some countries like Russia, Japan, and Hungary the population is even beginning to shrink because the birthrate is below 2.1 births per woman, the number needed to keep the population stable.

This cycle is linked to modernity.[10] Undeveloped societies, like many countries in sub-Saharan Africa, are in the first stage, with high birth rates and high death rates. But even Africa is changing. Death rates are falling across the continent despite the epidemics of HIV/AIDS, malaria and tuberculosis.[11] Developing countries are typically in the second stage with high birth rates and low death rates, and their populations are expanding rapidly, although China has had a rapid drop in its birth rate as a result of an aggressive birth control program. Developed countries are in the third stage, low birth rates and low death rates, and their populations are stable or falling.

As part of the process of demographic transition, the world's population is growing older. In developed countries the median age is between 35 and 45. In developing countries the median age is typically between 20 and 35, and the median age in all sub-Saharan underdeveloped countries is under 20. Gradually, as the population ages, it changes the politics of countries. The country becomes more conservative and much less prone to war. In many underdeveloped and developing societies the "youth bulge" of population has created political instability and contributes to war because young men are the recruits of armies.

Another important demographic change is rapid urbanization. In pre-industrial societies most people live in rural areas because production is located on farms, but in modern societies the population shifts to cities where jobs and economic opportunity are found. In 2007 for the first time in human history, the earth's population became more urban than rural.[12] By the year 2050 it is estimated that two-thirds of the world's population will live in urban centers. Some of the largest cities are in developing countries. Of the ten largest urban centers today, only two are in the developed world, Tokyo and New York. Three are in India, three in Latin America and one each in China and Indonesia. Today Africa and Asia have the most rapidly developing urban centers in the world.

As cities develop, the surrounding countryside also changes. There is less subsistence farming as agriculture is integrated into the broader economy of the region. Farmers become part of the cash economy, producing commodities to sell rather than production solely to feed their families.

Formal education of the young is essential for a developed society. Jobs demand literacy and an understanding of mathematics. Specialized jobs such as engineers, lawyers, health professionals or civil servants require post secondary or graduate education. In the most advanced societies innovation is linked to education because an understanding of science and technology is necessary for this work. Today all countries, even the poorest, are trying to provide universal education for their people, recognizing that this is the route to development and modernization. Education does more than teach skills. It is a vehicle for social change, because it teaches the young non-traditional ways of understanding the world.

Gender roles and family structures change with the rise of modernity. In most underdeveloped societies extended families are common, with three or more generations living together. Women do much of the manual labour and are expected to be the caregivers of children. Boys have greater prestige and are given special priority in many parts of the world. For example, in sub-Saharan Africa 110 boys attend elementary school for every 100 girls. In developed societies, nuclear families of parents and children are much more common. Females receive education, often work outside the home and have their own careers.

In developed societies the ideal of racial, ethnic and religious equality has emerged, although few modern societies escape the problems of prejudice and racism. But this is considerably different than in underdeveloped or developing societies. In sub-Saharan Africa ethnic and clan loyalties remain a serious issue as the genocides in Rwanda and Darfur have demonstrated. In Iraq a fundamental division is between Sunni, Shiite, and Kurd and in Afghanistan and Pakistan there is a sharp division between the Pashtun and other ethnic groups and even clans within tribes. Religious and ethnic differences remain a serious problem in former Yugoslavia and many other countries.

Perhaps the most fundamental cultural change brought on by the rise of modernity is the way that people understand their world. Many in underdeveloped societies interpret events as spiritual interventions by supernatural forces. A modern outlook provides "material" explanations of the natural world based on science. A person does not have to be an earth scientist to understand that earthquakes are caused by geological forces, not the intervention of the spiritual world. One explanation is rooted in tradition, and the other is rooted in modernity.

Many have pointed out that modernity is bringing a common culture and the spread of dominant languages such as English. There is some truth to that, although local culture remains strong everywhere. The mass media is pervasive in India. Education is improving in Africa. Despite government restrictions, many Chinese have access to the instant communications of the Internet and that is leading to political dissent. Millions of people are traveling and living in other cultures. Young people are growing up in a world that is radically different from that of their parents and grandparents. These cultural influences are changing the way that we understand our world.

Rapid social change is upsetting at any time, and modernity has brought great social instability around the world, particularly to people in the developing and underdeveloped world. It has uprooted rural people and cast many into urban slums. Unemployment in European cities of the 19th and early 20th centuries led to serious problems because workers had no way to support themselves or feed their families at times of mass unemployment. Deeply religious people are shocked and threatened by secular interpretations of the world. The demand for equal treatment of women is a serious challenge to traditional Muslim and many African societies. Many of the political upheavals of the last two centuries are rooted in the social changes that have been created by the forces of modernity.

The social instability of underdeveloped countries is striking, but as a country develops and becomes more prosperous, the growing middle class becomes more satisfied with their lives. Social change becomes less threatening and societies become less volatile and unstable. The Pew Research Center Global Attitudes Project conducted a study of thirteen middle income nations in different regions around the globe and found, "Compared with poorer people in emerging countries, members of the middle class assign more importance to democratic institutions and individual liberties, consider religion less central to their lives."[13]

The process of modernity is fundamentally changing the practice of politics around the world. Pre-modern societies can be ruled by kings or tribal and clan leaders. Most people in these societies live in isolated rural communities and have little idea what is going on in the next village, let alone the country or the world. When a society modernizes, these traditional forms of government cannot meet the economic and social needs of the people. The example of the events leading up to the French Revolution is instructive. The king had no knowledge or interest in the new economic order that was rapidly emerging and had no idea what types of policies were necessary to meet the needs of the middle class. The French royal family and the nobility paid a big price for their ignorance.

The same can be said about autocratic regimes everywhere. They simply are not able to deal with the complicated problems of modern societies. Fundamental to modernity is the need to have extensive participation in political life and in economic institutions. Autocratic governments drive dissent underground. Modern governments need the involvement of citizens in order to shape the policies that are necessary for the management of complicated societies and economies. Democracy is inherent in the rise of modernity.

The Rise of Democracies

Democracy is not only the establishment of democratic institutions and practices such as elections, parliaments, an independent judiciary and the rule of law; it is the establishment of individual rights such as freedom of speech and association, the right of assembly and equality of all citizens before the law. There are different types of democracy, such as direct democracy, town hall democracy or grassroots democracy, but what we usually mean when we use the word is representative democracy, the right of citizens to elect representatives who then are empowered to govern. The struggle for representative democracy has long and complicated historical roots. In England the struggle focused on parliament and the power of elected representatives of the people over the arbitrary power of the king and the aristocratic elite. There were similar developments in Switzerland and other places.

Americans point to their revolution as the moment they established democracy, but that is not exactly true. There were colonial assemblies before the revolution which provided a form of limited democracy over local affairs. The American Revolution was a struggle for independence against the arbitrary rule of Britain. "No taxation without representation," remains a classic democratic demand. It affirms the principle that only the people and their representatives have the right to levy taxes and govern. Since then there have been many such struggles against the arbitrary power of an empire, colonial rulers or dictators and they are all a part of the struggle of people for independence and democratic control.

There are many reasons why democracies are such a successful system of government, but the most important is that democratic practices suit complex modern societies that have many competing interests and groups. Democracy provides a system where political life is fought in public forums and decisions are made by the people's representatives in the open. Those who oppose the decisions can voice their objections, work to defeat the politicians in the next election and overturn the policies. All of this is legal and part of democratic rights of all citizens. There are restrictions to this rule but the most important is that dissent must be conducted without violence or intimidation. That is the brilliance of democracy and why the system works so well. Political debate, dissent and conflict are legitimate and even encouraged by those in authority.[14]

Democracies, for all of their messiness, scandals, demagoguery and controversies, are more stable than autocratic rule because the population accepts the fact that elections give the rulers legitimacy and provide the opportunity to replace the government. This legitimacy comes because the leaders can claim they have the support of the majority of the people. A modern country with a sophisticated economy and culture and with an educated population can only be governed by democratic forms of government. That is why most people in the developed world agree with Churchill's sage saying, "Democracy is the worst form of government, except for all the others."[15]

Democracy is on the move around the world. In 1998 U.S. President Bill Clinton claimed that, "For the first time in all history more people live under democracy than dictatorship."[16] The *New York Times* researched this statement and concluded that 3.1 billion people live in democratic countries while only 2.66 billion do not.[17] An academic group that studied the same question found that in 1950 only 14.3% of the world's population lived in democratic states but by 2000 this had risen to 62.5%.[18]

Today it is estimated that 120 countries have some form of representative democracy. Granted, there are many problems with many of these governments.[19] Some states categorized as democratic have very shallow democratic roots. In others elections are flawed by fraud and intimidation; but there is a perceptible growth in the number of people living in democratically governed countries.

Democratic practices are changing the politics of the globe. India has had a vigorous democratic form of government since independence in 1947. After the end of the Cold War the former Soviet Union was transformed into the democratic state of Russia, although strong leaders have created a very authoritarian form of democracy.[20] Most Eastern European Soviet satellites became democratic even before the collapse of the Soviet Union and a number of the Soviet Republics have broken away and established their own democratic forms of government. Indonesia, South Korea, Philippines, Thailand and other East Asian countries adopted democratic forms of government at about the same time. In 1980 there were only two elected civilian governments in South America. By 1990 there were no dictatorships left on the continent. The emergence of a democratic South Africa from the repressive apartheid regime was a stimulus for all sub-Saharan Africa, and now, despite problems with manipulated elections and authoritarian leaders trying to hold onto power, democracy has taken root in a number of African countries. It is a remarkable story of how representative democracy has spread around the world.

China remains the most populous developing country that does not have a democratic form of government and is the major exception to the rule that links modernity to democracy. But China is not ruled by a small autocratic elite. The Chinese Communist Party that formally governs the country has 70 million members. Political issues are discussed within the Party and decisions emerge from that process. That is hardly a democratic system of government as we know it, but it is not totally autocratic either.

Many observers believe that the Chinese government is taking gradual steps towards democracy and in time will evolve into a democratic state. At the end of the 1980s this seemed to be the case, but the repression of student protests in Tiananmen Square in 1989 reversed the movement for democratic reform. The army attacked the students and the death toll reached an unknown number that some estimate to be as high as 3,000 people. Thousands more were imprisoned. There are other examples of repression. There is little freedom of the press or free speech in the country and dissidents are regularly imprisoned. The suppression of Tibet by military force in 2008 was brutal, and during the Olympic Games that same year the government repressed various types of dissent to give the appearance that it had broad support from the people. But it is unlikely that the Chinese Communist Party can continue to deny people full political rights for much longer. Once the millions of young people who are being educated in universities join the work force, they will demand increased freedom and democratic rights.

But this optimistic discussion of democracy ignores fundamental problems. In the developed world democracy is now well established and supported by a variety of institutions, but in the new democracies the practice is still very fragile. Democracy has not stopped rampant corruption of elected officials in countries like India, Pakistan or sub-Saharan Africa. Elections are sometimes tampered with, as in the Ukraine in 2004 and 2005 and Kenya and Zimbabwe in 2008. In some democracies, such as those in Central America, armed militias mete out rough justice in an effort to suppress opposition. Several democracies, like Russia and countries in the Middle East, pose risks for journalists who try to cover events, and state control of the media has become a special problem. Opposition leaders who oppose the government are assassinated, imprisoned, or intimidated in places like Pakistan and Kenya. In many countries it takes real courage for individuals to stand up for their democratic rights.

In the United States, a country with a long and rich democratic tradition, there is vigorous democracy at the local level. People participate in issues and make their views known, but at a national level it is very difficult for ordinary citizens to participate. Incumbency gives sitting politicians a great advantage. Members of the House of Representatives and the Senate are re-elected over and over again. The average age of the members of the 110th Congress in November 2008 was 57.0 years. The average age in the House of Representatives was 55.9 years and in the Senate 61.7 years. Women and most minority groups are under-represented. The politicians in Washington are made up primarily of upper income, white, middle aged or elderly men who do not reflect the make up of the American population.[21] The enthusiastic welcome of Barack Obama's presidency reflected the hope that his election will bring about a new politics in America but that remains to be seen. Congress is still controlled by politicians who resist change.

In many democratic countries political leaders do not provide programs, policies or laws that reflect the views of the people they represent. Again, the United States is a convenient example. Polling data has consistently shown that the American people are in favour of higher government spending on social programs such as Medicare and less on the military but this has not changed government policies. By the spring of 2007 polling showed that 57% of citizens said that U.S. troops should be pulled out of Iraq,[22] but few of the leaders at that time advocated withdrawal. Politicians cannot make policy by polling, but if democracy is to be more than just window dressing, then government decisions must reflect the views of the citizens.

Empire and Democracy

The leaders of autocratic, undemocratic regimes tend to feel very insecure – and with good reason. They fear that their opponents are plotting against them; their neighbours often harbour opposition members living in exile as they wait for an opportunity to return and take power; they are often denounced for their undemocratic practices. In response they set up a police state to control their opponents and maintain power, but the feelings of insecurity remain. Because of their fears leaders of autocratic regimes look for support wherever they can find it, and often it is found in empires. The Soviet Union at the height of its power gave support to autocratic countries like Syria and Afghanistan, but the United States supported a far greater number of undemocratic regimes.

In South America, for example, when military regimes took power in Brazil, Argentina and Chile in the 1970s, 80s and 90s the United States gave them support. These military regimes tortured and murdered many of their own citizens. When democracy was re-established the politicians who came to power were the very people who had opposed the military leaders. They were well aware of the close co-operation between the military regimes in their own countries and the United States. Today anti-American feelings continue across Latin America and the reason is the close relationship between the U.S. and repressive regimes.

If there is one region where U.S. prestige is lower than in South America, it is in the Middle East, and the reasons are almost identical. The United States continues to give full backing to a number of authoritarian, repressive regimes such as Saudi Arabia, Jordan and Israel. The so called "Arab Spring" that suddenly sprang to life in early 2011, was led by young people who were resisting authoritarian regimes, but these movements also were strongly anti-American.

In supporting authoritarian regimes, Americans went against the fundamental political values and traditions of their own country. The U.S. chose to support insecure, weak regimes which relied on force to retain power, regimes willing to co-operate with American imperial aims, rather than politicians and political movements with democratic values. The "blowback," to use Chalmers Johnson's term,[23] has been disastrous for American prestige in the world. Americans have been finding it increasingly difficult to get the co-operation of democratic countries for their imperial projects. Democratic leaders feel much less insecure than dictators or military juntas. They get their support from the people, and it is characteristic of all free people to reject and resent foreign powers telling them what to do, especially if it is a superpower. The growth of democracy has meant the lessening of the power of empires and the greater autonomy of nations.

Democracy and War

The growth of democracy and democratic institutions and practices is an optimistic sign for the end of war. As long ago as 1795, Immanuel Kant argued that "republican" or democratic countries would never go to war against each other because war is against the interests of the people. In his view, democracy would lead to perpetual peace.[24] Both Bill Clinton and George W. Bush have made a similar point. "Democracies don't go to war with each other," Bush once said.[25] Others have refuted this by pointing out that some wars like the American Civil War are fought by democratic states, but even conceding that there are exceptions, it does seem to be the case that the risk of war is greatly reduced if the two sides, or even one side, are democratic countries. Today this point of view is called the "democratic peace theory."

The greatest exception to this rule is the United States. President George W. Bush justified the Iraq war by saying, "The United States will use this moment of opportunity to extend the benefits of freedom across the globe. We will work to bring the hope of democracy, development, free markets and free trade to every corner of the world."[26] This is saying, in effect, that the United States will impose democracy by military means. Military force is by definition an anti-democratic. His attempt to justify the war by reference to freedom and democracy fell flat. Few believed that American military intervention was inspired by such noble ideals.

Despite the practice of the United States, there is a something to the argument that democratic countries do not go to war. The majority of the wars of the past were promoted by dictators or imperial powers bent on using war as a tactic to dominate others. That pattern continues today. War is not in the interest of ordinary people. Their sons and daughters are the fodder of armies, they have little interest in dominating others, they have to pay for the military adventures and it is civilians who suffer the most when war ravages their country. It makes no sense for a democratically elected politician to advocate going to war unless it is to protect their own citizens.

Modernity and War

The process of modernity has diminished war in developed and developing societies. Wealthy, urbanized developed societies with an educated, aging population are much more likely to choose peace over war. People are still vulnerable to economic turmoil, but they are more secure and less prone to radical political appeals. They understand that war and all violent social disturbances are a threat to their way of life and the well being of their families, friends, communities and countries. As modernity advances and affects more and more people, the risk of war will be greatly diminished.

CHAPTER 6: THE DECLINE OF
THE AMERICAN ECONOMY

Rome's chronic leadership problems led to a decline in the economic prosperity of the empire, and soon the legions were unable to defeat the invading Germanic tribes seeking plunder. In time the whole edifice of the empire collapsed. Similarly, both the First and Second World Wars led to the economic decline of European powers and sealed the fate of colonial empires. The economic stagnation of the Soviet economy led to the implosion of their political system. The Soviet system collapsed, their empire was lost and a new economic system based on capitalist principles took its place. Economic decline is a certain indication of the decline of an empire.

The economic decline of the United States poses serious problems for the American Empire. The media covers the ongoing economic crisis in detail but what they fail to tell the public is the decline is political in origin, not economic. It can be traced back to the Reagan presidency if not beyond. One thing is certain. This decline spells the end of the American Empire, and that in turn will have an impact on the American use of war as a tactic of domination and the entire international system that has been in place since the end of the Second World War.

Forming the Neo-Liberal Ideology

Many Americans hold the belief that they are a pragmatic people open to new ideas and not constrained by political ideology. They point to the communists as shackled by a rigid ideology that warped decisions on economic and political issues and led to the demise of the Soviet Union itself. Even the Europeans, some Americans believe, are far too influenced by ideologies such as socialism or social-democracy. American pragmatism, on the other hand, they claim, helps them to respond and adapt to all situations in a practical, nimble way that is appropriate to conditions. This is a flattering image that Americans hold of themselves, but it has almost no semblance of truth.

American political life has been more driven by ideology than most countries in the world. The United States, like all developed countries, has been polarized on a left/right continuum. On the left are those who believe that the political system must be the instrument to ameliorate problems such as poverty and racism and provide programs to enhance education, health care and other social problems. The left advocates redistribution of income through the tax system so that the extremes of wealth and poverty are moderated, and believes that government must regulate business for the greater public good. In Europe the people with such beliefs are called social-democrats or socialists; in the United States they are called liberals.[1]

Those on the right of the political spectrum are strong believers in individualism. Small government, low or even no tax is their objective. To them private property is an expression of an individual's rights and its use should be exclusively up to the owner of the property. They believe government intervention in the market place is an unwarranted intrusion into the property rights of the individual. In both Europe and the United States people with these political beliefs are called conservatives, but the intellectual roots of this approach are in nineteenth century British liberalism. This is how Will Hutton expresses it:

> In this climate taxation is depicted as confiscation, a burden that must be reduced. The collective and public realms are portrayed as the enemies of property and individual autonomy and, worse, as opposed to the moral basis of society, grounded as it should be in the absolute responsibility of the individual.[2]

The United States is a country with a strong tradition of free enterprise and individualism, and American political life has tended to be on the conservative side of this left-right continuum. In the 1920s conservatives were clearly in control of the United States. An economic policy called *laissez-faire* capitalism was the ideology that shaped economic decision making.[3] *Laissez-faire* advocated that there be minimal government regulation of business, and that government must stay out of the economy. Taxes were low and often non-existent for business. But although the U.S. version of *laissez-faire* advocated minimal government intervention, in foreign trade there was an insistence on strong government action. The United States protected its industries in the 1920s with some to the highest tariff barriers in the world.

Laissez-faire came to an abrupt end in the depression of the 1930s and was blamed for much of the economic hardships of the period. President Franklin Delano Roosevelt and his supporters mounted the argument that only government could lift the economy out of depression. They believed that business must be regulated for the broader public good and that government must stimulate demand by providing welfare payments, unemployment insurance, make-work programs and public projects like the construction of dams and parks. The "New Deal," as it came to be called, did much to raise the United States out of the grip of depression. With the onset of the Second World War, the conscription of millions of men into the military and government spending on armaments, the depression was finally over.

Roosevelt was a liberal, and towards the end of the war he used his power and influence to set up institutions and agreements that reflected liberal beliefs. The most important of these institutions was the United Nations, but the economic arrangements worked out at the Bretton Woods Conference in 1944 were fundamental to this thinking. Bretton Woods was shaped by a new economic theory called Keynesianism named after John Maynard Keynes, an influential British economist who analyzed the catastrophe of the Great Depression. He advocated that governments should intervene in the economy to mitigate the problems of depressions and recessions by stimulating demand. They should do this by direct employment, like programs in the New Deal, but also by deficit spending to "prime the pump." In this way money would be pumped into the economy in times of need, which in turn would lead to increased economic activity and lower levels of unemployment.

In the era after the Second World War Keynesianism became the political and economic orthodoxy of most governments in the non-communist world. Dozens of elections were won or lost on the judgment of whether political leaders had been able to achieve the twin goals of economic growth and low levels of unemployment. Liberal ideology had triumphed in the United States. Both Democrats and Republicans followed Keynesian economics. Even a politician as conservative as Richard Nixon once said: "We are all Keynesians now."[4]

However, by the mid to late 1970s serious economic problems began to affect virtually all of the economies of the Western World. Deficit spending put more money into the economy and soon inflation became more and more common. Keynesian economics was blamed for this but it was hardly the fault of Keynes' theory. He had recommended that in order to smooth out the business cycle governments should run deficits in times of recession, but he also recommended that in times of prosperity and full employment governments should run surplus budgets to "dampen down" demand. Politicians welcomed the first part of this prescription but found it hard to follow the second. As is often pointed out, the careers of politicians are determined by the four or five year cycle of elections and they are always keen to have a prosperous economy when elections are called. That led to a series of deficit budgets but rarely surplus budgets.

Whether the fault lies in the political theory or political decisions, the deficit budgets of most western countries resulted in inflation. By the 1970s the yearly inflation rate of many currencies was reaching 10% and by the end of the 1970s "stagflation" – inflation as well as economic stagnation – had set in. This crisis led to a new set of economic policies that became the economic orthodoxy of the next decades.

There had always been a group of economists who rejected Keynesianism. They believed that the "invisible hand"[5] of the market should regulate the economy and that virtually all government intervention distorts the market place. The most influential member of this group in the United States was an academic named Milton Friedman who came to be regarded as the leader of the so called "Chicago School" of economists. Friedman argued that there was a close relationship between money supply and inflation, and that inflation could be controlled by the amount of money released by the central bank, accomplished by controlling interest rates. This is the reason these economists are often called "monetarists." Friedman went beyond economics to argue that free markets lead to political and social freedoms, and that true democracy could only be achieved with a free enterprise capitalist system.[6]

The members of the Chicago School are essentially *laissez-faire* conservative economists who believe that free markets are self-regulating. They stand in the classical nineteenth century liberal tradition of limited government and the non-regulation of the economy by government. Unlike the American followers of *laissez-faire* in the 1920s, who supported high tariffs, the Chicago School advocated free trade, like the classical British liberals of the nineteenth century. That is why they are sometimes called "neo-liberals."

In the late 1970s a new political movement was being constructed based on neo-liberal economic theory. This group advocated that the economy should be regulated by monetary policy rather than government regulation, that taxes should be slashed and government intervention minimized. The anti-government rhetoric that went along with neo-liberalism had great appeal, particularly in the rural and small towns of America that valued individualism, but most of the financial support for the movement came from the wealthy that stood to financially benefit from these policies. A new conservative movement was born out of neo-liberal economic policies and the yearning for the reduction of government and taxation.

The political impact of these ideas on government policies was profound. In 1979 Margaret Thatcher was elected Prime Minister of Britain, and in 1980 Ronald Reagan became President of the United States. Both of these politicians were strong advocates of Friedman and neo-liberal economic policies. They both led governments that slashed government programs, reduced taxes, attacked the so-called privileges of trade unions and deregulated industry and the financial institutions. Free trade policies had already been established, and Reagan and Thatcher supported and promoted them. In his first inaugural address on January 20, 1981, Ronald Reagan said, "Government is not the solution to our problem; government is the problem."[7] Margaret Thatcher once said there is no such thing as society, only individuals.[8]

The consequences of these policies were widespread in both Britain and the United States. In the U.S. Ronald Reagan used the term "supply side economics" to describe his economic policies. Taxes were slashed for upper income groups. The top tax bracket was cut from 70% to 50% in 1981 and then to 38% in 1986. As a result the gap of income between the rich and everyone else exploded. The middle class shrank, and incomes of working people stagnated or declined.[9] Much of the regulation of business was removed, but there were increased controls on trade unions. Finance capital was favoured over manufacturing. Many industries shifted from the northeast of the United States, the so-called "rust belt," to the south and west, where labour was less expensive and unions not so powerful. In Britain there has been a shift from the industrial north of the country to London and the south.

But one U.S. government program was sacrosanct: the military. Reagan and the conservatives around him believed that military power was essential for America's superpower status and imperial ambitions. Military spending increased 40% between 1981 and 1985. The combination of lower taxes and increased military spending resulted in a soaring U.S. deficit. Economic conditions in the United States improved, but this was more because of deficit spending, a policy advocated by Keynesian economics in times of recession, than it was monetary policy.[10] Reagan was unconcerned about the rising debt and in his administration and during the presidency of George H. W. Bush, who succeeded him, the U.S. debt ballooned.

With the election of Democrat Bill Clinton in 1992 there was the opportunity to reverse these policies of neo-liberalism, but he continued and strengthened them. By the end of the 1990s trade had liberalized and most governments had removed the barriers to the free flow of money. Financial markets had become so integrated that essentially there was only one global financial system. Hundreds of billions of dollars were regularly flying around the world in fierce speculation on currencies. This was summarized as "the Washington Consensus," a free market approach to economic management, an ideology that the United States exported to the developing world. Globalization had arrived.[11]

This international free trade system led to significant problems. Money rushing from one currency to another resulted in the rapid devaluation of many currencies, which in turn led to credit squeeze, financial crisis and even collapse. The free trade in goods led to significant job losses in developed countries and the stagnation if not deterioration of wages. This came to be called "the race to the bottom," by trade unionists, but the leaders of U.S. business supported these policies. Corporations were able to reduce costs and at the same time rapidly expand their markets. Corporate profits were spectacular, contributing to the rise in the value of the stock of these companies.

Environmental concerns were another serious problem. The environmental movement in the developed world has led to much stronger environmental laws in those countries. Corporations, in some instances, located their manufacturing in developing countries to avoid these environmental regulations. Countries or groups that tried to stop the importation of goods on environmental grounds were stopped by the WTO with the legal argument that environmental regulations were an impediment to trade.

These problems led to the development of a strong "anti-globalization" movement that had a political impact with the protests at the Seattle Ministerial conference of the WTO in 1999. But while globalization led to serious problems among middle and low income people in the developed world, and serious environmental problems, increased trade contributed to unprecedented improvements of the economic prospects in the developing world and the living standard of millions of people. Rapid economic growth of developing countries – with the notable exception of sub-Saharan Africa – is creating a different world.

From Neo-Liberal to Neo-Conservative

In the year 2000, the beginning of the new millennium, the United States was at the height of its power. After the collapse of the Soviet Union it was the only remaining superpower with a network of semi-independent countries that constituted its empire. It was at this moment that a small number of conservatives found themselves in control of the United States government, and changed the political direction of the country.

Through the 1990s a group of conservatives had gradually taken control of the American Republican Party. They built a coalition made up of the business and corporate elite, evangelical Protestants, rural and small town voters and a sizable number of middle and lower income people concerned with issues of race, crime and immigration. It was a coalition built on fear: fear of the loss of wealth, fear of "modern ideas" like the Theory of Evolution, fear of government intervention and high taxes and fear of being overwhelmed by people different than themselves.

This conservative group supported and promoted the neo-liberal economic agenda, but within this coalition was another group who were primarily interested in American foreign policy.[12] They believed the United States should project American interests abroad; military power was essential to promote these interests. They were strong supporters of the State of Israel and various right wing regimes. The group often opposed the efforts of the United Nations because this multilateral influence on international affairs might curtail American power. Neo-liberalism was an economic policy; neo-conservatism was a set of political policies that supported the American Empire. The two approaches were united in the George W. Bush White House that took office in January 2001 and so the term "neo-conservative" or "neo-con" was coined to describe them.

Once the Republican administration took control in Washington the neo-cons set a more aggressive foreign policy. They quickly abandoned any pretext of balancing economic interests and became strident defenders of corporations, private property and the interests of the wealthy. Neo-liberal ideology was opposed to special interest groups in politics because they distorted the market place, but in practice Washington became a place where armies of lobbyists and special interest groups became so powerful that they wrote legislation and advocated the dismantling of environmental protection and labour laws.[13] Americans, who prided themselves as political pragmatists, now found themselves governed by the most ideological government in America's history.

The United States and the World

Percentage of World Gross Domestic Product by country or region

YEAR	1950	1960	1970	1980	1990	2000	2006
World	100.0%	100.0%	100.0%	100.0%	100.0%	100.0%	100.0%
United States	27.2	24.2	22.3	21.1	21.4	21.8	19.6
Western Europe, 30 Countries	26.2	26.7	26.1	24.2	22.2	20.5	17.8
Eastern Europe, 14 Countries	3.5	3.6	3.4	3.4	2.4	2.0	2.6
Former USSR	9.6	10.0	9.8	8.5	7.3	3.5	4.1
Canada, Australia, N.Z.	3.4	3.2	3.2	3.2	3.2	3.2	2.9
Japan	3.0	4.4	7.4	7.8	8.6	7.3	6.1
China	4.5	5.2	4.4	5.2	7.8	11.8	16.7
India	4.2	3.9	3.4	3.2	4.1	5.2	6.1
42 East Asian Counties	4.8	4.6	4.9	6.2	8.0	9.5	9.2
Latin America and Caribbean	7.8	8.1	8.3	9.8	8.6	8.3	7.7
Middle East	2.0	2.3	3.0	3.8	3.4	3.7	3.6
Africa	3.7	3.5	3.5	3.6	2.6	3.1	3.2

Source: http://www.ggdc.net/Maddison/historical_statistics/horizontal-file_03-2007.xls

The Gross Domestic Product of the world has increased almost eight fold from 1950 to 2006. That increase in wealth has happened on every continent and in almost every country. But the figures also illustrate a gradual shift in economic power in the world. In 1950 the developed world (United States, Western Europe, Canada, Australia, New Zealand and Japan) had 59.8% of the world's Gross Domestic Product. By 2006 this had slipped to 46.4%. The former USSR countries and Eastern Europe had 13.0% of the world's GDP in 1950, but by 2006 that had dropped to 6.7%. The most dramatic rise of wealth has been in the developing world: China, India, other East

Asian countries, Latin America and the Middle East. Their percentage of the world's GDP has risen from 23.3% in 1950 to 43.3% in 2006. The rate of economic growth of China and India suggests that they will play a major role in world affairs in coming years.

In the 2008 Fortune Global 500[14] list of multi-national corporations, measured by revenue, the headquarters of the top companies are located as follows:

European Union	184 companies
United States	153 companies
Japan	64 companies
China	29 companies
South Korea	15 companies
Canada	14 companies
Australia	8 companies
India	7 companies
Taiwan	6 companies
Brazil	5 companies
Mexico	5 companies
Russia	5 companies
Singapore, Malaysia, Thailand	3 companies
Saudi Arabia, Turkey	2 companies
	500 companies

Among the top ten companies in 2008, five are American. The largest is Walmart, a retail chain. Four out of the ten are oil companies and three are automobile companies. The United States has now been displaced as the country with the largest number of companies in the top 500 and replaced by the fast-growing European Union corporations. In 2005 the U.S. had 176 corporations in the Fortune 500 list, falling to 153 by 2008. Russia, with only five companies in the top 500, all of them energy companies, reflects how far that country has fallen since the end of the Cold War. China, with 29 companies on the list, and India, with seven, are still small in terms of economic power compared with the developed world, but that is about to change.

China's economy has grown more than any other country's. In 1950 China had only 4.5% of the world economy but by 2006 they had 16.7% of the world's GDP. What is more remarkable is that most of this economic growth has come in little more than thirty years, since Mao's death in 1976. While the annual economic growth rate of the United States and Western Europe is currently between two and three percent, the growth rate of China is between nine and eleven percent. China's economy continued to expand at these levels through the recession that began in 2008. There is considerable untapped economic potential in the country. About 800 million Chinese continue to work in agriculture. Once that population changes to industrial production, the GDP of China will be larger than the United States and the European Union.

The economic rise of China, and to a lesser extent India, the Middle East and South America, signals that the world will radically change over the next fifty years. As the American economy declines relative to others, so will its empire decline. The U.S. will not be able to continue to achieve its economic and political objectives by military means, as they have recently done in both Iraq and Afghanistan, because other powerful nations will not allow it to happen if it interferes with their political or economic objectives. A quick tour of the world shows how much the American decline has already set in, and their power and influence has eroded.

In South America, a part of the world that has been dominated by the United States since the Monroe Doctrine was proclaimed in 1823, several socialist and left-leaning governments have come to power in the most important countries. Many have made links with Cuba and Venezuela in outright defiance of the U.S. A goal for these countries is to free themselves from American domination. They are working together to promote regional trade and have made trade links with China, India and South Africa. Recently they launched the "Bank of the South" to play a central role in promoting the economy of the region and as an alternative to the World Bank and the IMF. That has given them even greater independence from the United States. South American countries plan to launch a co-operative news service so they are freed from CNN and the American domination of the news.

The growth of the economies of the Far East is nothing short of phenomenal. China and the Asian Tigers of South Korea, Taiwan, Hong Kong and Singapore have become the manufacturing centers of the world and that growth has brought increased prosperity and stability and has lessened the number of wars in the region. There are still millions of people who live in poverty but the region is changing so rapidly and the wealth is accumulating at such a rate that soon extreme poverty will be a thing of the past. China has 2.25 million in their military, almost a million more than the United States.[15] Their troops are not as well armed as the Americans and the Chinese leadership have said they have no intention of challenging the military supremacy of the United States, but the country has clearly emerged as an important leader in international affairs. As problems resurfaced with North Korea, it was China that used its influence to bring them to the negotiating table because the United States had little ability to influence events.

The growth rate of India, another country with over a billion people, is not as high as China's, but it is impressive none the less. India is taking over many information technology jobs and is following an independent foreign policy. With increased trade and wealth, India has become the dominant economic power in the region. Its military is almost as large as that of the United States, and its equipment is improving.

The Russian Federation has been transformed from the stodgy days when the Soviet Union was driven to the point of collapse by the bureaucracy. Russia has reinvented itself as an energy rich powerhouse that exports oil and other commodities to Western Europe, but there is still considerable poverty particularly in the rural areas of the country. Russia is one of the few states to openly challenge the United States. In 2007 President Vladimir Putin attacked the policies of the U.S. for using force to solve problems and having "disdain for the basic principles of international law."[16] Russia is making economic links to Iran and other Middle Eastern countries in defiance of American objections.

The European Union now is composed of twenty-seven member states. Its population of 502.5 million people is almost 200 million larger than the population of the United States. Most E.U. counties are members of NATO, and NATO membership is growing. The Western European countries have been close allies with the Americans for decades, but the Europeans were deeply disturbed by the American invasion of Iraq, and U.S. prestige in Europe was at an all time low during the George W. Bush Presidency. Even conservative leaders such as German Chancellor Angela Merkel and French President Nicolas Sarkozy have gone out of their way to distance themselves from U.S. foreign policy. The debt crisis in Greece, Ireland, Portugal, Spain and Italy has recently shaken the euro, but in the most prosperous countries of Europe standards of living are on a par or above the United States.

The Middle East – that part of the world the United States has been preoccupied with for decades – continues in crisis with no signs of resolution to fundamental problems. Oil is the basis of the economy in the region but political instability and war are hindering economic development. In the past the U.S. has supported blatantly anti-democratic governments like Egypt and Saudi Arabia, and the uprisings of the Arab Spring in 2011 against autocratic regimes in the region demonstrated the pitfalls of that policy. The Israeli-Palestinian crisis remains a major problem. Many in the region and in Europe blame the United States because of its unwavering support of Israel. The Americans refuse to use their power and influence to force the Israelis to make reasonable accommodations with Palestinians. If one thing has been learned from the invasion of Iraq it is that the problems of the region cannot be solved by military force, yet the Israelis continue to rely on their superior military.

Only Africa appears to favour the Americans, largely because the United States has not played a major role on the continent. For a century and a half Africa has been dominated by Europeans and subject to their imperial colonial ambitions. Even today the Americans remain largely irrelevant in Africa. There is little trade between the United States and African countries, and Americans give relatively little in aid. In recent years the Chinese have been courting the African states in order to gain access to their rich raw materials. The European

Union, India and other countries are likely to join the efforts to exploit this underdeveloped continent.

The American Debt Crisis

There is a complex group of reasons for the relative decline of the United States, but the key ones are the accumulating American debt and the U.S. balance of payment problems. Governments, like individuals and families, cannot ignore debt. If they do, more and more of the revenue that they raise must go to pay the interest on the debt and ultimately the country is in ruin. That is what has been happening in the United States. From George Washington to Dwight Eisenhower, a period of 160 years, the country had little public debt. The largest debt was $200 billion from the Second World War, but that was easily managed by the enormous American economy and tax base. The serious debt problems of the U.S. began in Lyndon Johnson's presidency. During the Vietnam War Johnson said that "we can have guns and butter," and this belief resulted in deficit budgets.[17] But U.S. debt grew much worse in the Reagan years when tax reductions and massive spending increases for the military sent deficits soaring, adding billions of dollars to the U.S. debt. Large deficits continued in the George H. W. Bush years and during early years of the Bill Clinton presidency. Clinton did not raise taxes but he held down the costs of the military. The expanding economy in the mid and late 1990s resulted in more tax revenues, and in the last three years of Clinton's presidency, 1998 to 2000, there were balanced budgets, the first time since 1975.

With the election of George W. Bush the U.S. deficit soared much higher. Vice President Dick Cheney, the major policy maker of the administration, once said, "Reagan taught us that deficits don't matter."[18] The administration took this advice literally. Bush had promised to strengthen the military and after 9/11 the President had all of the justification needed to swell military budgets. Soon the United States was engaged in the War on Terror, and wars in Afghanistan and Iraq. Spending on the military increased substantially. The 2009 military budget was set at $515.4 billion but altogether the United

States was spending about $1 trillion on defence-related purposes. To this day the United States spends more on its military than all other countries combined.[19]

While military spending was skyrocketing the neo-cons also delivered on another part of their agenda, cutting taxes. In both 2001 and 2003 the Bush administration introduced major tax cuts, justifying them by saying that the cuts were needed to stimulate the economy, even though the economy was at almost full employment. The 2003 tax cut alone took $550 billion out of the budget. These tax cuts, like the cuts brought in by Reagan, benefited only the rich and contributed to income inequality.

By May 2011 the U.S. national debt had risen to almost $14.5 trillion or $45,939 per person – roughly $183,756 for a family of four.[20] The economic emergency package put together by the American government in late 2008 and early 2009 added another $1.75 trillion to the debt. Barrack Obama has said that he sees years of trillion dollar deficits to deal with the economic crisis.[21] This debt will be increasingly difficult to pay off. The American population is aging and the costs of long term entitlement programs like social security and Medicare[22] are unsustainable. Adding to the crisis, total personal household debt in the United States, including mortgages and consumer debt, was $11.4 trillion in 2005. $2.55 trillion of that amount is credit card debt with high interest rates.

War has played an important part in this accumulating debt. "Some … suggest that capitalism needs wars, that without them, recession would always lurk on the horizon. Today, we know that is nonsense… Peace is economically far better than war."[23] Those are the words of Joseph Stiglitz, the 2001 winner of the Nobel Prize in Economics and a former chief economist at the World Bank. Stiglitz has estimated the cost of the Iraq War to American people will be between $3 and $5 trillion.[24]

The U.S. debt crisis came to a head in the July 2011 debate on the expansion of government debt limits. Conservatives, led by Tea Party Movement members of Congress, refused to consider tax increases of any kind and President Obama caved in to their demands, agreeing to reduce the U.S. budget by cutting services. This stunning decision illustrates the inability of U.S. political leaders to cope with debt problems. The U.S. financial problems are not economic, they are political problems.

The United States can no longer afford war. Even the costs of the Iraq and Afghan Wars have pushed the country to the point of insolvency. The only solutions are a combination of higher taxes and cut backs on spending, particularly military spending, but that seems unlikely to happen. The U.S. debt is a train wreck that has already created injury to the American people and yet the political system defies solution to basic economic problems.

The United States and Free Trade

The accelerating level of the national debt is only one of the economic problems facing the United States. The balance of payments problem promises to be equally serious. The United States has promoted free trade since the end of the Second World War, and it continues to have strong support from the public around the world. The Pew Global Attitudes Project found that 59% of U.S. respondents to a survey in 2007 supported free trade.[25] The difficulty is that the United States is losing the economic contest in the international market place that has been created by free trade, and that is leading to a loss of economic and political power.

Free trade policies have benefited some Americans because they have resulted in high profits and soaring stocks for corporations. For others in the U.S. free trade has been a disaster. American made products cannot compete against products made in the developing world because wages and the costs of production in the U.S. are much higher. Plants have closed across the United States and workers have been laid off. It is estimated that at least two million jobs have been lost, many of those highly paid unionized jobs. Alan Binder, a Princeton economist and a former vice-chair of the Federal Reserve Bank, estimates that as many as 40 million American jobs could be lost as a result of free trade if the policy continues.[26]

There is one commodity that has created special problems for the Americans and that, of course, is oil. There is much talk about the oil crisis and the need to cut back on fossil fuels because of its rising cost and for environmental reasons. The end of cheap oil has arrived and it is predicted to increase in price for the foreseeable future. There are three basic reasons: oil reserves are being depleted, the new reserves that are coming on stream are more expensive to exploit and the demand for oil is exploding as countries like China and India grow wealthier and their citizens buy cars. Some analysts believe that 2005 was the point of "peak oil," and although the price will fluctuate, over time oil will become more expensive.[27] When that happens prices will rise rapidly at the gas pump. That will result in lowering the standard of living for most Americans because they depend on their cars for so many of their activities, and trucking is the major way that goods are delivered across the North American continent.

The Middle East is the largest source of oil deposits and the need to import oil by developed countries is the reason the Americans have been so active in the region. As long ago as 1980 President Jimmy Carter declared that Persian Gulf oil was vital to the interests of the United States. Both the Persian Gulf War of 1991 and the invasion of Iraq in 2003 were motivated by the need to ensure access to Middle Eastern oil. None other than Alan Greenspan, the former chair of the Federal Reserve, with close connections to the neo-cons in the government, said, "I am saddened that it is politically inconvenient to acknowledge what everyone knows. The Iraq War is largely about oil."[28] Like the British Navy's protection of trade in the nineteenth century, the U.S. military is providing access and security to the oil of countries like Saudi Arabia and Iraq for the United States and its empire. People are dying so the U.S. and its allies can have access to oil.

The American trade crisis is deepening. In 2006 the United States imported $857 billion worth of goods more than they exported. In 2010 it was $497.8 billion.[29] With smaller countries a trade deficit of that relative size, occurring year after year, would lead to a fiscal crisis and the value of their currency would drop precipitously, but because of its size and economic leadership, the United States has advantages that other countries do not share. The U.S. dollar is the world's reserve currency (the dollar hegemony) and virtually all countries have large dollar reserves. That helps to keep the American dollar high.

But can this situation continue? The United States needs an inflow of $65 to $75 billion a month to finance the current account deficit. Anything less will lead to a shortfall and the U.S. dollar will weaken and begin to fall in value.[30] Up until now the U.S. Treasury has been printing treasury bills and using them to settle their balance of payments accounts. Essentially Americans have been creating money to buy imports, but countries, corporations and individuals who hold U.S. dollars are beginning to get nervous. A substantial number of investors are moving away from the U.S. dollar and holding their reserves in euros. Saudi Arabia, which earns billions of U.S. dollars from its oil revenues, is now holding some of its reserves in euros. Russia holds all of its reserves in euros, and Qatar and Kuwait have been shifting their reserves to euros and Asian currencies. The euro is becoming a favoured currency and the era of the dollar hegemony may be coming to an end.

The wild card in this crisis is China. China now has $1.7 trillion in U.S. government debt,[31] by far the largest in the world, and the reserves are continuing to grow. China's reserves are so huge that it no longer has to be concerned about protecting its own currency. Recently the China Investment Fund was set up, and the government has announced that they are planning to invest the reserves around the world to make higher returns.[32] This is motivated by the fact that they have lost 20% of the value of their reserves by the decrease in the American dollar. In November 2007 Xu Jian, a Chinese central banker, announced officially that China would no longer keep just American dollars in its reserves but would diversify its holdings to include other currencies.[33] In time this will hasten the downward slide of the dollar.[34]

Experts are divided on the outcome. Some predict a drop of 30% in the value of the dollar, others even more, but all agree that the direction is inexorably away from the U.S. currency. When the dollar falls it will make American manufactured products more affordable and improve employment, but it will make foreign investments for American companies more expensive. It will increase the costs of imports and it will mean a drop in the standard of living of Americans.[35]

Perhaps the only good news is that it is in no one's interest to see the collapse of the American dollar because that would plunge the entire world into depression. It is more likely that the shift away from the American dollar will happen gradually. That will give the world time to adjust to the new economic reality, but the indications are clear. The preeminent position the U.S. economy has held since the end of the Second World War is over. The best guess is that the euro will appreciate and become the world reserve currency. The other possibility is that countries will hold reserves in a basket of stable currencies. Whatever the case, the advantages that the United States reaped from the dollar hegemony are coming to an end.

Global Impact of Free Trade

Free trade has been a mixed blessing for the United States, and the results internationally have been mixed as well. Developing countries like China, India, South Korea, Indonesia, Brazil and others have benefited because free trade has stimulated their exports and led to rapid economic growth, but underdeveloped countries with agricultural economies have been harmed by free trade practices and policies. In the undeveloped world the complaint is that the rules of the international economic system are biased in favour of the rich developed world, giving the multi-nationals complete access to their markets and ruining their local industries, while excluding their agricultural products from the markets of the developed world. The economist Joseph Stiglitz writes: "The international trade agreements, that the United States was so proud of a few years ago, were grossly unfair to the countries of the Third World."

Farm subsidies are a special problem. In the developing world the majority of people are subsistence farmers who try to grow a little extra beyond their own needs to sell on the market so they can get the cash to buy things they need to survive. The United States, countries in the E.U. and other developed countries have a small portion of their workforce in agriculture, but these governments provide massive subsidies to farmers. In 2007 the U.S. government provided $18 billion to farmers in the form of agricultural subsidies.[36] In 2002 European Union subsidies to agriculture were six times the total amount of foreign aid that all rich countries gave to the poor.[37] Not only is this against the rules of the WTO, not only does it give benefit to already wealthy farmers, but it disrupts agricultural production in the developing world.[38]

As an example, the United States is the largest cotton producer in the world. About 12,000 U.S. cotton growers receive between $2 and $3 billion a year in subsidies. This is a huge incentive and American growers flood the markets around the world with their subsidized cotton. It is estimated that this reduces the price of cotton about 14% below the price it would otherwise have, making it impossible for even the poorest countries in the world to grow cotton at a profit. "Subsidies are a catastrophe for us," said Zakariyaou Diawara, the head of the cotton farmer's union in the impoverished West African country of Mali. "Our cotton is of better quality; it's the subsidies that crush us."

When the WTO found the U.S. and other countries that subsidize their agricultural industries contravened international trade laws, the American government made minor changes to the way the subsidies were administered and kept them in place. Again there was a complaint to the WTO, but the Americans have appealed and the slow WTO dispute process means that it will be years before this issue is resolved, if ever. Meanwhile, as a condition of receiving aid, Mali and other West African nations are not allowed to subsidize their farmers.

If there were no subsidies, it is estimated that this would improve the living standards of these desperately poor farmers in Mali. At least three million people depend on cotton in the country. In a country like Mali, where farmers earn about $2,000 a year and about 40 percent of the children under the age of five are malnourished, an increase in income would make an enormous difference in the living standards of the entire country[39] and decrease the chance of war and civil and political unrest.[40] But nothing is done. The Americans and other developed countries dominate the world trading system and small impoverished countries like Mali are ignored.

Poor agricultural countries have special problems with free trade but some developing countries have also had serious problems. With the collapse of the Soviet Union in 1991 the economic crisis of the former superpower was severe. Unemployment soared; people were on the verge of starvation; crime increased alarmingly. The International Monetary Fund and the World Bank offered loans to Russia, but demanded in return that government owned assets be sold and services like education and health care cut back. In the aftermath, billions of dollars of state assets were sold at fire sale prices, enriching a small number of people called the "oligarchs," but leaving the majority of the population in poverty. Vladimir Putin has managed to deal with the crisis by selling oil and gas to the European Union, gaining foreign exchange, and clawing back some of the assets from the oligarchs by legal and semi-legal means. In the process Russia has abandoned neo-liberalism and developed a state directed economy.

In 1995 the "tequila crisis" hit Mexico, spread almost immediately to Brazil and Argentina, and was felt in Chile, The Philippines, Thailand, Poland, South Korea and Sweden. The currency reserves of these countries were low and the unregulated monetary markets led to a flight of capital. The reason for the crisis was different with each country but the pattern was similar. Problems began when the country did not hold enough reserves and there was a run on the currency, driving down its value. Factories closed, unemployment increased, driving down wages and creating misery for the poor. In Argentina a serious banking crisis led to the freezing of all bank accounts. No one could access his own money. The IMF and the World Bank were asked for help by the governments of these countries and their prescription was the same: loans would be given only on the condition that government owned assets were sold and vital services like education and health care were rolled back. In the meantime the wealthy, who were able to use the crisis to purchase devalued assets, increased their wealth.

Naomi Klein's book, *The Shock Doctrine*,[41] shows how in country after country neo-liberal economic policies have led to mass unemployment, a decrease in economic activity and real hardships for the poorest people. The insistence on privatization has led to the sale of state assets in developing countries. Many of these sales have gone to multi-national corporations, which take a high rate of profit out of them. But most serious of all, the insistence on the reduction of social spending has led to cuts in education, health and a raft of social programs that are essential if the people of the developing world are to gain the skills necessary for economic development. These policies hurt many developing countries but they were a disaster to poor underdeveloped nations.

Today many countries have taken steps to avoid being vulnerable. Almost all of the developing countries outside sub-Saharan Africa have substantial reserves to make their currencies immune from attack. Some, like Brazil and Argentina, have announced that they will never put themselves in the position where they will be dictated to by the IMF and the World Bank again. This is yet another indication of the diminished power of the U.S. The IMF and the World Bank are institutions that are run by policies dictated by the United States. Countries now are turning their back on them because they do not meet their needs.

The Crisis of 2008-09

Neo-liberal economic policies are built on an ideology that the best government is the least government. They advocate low taxes, privatization and deregulation. During the term of George W. Bush the neo-cons toured the world, proselytizing the benefits of the Washington consensus approach like evangelical true believers.[42] Then, in 2008, the entire U.S. neo-liberal economic program unravelled. The American financial sector had been deregulated to the point where there was no or little government oversight. Clever Wall Street brokers and investment houses packaged various debts into "structured debt derivatives" and then sold them to investors and financial institutions in the United States and around the world. The problem was that these derivatives were virtually worthless.

This is the assessment of Uwe E. Reinhardt, an economist who was involved in these financial institutions:

Our entire 21st-century banking sector, managed as it is by graduates of the nation's top business schools, supported by highly trained financial engineers, and monitored around the clock by thousands of allegedly bright financial analysts, immolated itself with highly toxic assets, purchased with borrowed money, and in the process infected the entire world economy.[43]

Most of this debt was in sub-prime mortgages and adjustable rate mortgages that had been granted to high risk borrowers to buy houses. The mortgages had value as long as the value of the property was maintained and the owners continued to pay, but in 2006 and 2007 house prices in the United States began to decline. People wanted to get out of these mortgages because the houses were not worth what they were paying for them. Many also found that they could not afford the escalating interest rates of the adjustable mortgages. People refused to pay or were unable to pay, foreclosures increased, bankruptcies accelerated and then the investors who had bought the derivatives realized that they held investments with very little real value.

Panic set in to the American financial markets. Credit tightened because banks and financial institutions did not have the money to lend or were holding on to their money in case of future needs. This lack of credit affected companies across the country. Lay-offs multiplied, there were bank failures and bankruptcies and restructuring of major Wall Street financial institutions, talk of recession turned to predictions of depression, and then the government began to act.

The large mortgage companies Fannie Mae and Freddie Mac and the insurer American International Group Inc. were essentially nationalized by the federal government. The lack of credit was a serious problem and it was announced that the government would provide $700 billion in a bailout package, an incredible amount of money, while some analyses say the total amount of the bailout exceeds $1.5 trillion. In the summer of 2008 the big three auto companies said they faced bankruptcy and demanded help. Then, in September and October 2008, the Dow Jones Industrial average lost 40%, the stock market crashed and trillions of dollars of value were wiped out in a few days. Pension funds suddenly found their assets could not meet their obligations.

The crisis quickly migrated to Europe, Japan and the rest of the world. Britain was particularly vulnerable because it had followed the American practice of deregulation of financial institutions. The British government was forced to nationalize the Northern Rock bank because thousands would have lost their deposits if the bank had failed. International trade dropped because letters of credit were not available, stock markets plummeted and the withdrawal of credit crippled companies.

Many Americans were angry with their government because they felt that the bailout was rewarding the very people who had caused the problem in the first place. Around the world the anger was directed at the U.S. For decades the Americans had used their influence and control of institutions such as the IMF, the World Bank and the WTO to propagate their neo-liberal economic policies. These policies had caused considerable hardships in developing countries, particularly the poorest and most vulnerable. Now the Americans had completely reversed themselves by adopting policies of state intervention that only socialists advocated, and this was being done by the administration of George W. Bush, the most ideological conservative to ever occupy the presidency.

The French Prime Minister François Fillon said, "The world is on the edge of the abyss because of the irresponsible system." German Finance Minister Peer Steinbrueck predicted the end of the U.S. status as the "superpower of the global financial system." Glen Hodgson, chief economist of the Conference Board of Canada, said, "You only have moral authority when you have your own house in order."[44] These are very strong words coming from political leaders of the closest allies of the United States.

The Consequences of Neo-Con Policies

Since Ronald Reagan was President, most Americans and their political and economic leaders have been guided by the myth of invincibility and the myth of unending wealth. Americans have been politically paralyzed, unable to raise taxes to pay for the high level of consumption that they demand and running up debt to unsustainable levels. It was neo-liberal economic policies that led to the economic crisis of 2008-2009 and though Barack Obama, a liberal, has been elected President, he continues to pile up the debt and has been unable to raise taxes because of the Republican control of Congress. These policies have had a devastating impact on the lives of American people.

The United States now has a greater division of income and wealth than any other developed country. The richest 10% of the population have prospered as a result of neo-liberal policies, but 90% of Americans have seen their incomes stagnate or fall, and 36 million people live below the poverty line. The poor live in deteriorated neighbourhoods with ever-diminishing employment opportunities, while the rich have access to staggering amenities. This inequality has ossified into a class structure with an elite who not only control unprecedented wealth but also with their money give their children access to expensive educational institutions, the training grounds and clubs of the elite of the next generation. Meanwhile the poor are trapped, angry and frustrated.

The figures tell the story. Middle class income is no higher today than it was in 1970. "The income of a young man in his 30s is 12% below that of a man his age three decades ago."[45] One way that families are compensating for this loss of income is that more women are going into the workforce. In 1970 only 38% of women with school aged children were working; now the figure is close to 70%. The typical American now works two weeks more a year than 30 years ago. Until now Americans had higher incomes than workers in Western Europe, but that is primarily because they work longer hours. Europeans typically have four week's holiday a year while Americans have two.

In recent years the wealthy have been involved in a corporate game of free market capitalism where the emphasis is on the stock market rather than building companies. In search of corporate profits, the top executives attacked their very own employees with lay-offs in the hundreds of thousands. This balloons the bottom line because labour is a major cost of business, but it attacks the long term viability of the company because its operations are dependent on the middle-managers and workers who have the knowledge and history to run the enterprise. The top executives – those with stock options – make windfall gains because the price of the stock spikes upwards on news of high profits, but the long term viability of company is put in jeopardy.

The unregulated markets in the United States led to an unprecedented level of unethical behaviour by people in the finance industry, the richest in the country. The people who created this situation walked away with hundreds of millions of dollars in fees and stock options. The average chief executive's pay was 275% higher than the average worker. Is it any wonder that the American public was furious that the Bush administration was bailing out the very people who had created the crisis and made all of the profits?

The implications are devastating to the American people and the economy. The decline of the dollar is a sure sign of the decline of the American Empire. During the Roman Empire the denarius, the Roman currency, dominated trade and stimulated economic activity across the empire, but as Roman military adventures became overextended the denarius declined in value. Soon the empire found it difficult to pay for the legions. Roads and services deteriorated and in time the empire fell apart. After 1500 the powerful European colonial empires had strong, centralized governments that funded, directed and reaped the rewards of their colonies. The British pound sterling was the commanding world currency during the nineteenth century. Because of the strength of the pound, London was the center of the world commerce, British ships transported goods to every corner of the globe and the British funded and owned railways and other enterprises around the globe. The First and Second World Wars ended the strength and domination of the British pound and soon their empire could not be sustained.

Those who think this could not happen to the American Empire are ignoring history. An economic crisis can happen overnight with cruel consequences. When traders lose confidence in a currency they will dump it regardless of the impact on the economy. In this electronic age billions of dollars can move in a blink of an eye with immediate consequences. A lower U.S. dollar will affect everything in the country. American wealth will be devalued, the value of American companies will deteriorate, imported goods will become more expensive, the standard of living of Americans will shrink dramatically, foreign wars will be unaffordable and the American Empire will come to an end.

Not only is the United States in grave economic danger but it is rapidly declining relative to other countries. China has now overtaken Germany as the third largest economy, and if its growth rate continues, Goldman and Sachs predict it will overtake the U.S. by 2035.[46] By 2040 it is predicted that China, India, Russia, Brazil and Mexico will hold economic leadership.[47] This will force a reordering of the international order.

The social indicators comparing different countries illustrate that the United States is a society with serious social problems.

- The United States is 49th in world literacy.[48]

- The United States ranked 28th out of 40 countries in mathematical literacy.[49]

- Europe surpassed the United States in the mid-1990s as the largest producer of scientific literature.[50]

- China now produces almost three times the number of engineers as the United States. Increasingly western companies are locating their research and development divisions in China.[51]

- The World Health Organization ranked the U.S. overall health performance as 54th in all countries. At the same time, the U.S. spends more on health care per capita than any other country.[52]

- Lack of health insurance coverage causes 18,000 unnecessary American deaths a year.[53]

- U.S. childhood poverty per capita now ranks 22nd, second to last among the developed nations. Only Mexico has a lower ranking.[54]

- The United States has greater income inequality than any other developed country. "America, with 36.5 million poor and hundreds of billionaires, is becoming the world's richest Third World nation."[55]

- Between 1980, when Ronald Reagan was elected president, and 2004, the mid-point of George W. Bush's presidency, the proportion of income earned by the top one percent of U.S. households more than doubled from 10% to 22%. The combined net worth of the top one percent today is higher than the total for the bottom 90%.[56]

- The Gini Index Score of Income Inequality shows the distribution of income of the United States is more like a developing country than other developed countries.[57]

- The United States is 41st in infant mortality. Cuba has a higher ranking.[58]

- Women are 70% more likely to die in childbirth in the United States than in Europe.[59]

- Americans now spend more money on gambling than on movies, videos, DVDs, music and books combined.[60]

- One half of all U.S. children live in a one parent household.[61]

- The average Japanese family has savings equivalent to $117,000.[62] American families average $85,000 in debt.[63]

- The United States had 715 per 100,000 people in jail, the highest rate of incarceration of any nation in the world. Canada and Australia, by comparison each have 116 per 100,000 people in jail. The weighted average of all countries surveyed was 147.9 per 100,000 people.[64]

The End of Empire

The end of the Cold War brought a moment of sole superpower status to the United States – "hyper-power" as a French Foreign Minister once called it. And yet, after less than two decades of American political ascendancy, the evidence of decline is everywhere. The end of U.S. economic supremacy is a sure sign of the end of empire and the end of the American policy of imposing its will by the power of its military. Today economic power is much more evenly distributed among the nations of the world than it has been for the last 100 years and that will be reflected in the international political arena. The United States will still be a major power in the world, but no longer will it be the sole superpower imposing its will on others. The American empire is finished. Economic conditions are creating a multilateral world where war, as a tactic of domination, is no longer acceptable.

CHAPTER 7: TACTICS AND TECHNOLOGY

> "Afghans don't understand any more how come a little force like the Taliban can continue to exist, can continue to flourish, can continue to launch attacks, with [troops from] 40 countries in Afghanistan, with entire NATO force in Afghanistan, with entire international community behind them, still we are not able to defeat the Taliban. There must be a problem somewhere."[1] *(Afghan President Hamid Karzai, November 2008)*

The reality is that, with all of its firepower, equipment and the most sophisticated military the world has ever seen, the United States, along with its coalition partners totalling over 100,000 troops on the ground, cannot defeat Taliban insurgents in Afghanistan amounting to no more than 10,000 fighters. Of that number it is estimated that only between 2,000 and 3,000 of the Taliban fighters are highly motivated.[2] The rest are part-timers made up mainly of rootless young men. The reasons for this failure explain why war is no longer an effective means of domination in the twenty-first century.

Changes in the Nature of War

Wars in Europe during the Middle Ages were fought with very small armies. Each soldier had to outfit, arm and feed himself. The knights were resplendent in their armour, mounted on powerful warhorses while the infantry soldiers were impoverished peasants and townsmen armed with pikes and swords that often shattered in battle. Ordinary soldiers had little interest in the objectives of the war. They were there for the plunder.

In the Battle of Agincourt in 1415, one of the key battles of the Hundred Years War, the English had around 5,000 men in the field and the French 15,000. The English prevailed in the Battle of Agincourt because they introduced the long bow, a powerful new weapon that shattered the French. That weapon illustrates the relationship between the technological advances in weaponry and victory on the battlefield that has held since the beginning of warfare: the force with the most technologically advanced weapons always prevails on the battlefield. That rule has been challenged with modern warfare.

It was around the beginning of the sixteenth century that warfare began to significantly change. What caused that change was the introduction of gunpowder. At first cannons were developed and used to shatter the walls of forts and castles but then hand held muskets were introduced. By 1501 the Spanish had developed the "fire stick," a type of musket that could fire a 20 ounce iron ball a range of 100 yards. By 1525 they had improved the weapon so that it could be hand held, or more often held in a forked stick, when it was fired. The projectiles fired from the first muskets traveled at speeds that made them invisible to the human eye.

War had changed forever in Europe. Battles were fought using muskets and the army that almost always prevailed was the one that was best armed and disciplined. Gunpowder had a profound effect on the expansion of European empires. Cannon and muskets gave Europeans an overwhelming advantage when their armies came up against the armies of indigenous people armed with spears and bows and arrows. Rarely could native people prevail in battles against the Europeans for the next 500 years, and that led to European colonialism and world domination.

Gunpowder, cannon, and muskets revolutionized warfare in Europe. Battles were not won by the bravery of individual warriors: it was the training and discipline of the armies that led to victory in warfare. Muskets were inaccurate and useless beyond the range of 100 paces. In battle the armies stood facing each other in double rows, exchanging musket volley after musket volley until one side was so decimated that they were overwhelmed with a final charge. Victory went to the army that could withstand withering fire and not turn tail and run. Only an army that had been instilled with the most rigid discipline could emerge the victor under battlefield conditions like that.

By the early eighteenth century the military and war itself had become professionalized. No longer did the rank and file have to depend on plunder to survive. Soldiers were paid according to their rank and the military supplied them with food, uniforms and weapons. This was the industrialization of war. Weapons were improved and manufactured in great quantities. During the Napoleonic War British industrial production was so great and the country's wealth so enormous that they supplied weapons and uniforms to their troops and all of their allies.

From the beginning of the Seven Years War in 1756 to the Battle of Waterloo in 1815, a period of almost sixty years, Europe was almost continuously at war. The scale of war changed. In the Seven Years War, from 1756 to 1763, there were hundreds of thousands of troops on both sides of the conflict. It is estimated that between 900,000 and 1,400,000 died in that war. In the Napoleonic Wars there were at least 3,250,000 casualties of combatants and some estimates put the number of casualties in the wars at over 6 million.

Recruiting became an especially difficult problem. Soldiers were paid a shilling if they signed up with the British army. "The king's shilling," it came to be called. Often possible recruits were tricked to take the king's shilling. Recruiters got men drunk, and they sobered up only to find they had joined the army. Press gangs even kidnapped men off the streets.[3] Once they were in the military, ordinary soldiers or seamen were treated brutally in order to maintain discipline. Flogging for minor infractions was not unusual and capital punishment was meted out for the more serious offences.[4]

These types of practices were common in all of the armies of Europe at the time, and yet these same armies became highly disciplined and effective.[5] Napoleon built the largest and most powerful military force of his day, *"la Grande Armée."* The French won battle after battle and the French Empire extended further and further until France dominated virtually the whole European continent. Napoleon was the strategic master of conventional warfare. He had been an artillery officer and in battle he concentrated artillery fire on a weak section of the enemy's line to force a breakthrough. It seemed no army could defeat *la Grande Armée* on the battlefield. Out of desperation, a new strategy emerged to challenge the French and change the conduct of war.

In 1808 French troops were sent into Spain, a country that was a French protectorate. At first the troops were welcomed by the Spanish people, but soon it became obvious that Napoleon was intent on taking over the country and making it a vassal state. He removed the Spanish king and put his brother, Joseph, on the throne. Spanish nationalists were infuriated. Citizens of Madrid rose up and some 150 French soldiers were killed in a riot. The next day the French army shot hundreds of people in retaliation. (This massacre of Spanish civilians is the subject of Goya's famous painting called "The Third of May, 1808." A reproduction of the painting is on the cover of this book.)

Spontaneous opposition to the French broke out in much of Spain. Spanish provinces threw out their French governors. Attacks on the French troops multiplied and the French could not predict where or when the raids would come. Supply trains were attacked. French citizens were killed. Guerrilla war – or "little war" to translate the Spanish word – had been born.[6] Napoleon reinforced his army in Spain, but the attacks only increased. Spanish volunteer militia overran French positions and the casualties mounted. It was a catastrophe for the strongest, largest and best equipped fighting force in the world at that time. Twenty-four thousand French troops were lost. The French command panicked and ordered a general retreat.

For the first time Napoleon's *Grande Armée* had faced a defeat of this magnitude, and it had happened with uncoordinated attacks by undisciplined groups of militia who could barely be called an army. The Spanish guerrilla forces were not motivated by plunder; they were not trained, disciplined or paid; they even provided their own weapons. These were ordinary citizens motivated by nationalism, and the desire to throw out a foreign oppressor. A new military strategy had emerged.

This was not to be the last defeat for Napoleon at the hands of an army using unconventional tactics. In 1812 Napoleon invaded Russia with 700,000 men of the *Grande Armée*. This vast army was invincible on the battlefield and the Russians, with only 488,000 troops in their army, knew it. Rather than engaging the French, the Russians fell back, burning their villages and crops as they retreated. There were some battles and in every one the French were the victors. Napoleon fully expected the Russian Czar to surrender, and for Russia to become another vassal state of France, but all that happened was that the Russians fell back further and the *Grande Armée* advanced through burnt fields and deserted villages. Finally on September 14, 1812 the French army reached Moscow. The city was empty, but still Napoleon did not receive the surrender of the Czar.

Napoleon waited. His troops were hungry. The supply trains were unable to get through and the men were unable to live off the scorched, empty land. Winter was closing in. Finally Napoleon had no choice but to order a retreat. The *Grande Armée* left Moscow as winter was beginning. The Russians waited for them, attacking the stragglers, striking when the French were at their weakest. Starvation took the worst toll of all. By the time the remnants of the French army were finally out of Russia there were only 27,000 fit men left of the *Grande Armée*.

In 1815, two and a half years later, Napoleon finally met his Waterloo, when the French were defeated by the British and Prussian forces that faced them in that conventional battle, but the unconventional guerrilla warfare of the Spanish and Russian campaigns were what led to that final defeat. Those campaigns are the key to understanding modern warfare.

The First and Second World Wars, as well as the Korean War were all fought using conventional tactics. Technology played the decisive role in determining the final victor in these conflicts. During the First World War the machine gun and artillery were the dominant weapons. They were so lethal that attacking troops exposed on open ground were quickly annihilated. These weapons gave defence the advantage over attacking forces and led to trench warfare. On both sides soldiers huddled deep in trenches, trying to keep away from the murderous fire and exploding artillery shells. It was only in the last few months of the war that tanks and aircraft gave attacking forces some advantages and finally the impasse of trench warfare was broken.

Again, what determined the course of the Second World War was technology. The classic land battle of this war was the German *blitzkrieg* tank attack. In 1940 the German tanks smashed through the

French and British lines in northern France, routing them within hours. Tanks became the chief assault weapon of the war, and the use of aircraft also changed the way the war was fought. Bombing raids against British and German cities were indiscriminate attacks on citizens in order to attack the centers of industrial production and terrorize the population. In the war in the Pacific the American navy and air force were the dominant weapons that defeated the Japanese.

The First and Second World Wars were massive struggles that pitted whole societies and their entire industrial capability against each other. In the First World War over eight and a half million combatants were killed in the trenches and four times that number wounded.[7] In the Second World War 61 million people were killed. Twenty-two million were combatants and 39 million were civilians.[8]

The lesson that military planners drew from these conflicts was that the most advanced and effective technology helped to create the most destructive weapons and those weapons won wars. This belief led to the development of nuclear weapons, the ultimate weapons of mass destruction. The weapons of war now could literally end the human race. The fear that this might happen has led to efforts to avoid large scale conventional warfare and above all to ensure that nuclear war does not happen.

The struggle of the world wars and the Korean War was over land, and the progress of these wars was marked by the position of the front – the place where the two armies confronted each other. But since Korea, wars have not had a front, and although they have been fought using conventional weapons, they are not conventional wars at all. As well, the belief that technology wins wars has also been challenged. The significant wars since Korea have been called "asymmetrical wars" and these wars are much more like the Spanish and Russian campaigns in the Napoleonic Wars than the conventional wars of the first half of the twentieth century.

Asymmetrical Warfare

Asymmetrical warfare goes by different names such as unconventional war, guerrilla warfare or insurrection. In such conflicts a well armed and supplied military force is pitted against an enemy that is much weaker militarily. The war takes place on the home territory of the weaker force. Vietnam is a classic example of an asymmetrical war. The Viet Cong were native to Vietnam, and the Americans occupied the country with a much superior military force, but victory did not go to the superior force as would be expected in a conventional war. Since Korea there have been many such conflicts: the French in Vietnam and Algeria, the British in Malaya, Kenya and Northern Ireland, the South African apartheid regime against the ANC, the Colombian government against FARC, the Soviets in Afghanistan and Chechnya, the Americans in Vietnam, Afghanistan and Iraq and the Israeli-Palestinian conflict in the Middle East. In all of these wars the developed countries had far greater firepower than their enemies, but ultimately they were either defeated, forced to withdraw, or change their policies to accommodate the enemy.

In asymmetrical wars the guerrillas are organized into small groups of lightly armed, mobile fighters. They use their knowledge of the country and the support of the local people to ambush and attack their better armed and equipped enemy, much like the way the Spanish and Russians attacked and defeated Napoleon's troops. Even a small number of attackers using modern, hand held weapons can inflict heavy casualties on the enemy within seconds, especially if the forces attacked are in the open and the guerrilla fighters are concealed. Large numbers of attackers in a battle are a disadvantage in an asymmetrical war because they can be spotted and eliminated by air strikes. The aim of the attackers is not to defeat the enemy in each battle. It is to inflict casualties, harass the enemy and reduce their morale and commitment to the war.

In asymmetrical warfare the guerrilla group must keep the support of the local population. That allows the fighters to merge with the people, get supplies, rest, plan the next operation and then strike again. It is estimated that two percent of the population can lead a successful insurrection, if they have the sympathy of the other ninety-eight percent of the population. During the Vietnam War, President Lyndon Johnson spoke about the importance of winning the "hearts and minds" of the Vietnamese people. He understood that if the Americans were to win the war they had to have the support of the Vietnamese people. The Americans never won the hearts and minds of the Vietnamese and ultimately lost the war.

One of the difficulties of fighting an asymmetrical war is controlling the troops. With a mounting insurrection the occupying army comes to feel threatened and lashes back with increasing ferocity.

> So the occupiers break down doors and search for weapons, terrorizing and humiliating people in the process. They call in air strikes, which kill innocent bystanders. They choke off commerce and impose curfews to teach the locals a lesson, lessons that are never learned. For over 800 years the English beat, imprisoned, transported, shot and hung hundreds of thousands of Irish, and it made the natives not the slightest bit quieter or more respectful. Indeed it made them quite the opposite.[9]

Similar things happened in Vietnam and are continuing to happen in Iraq, the Israeli-Palestinian conflict, Afghanistan and the so called "tribal lands" in Pakistan along the border with Afghanistan. Fear and anger lead soldiers to commit atrocities. That in turn makes the population angry at the occupying army, which leads to an increase in the recruits of the insurgents. Over time the number and intensity of the insurgent attacks increases. This is how David Halberstam describes the process:

> [In Vietnam] the sheer ferocity of our firepower created enemies of people who were then on the sidelines, thereby doing our enemies' recruiting for them... What is now called collateral killing creates a growing resentment among civilians, who may decide that whatever values we bring are not in the end worth it, because we have also brought too much killing and destruction to their country.[10]

Since Vietnam the American public has shown a reluctance to support wars where there are high casualties of American troops. As a result the Pentagon entered into an expensive and complicated program of computerization of the battlefield. This high tech warfare is designed to keep troops out of harm's way.

> Many soldiers...are now in considerably less danger than they would be in their automobiles at home. Working in front of computer screens in air-conditioned tents miles from the battlefield or at 35,000 feet in a B-2 bomber, they have no more sense of combat than teenagers in a video arcade.[11]

In the last three years the Americans fighting the war in Afghanistan have gone one step further to bomb targets in Afghanistan and the tribal regions of Pakistan with unmanned drone aircraft, computer controlled by technicians in Arizona, half a world away. The problem with this reliance on high tech weapons is that it often does not work. There are computer failures and more often technical incompetence on the part of the people operating the equipment. The major problem has been that the computers and their operators find it impossible to differentiate between friend and foe. As a consequence the American military have killed a large number of non-combatants. This, in turn, fuels the anger of the local population and swells the ranks of the insurgents.

Asymmetrical wars were spawned out of an understanding that poorly equipped groups could never defeat well armed troops by using conventional tactics. There is not a military force in the world that could defeat the Americans in a conventional battle today. This has led to a change in the very nature of the practice of war. Insurgents have rejected conventional warfare. No longer are there huge armies confronting each other on the battlefield. Victory in an asymmetrical war comes not from winning battles; it is the result of attrition. The struggle continues until the dominant side realizes that they cannot sustain the casualties and is losing the support of the people at home. Finally political leaders make the decision to withdraw. Victory is the reward of stubborn perseverance, and the ability to continue the struggle despite the casualties and hardships.

The success of putting down insurgencies since the Korean War has been dismal. The French lost wars in both Vietnam and Algeria. The British had some success in Malaya and Kenya. In both cases some of the British officers knew the countryside and culture of the local people, but when the war subsided, the British granted independence and got out of both countries as quickly as they could without losing face because they knew that if the wars were to resume they would have no chance of winning. The Soviets lost in Afghanistan after a nine year war that contributed to the collapse of the Soviet Union itself. The Russians appear to have put down the insurrection in Chechnya, but critics claim their victory is largely the result of the brutal tactics of the Russian soldiers. The Israelis continue to prevail against the Palestinian insurrection in the West Bank and Gaza, but they have not defeated their enemies. In time it seems likely that the Israelis will be forced to recognize a Palestinian state. The Americans lost in Vietnam, the most important asymmetrical war ever fought; Iraq has been a debacle; and the prospect of victory in Afghanistan appears slim. Thomas Johnson, professor of national security at the Naval Postgraduate School in Monterey, California writes, "Since World War Two, has there been one successful counter-insurgency? The answer is none. This war [Iraq] will never be won militarily."[12]

Terrorism

Terrorism is a tactic in an asymmetrical war.[13] It is a sure sign that the terrorist side is very weak. The group does not even have the strength to mount guerrilla attacks, let alone carry out a campaign of conventional warfare. But terrorism also indicates the group is deeply committed to their cause, even to the point where individuals are willing to give up their lives. Terrorism has proven to be a very effective tactic in frightening the population, and shaping political decisions, but the use of terror has never won a war.

Terrorism has long historical roots that go back at least to ancient times. In the nineteenth and early twentieth centuries radical political theories led to the formation of a number of groups who saw terror as a legitimate tactic. Anarchists were successful in assassinating heads of state in Russia, France, Spain, Italy and the United States. The most famous terrorist attack before 9/11 was the assassination of the Austrian Archduke Franz Ferdinand in Sarajevo, the capital of Bosnia Herzegovina, by a terrorist. This attack was the incident that led to the First World War and the deaths of millions in the trenches. It also set in process the events that led to the Second World War. It is no exaggeration to say the pistol shots of a terrorist in Sarajevo, almost one hundred years ago, have shaped world history from that day to this.

In our day the widest use of terrorism has been by the Palestinians in their struggle against the Israeli army. This is a classical asymmetrical war. Israel has the best equipped army in the Middle East, and has won a number of wars against their Arab neighbours. Israel buys or is given modern military equipment by the Americans, their closest ally, and they have a sophisticated arms industry themselves. Their conscripted army has high moral, is well disciplined and has a high calibre of officers. Man for man the Israeli army is probably the best in the world.

By contrast the Palestinians have virtually no military capability and few weapons. Politically they are deeply divided by competing political and religious factions. The Israeli intelligence has infiltrated Palestinian society so thoroughly that there is little that they do not know about their enemies. Palestinian militants are harassed constantly and frequently imprisoned. The living conditions of the Palestinians are almost intolerable. The tiny Gaza Strip is the home to 1.4 million people living in poverty. It is regularly called an open air prison, and the West Bank conditions are little better. Adding to the trouble, Israelis have built settlements in the West Bank, violating U.N. resolutions and ignoring the outrage of the local population, but the Palestinians remain powerless to stop them.

The terrorist campaign of the Palestinians grew out of their military weakness and the anger and frustration of their daily lives. To many Palestinians, terrorism was the only way that they could express their feelings about their desperate situation. Terrorist attacks in Palestine go back to the 1970s with scores of incidents. The "intifada" campaign started as stone throwing attacks by young Palestinians on Israeli army units, but the length and duration of the attacks alarmed the Israelis. Then the attacks escalated into suicide bombings. From 1993 to 2003 there were at least 155 suicide attacks, killing scores of Israelis.

The impact of these terrorist attacks was immediate. Fear and anger consumed the Israeli population. Yasser Arafat and the Palestinian Authority that he led were blamed, but it seems much more likely that this was the work of small cells of militants. There were intense debates in Israel about what was motivating the attacks and what should be done to stop them.[14] Control by the armed forces was increased. More young Palestinians were held in prison, and that in turn led to accusations that Israel was turning into a police state. The terrorist attacks escalated into rocket attacks from southern Lebanon and the Gaza Strip. The Israeli army attacked the southern part of Lebanon in July 2006 and Gaza in December 2008 and 2009 but still the campaign of terror continues.

The reaction of the Palestinians to the repression was even more remarkable. After a suicide bombing there was dancing in the streets. The bombers were called martyrs and their families were honoured and given money as compensation for their loss. Across the Muslim world their sacrifice was praised by political and religious leaders. In the eyes of many in the Middle East, terrorism had become a legitimate political tactic, and support for radical Islamic groups like Hezbollah in southern Lebanon and Hamas in the Gaza Strip has broadened. The powerful conventional army of the Israelis has not been able to stop the attacks, and their use of force has only strengthened the terrorist campaigns.

The Israeli-Palestinian conflict is one of the major reasons for political turmoil in the Middle East, but there are other underlying sources of political instability. The rapid social changes that challenged the traditional way of life have had an unsettling effect on the region. Parts of the Muslim world, and powerful families and political elites, became wealthy as a result of oil money while poverty continues to be widespread in the region. Religious conflict between Sunni and Shiite Muslim groups is common and both have been threatened by the rise of secularism. Above all nationalism has become a powerful political force. Many in the Middle East decried the influence of Americans, British and French who have meddled in the politics of the region since the collapse of the Ottoman Empire. In recent years Western support for reactionary authoritarian regimes that control the oil of the region has added to the problems.

This is the background to the rising level of anger of many in the Middle East. That anger has led to such events as the Islamic Revolution in Iran in 1979, political instability across the region, terrorist attacks in the Middle East and Europe against American and European symbols of power, and the 9/11 terrorist attacks. Osama bin Laden and members of al-Qaeda struck against the symbols of U.S. power, the World Trade Center and the Pentagon, in order to show the vulnerability of the Americans and draw them into a broader Middle Eastern conflict.

These terrorist attacks launched the United States, Britain and their allies into what has come to be called the "Long War," the war against Islamic fundamentalism in Afghanistan and Iraq and the scores of attacks by American intelligence agents in Pakistan, Yemen and Somalia. The Long War is an imperial war waged by the American Empire and justified by the dubious claim that it is necessary to protect the American homeland against terrorism. The real or hidden reasons for the wars are to pacify the Islamic world so that developed countries can continue to have access to oil from the Middle East and to protect and enhance the security of Israel, the major U.S. ally in the region. The wars are an attempt to impose American values and political and economic practices on the Islamic world. What they did, in fact, was play into the hands of their enemies. The United States fell into bin Laden's well laid trap.

> Captured al-Qaeda documents reveal that Osama bin Laden's principal goal in the 9/11 attacks was to lure the United States into a clumsy counterattack in the

Middle East that would alienate Muslims, help al-Qaeda recruit more jihadists and bog down the American military in a no-win war.[15]

Like the terrorist killing of the Crown Prince of Austria in 1914, the 9/11 attacks were a reflection of the intense anger and frustration of the terrorists, but also a response to their weakness. These groups felt they had no alternative but to lash out with violence, killing innocent people as well as themselves. In both cases the terrorists not only achieved their objectives, they gained far more than they could have imagined by driving their enemies into war.

Terrorism cannot be dealt with by military force. The military is much too blunt an instrument. Terrorists carry out their attacks either alone or they are organized in small, secret cells. Armies cannot be expected to defend against attacks such as this, and they cannot stamp out terrorism. The only defence is sophisticated police intelligence work that understands the culture of the terrorists, and has sources within the militant groups carrying out the attacks. Even then it is very difficult to head off all terrorist attacks. The greatest failure of the Americans, in both the Cold War and in the post Cold War era, has been the failure of their intelligence community. The Europeans have much more sophisticated intelligence agencies than the United States, and they have been more successful in countering terrorism.

If terrorism is to be challenged, the grievances of the terrorists have to be addressed. This is something that the Americans and their allies like the Israelis have refused to do in the Middle East because their solution is a military one – trying to put down the jihadists and insurgents by force of arms. In the process they have become aggressors, invaders and occupiers and they have created more enemies in these regions than ever before.

War in Afghanistan

The Americans and their allies have fought two asymmetrical wars: Iraq and Afghanistan. There are significant differences in these conflicts but striking similarities. In both wars the American military are seen as Christian invaders of Muslim countries. They arrived with the overwhelming firepower of the American military machine in the belief that the wars would be easy, only to discover that their invasion resulted in insurrections and guerrilla wars where their forces had become the major targets. Both wars have become long, unwinnable conflicts that sapped the power of the military and prestige of the American Empire.

The war in Afghanistan began weeks after the 9/11 terrorist attack and progressed very quickly. The Americans received authorization from the United Nations for limited action to go after al-Qaeda and Osama bin Laden and they used that legitimacy to bomb and attack the al-Qaeda training camps. The Taliban regime quickly collapsed after the American initial attacks and its leadership scattered. Osama bin Laden and other terrorist leaders escaped into the tribal region of Pakistan. The Americans then widened their involvement much beyond the original U.N. resolution. They and their allies chose a new leader for Afghanistan, Hamid Karzai, whom they installed in as president in the capital of Kabul. Later his presidency was confirmed with an election. It was reported in the western press that the Afghan people were happy that the conservative Taliban government was vanquished, and by the spring and summer of 2002 it appeared that Afghanistan was pacified – but appearances were deceiving.

Afghanistan is a country of 32 million people. It is remote with high mountain ranges, fertile plains and valleys. The people are a complex mix of different nationalities, tribes and sub-tribal groups. About 42% of the population is Pashtun, making up 13 million people. They live in the southern part of the country, and just across the border, in the tribal areas of Pakistan, live another 27 million Pashtuns. In total there are over 40 million Pashtuns.

The Pashtuns are deeply conservative Sunni Muslims. They have a system of tribes and clans that are interdependent but retain considerable autonomy. In Afghanistan the Pashtuns traditionally recognize the authority of the Kabul government, but the real power rests with local warlords and clan chiefs. They have a long history of resisting foreign invaders. Alexander the Great could not defeat them when he invaded in 327 BC. The Pashtuns resisted the Mongol invaders of the 12th century. The British invaded Afghanistan on three occasions and were driven out each time, and the Soviet Red Army was defeated by the Pashtun-led Mujahideen in their Afghan War from 1980 to 1989. After the Soviets withdrew a civil war broke out and by 1996 the Taliban controlled 80% of the country.

After the American invasion and war of 2001, the Taliban leaders and their supporters retreated from Afghanistan into the tribal regions of Pakistan where they could merge into the population of other Pashtuns and find safety and protection. There they regrouped and began to plan for the next stage in their struggle against what they saw as Christian foreign invaders led by the Americans. Through the summer and fall of 2002 young Pashtun men were recruited into a guerrilla force. The local Pakistan authorities posed no threat. The Inter-Services Intelligence (ISI), the Pakistan secret service, gave support to the Taliban because many in the secret service were of Pashtun origin. Training camps were set up in remote regions of Pakistan. The Americans had flooded the region with weapons when they supported the Mujahideen in their fight against the Soviets. Armaments were gathered and soon this new force began to infiltrate into Afghanistan in an attempt to rid their country of foreign invaders. By 2003 the insurrection picked up in intensity.

The Taliban are organized into groups of about fifty fighters. They infiltrate into Afghanistan from Pakistan in groups of between five and ten fighters and then regroup and launch their attacks. There are three major Taliban insurgent groups that operate in Afghanistan. "These groups co-ordinate activities loosely, often achieving significant unity of purpose and even some unity of effort, but they do not share a formal command-and-control structure. They also do not have a single overarching strategy or campaign plan."[16]

Some of these attacks are ambushes of coalition forces. At other times they use improvised explosive devices that they plant in roads or suicide attacks. Most of the casualties suffered by the Americans and their allies have been from the improvised explosives. Part of the Taliban strategy is a campaign of assassinations of their Afghan enemies, like teachers, police officers, community and political leaders. The Taliban long term objective is to control the population and displace the national government, but they are patient, believing that in time the invaders will tire of the war and finally withdraw. The insurgent military operations are only part of their efforts to control the population through fear and intimidation, but violent attacks demonstrate the government's inability to provide security; that helps the Taliban recruit more fighters and raise money. The attacks also provoke reactions that further alienate the population and undermine the political support for the coalition.

The Taliban are a complex mix of fighters drawn from many different factions of Afghan society. This is a description by Anad Gopal, a Pakistani journalist:

> Every suicide attack and kidnapping is usually attributed to 'the Taliban.' In reality, however, the insurgency is far from monolithic. There are the shadowy, kohl-eyed mullahs and head-bobbing religious students, of course, but there are also erudite university students, poor, illiterate farmers, and veteran anti-Soviet commanders. The movement is a *mélange* of nationalists, Islamists, and bandits that fall uneasily into three or four main factions. The factions themselves are made up of competing commanders with differing ideologies and strategies, who nonetheless agree on one essential goal: kicking out the foreigners.[17]

The Taliban know the country and have the support of the local people, particularly people that live in the countryside. They can merge into the population, rest and plan their next attack. This is a war of attrition. Individual battles are of little account. The objective of the Taliban is to wear down the enemy and weaken their resolve. A classic asymmetrical war has emerged.

Complicating matters, after the fall of the Taliban many Afghans farmers resumed growing poppy plants, the source of opium for the illegal heroin trade. Opium production had been stamped out during the Taliban regime. Now it has returned with a vengeance. Today it is estimated over 90% of the world's opium comes from Afghanistan. Local warlords control the drug trade. The Americans have made an attempt to stop the production of opium, but with little success. Today the Taliban give protection to opium production but so does the government in Kabul. For both sides the narcotics trade was a powerful incentive to continue the war.

As the Taliban insurgency increased in intensity a multinational coalition called the International Security Assistance Force (ISAF) was organized by the Americans to support the Afghan government. The largest groups in the coalition are Americans and British troops. It also includes other NATO members such as the Canadians, Germans, Dutch and French along with some non-NATO troops. The armies of each national force in the ISAF were given specific responsibilities in Afghan provinces. Most of the troops are deployed in the southern part of the country along the boarder with Pakistan. The Afghan National Army supports the coalition and fights alongside them. It is to expand to 200,000 by 2015.

The coalition forces face many problems. U.S. General Stanley McChrystal, a leading expert on insurgencies and a one time commanding U.S. general in Afghanistan, says that the ISAF is a "conventional force that is poorly configured...inexperienced in local languages and culture and struggling with challenges inherent to coalition warfare." The enemy is elusive and coalition troops find it difficult to track them down and eliminate them. Many of the coalition casualties are from improvised explosive devices, a very difficult weapon to detect.[18]

The Globe and Mail printed this description of a firefight that a Canadian platoon fought against the Taliban in March 2009:

> "We carry a lot of kit and do not move very easily. They carry almost no kit and move incredibly fast," said Lieutenant Jeff Lloyd. The Taliban began maneuvering around the (platoon) and taking shots. "They just seemed to be popping their heads up now and then."[19]

The platoon survived the ambush with no casualties, but on the way back to their base four exhausted Canadian soldiers were killed and another eight wounded in two separate roadside bomb incidents.

Soldiers feel safe in their camps but know that out in the field attack can come at any moment. Suicide bombers are a constant threat. Soldiers get frustrated and nervous and respond too quickly, often killing ordinary Afghans. The Americans continue to put their faith in their superior technology and that has led to tragic results. Soldiers on the ground select targets, or technicians thousands of miles away pinpoint targets using electronic equipment carried by unmanned drone aircraft. Once the targets are set, aircraft or armed drones are sent in to drop bombs. Sometimes Taliban are killed but often it is innocent Afghans who die. Weddings celebrations in this culture are commonly marked by firing machine guns into the air. More than one Afghan wedding has been mistaken for a Taliban attack. American bombers were called in and the result was tragedy, with dozens of deaths. By 2009 over 60% of the deaths of Afghan people were the result of bombing raids, not insurgent attacks, and this is turning the local population against the coalition forces. Some generals feel that air attacks are a serious problem and advocate that they be stopped; but they continue.

The presence of large numbers of foreign troops is fuelling the conflict by providing the Taliban with a convenient enemy of foreigners.[20] War has been going on in Afghanistan almost continuously for thirty years. People are tired of the constant conflict, but there is no sign that the Taliban are ready to come to the peace table. They see their struggle as having a holy purpose to impose sharia law and cleanse society of decadent foreign influence such as women's rights, western music, films and magazines. The ISAF forces have put their hopes on the overwhelming strength of the military, but what they have completely underestimated is the dedication of the Taliban and their commitment to their cause. Because they are willing to take punishment and continue their fight regardless of the odds, the Taliban are in ascendency.

Today the Taliban control a large percentage of the countryside; outside of the capital, the central government has little power or influence. President Hamid Karzai is now called the "Mayor of Kabul," suggesting that he only controls the capital city, and in fact even the capital has come under attack. War lords supporting the drug trade and various other criminals operate openly. Even President Karzai's brother has been accused of being part of the heroin trade. Afghanistan is ranked 176 out of 180 countries that were surveyed by the corruption watch group Transparency International.[21] Surveys show that 9 out of 10 Afghans disapprove of the Taliban, but they do not like the central government either, and they are deeply suspicious of the foreign troops on their soil.[22] The local people are wary, waiting to see which group emerges as the victor before committing themselves to one side or another.

Corruption of the Karzai government is a huge problem. Aid funds have simply disappeared. Members of the government are involved in the international trade in narcotics and the corruption of the police and government officials is widespread. The most dramatic example of corruption was the collapse of the Kabul Bank. It was discovered that $900 million had simply disappeared. It has been alleged that President Karzai, his family and friends had used the bank for unsecured personal loans which were never repaid. Over $22 million was given to Karzai's half-brother and $78 million went to the brother of Karzai's vice-president. The president of the bank was charged but others who benefited were never prosecuted.[23]

As these and other examples of corruption became known international support for the war diminished. People in countries who had contributed troops to the ISAF became increasingly sceptical. Their troops were in the front lines, sustaining casualties while their efforts seemed to be doing little more than supporting a corrupt regime that was doing nothing to help or improve the lot of their own people. By 2011 the war had been going on for ten years and it was only getting worse. The Canadians and Dutch withdrew their forces and others considered doing the same.

Increasing numbers of experts and politicians are now saying the war cannot be won. The British Ambassador to Kabul has said the war has already been lost.[24] In an interview with CNN on March 1, 2009 Stephen Harper, the Prime Minister of Canada, said, "We are not ever going to defeat the insurgency. My reading of Afghanistan's history is that they've probably had an insurrection forever of some kind."[25] Military experts argue that the situation is salvageable, but others say that it would take 200,000 troops and carpet bombing of Pashtun towns and villages, killing untold numbers.[26]

In May of 2009 the Pakistan army launched an attack on Taliban militants in the Swat Valley and Waziristan area along the border called the tribal areas. This coordinated strategy, with a pincer movement of two armies, the Pakistanis from the south and the Americans and the ISAF from the north, is designed to punish the Taliban and to force them to the peace table to negotiate a settlement of the war. The Obama administration has escalated the American commitment and has committed an additional 60,000 troops. A key part of this plan is the use of drone aircraft to bomb and assassinate Taliban leaders in Pakistan. The plan is to take the war to the Taliban and inflict heavy casualties on the enemy in the hopes of gaining victory.

But now some top American military planners are questioning the military tactics of the coalition forces and even predicting that it is doomed to failure. General Stanley McChrystal, once the American commander in Afghanistan, wrote a report for the President, published in August 2009, which questions the entire military operation and advocates a complete change in strategy. He understands that the ISAF operations are alienating the Afghan population and the coalition forces are seen as an occupying army. McChrystal believes that the objective of the coalition effort should be to provide stability in the country so Afghanistan does not once again become a base of operations for al-Qaeda. In order to achieve that objective he believes that the ISAF forces must shift from a tactic of killing the enemy to protecting the civilian population from the Taliban. The coalition troops must live with the Afghan people and protect them. In order to do that there must be a substantial surge in the size and effectiveness of the ISAF forces. McChrystal recognizes that the ISAF cannot defeat the Taliban militarily; the only group that possibly can do that is the

Afghan Army, and they are a long way from having the capability of doing that.[27]

It will be a tall order to change the military tactics of modern armies from attack and kill to protecting the civilian population. It goes against all military training and tactics, which emphasize that soldiers operate as co-ordinated units and defeat their enemies by delivering overwhelming firepower. McChrystal's tactics would convert soldiers into policemen and position them in isolated villages where they would operate alone or in small groups, subject to ambush or even betrayal by the villagers. It will be very difficult to convert conventional armies who do not understand the language, culture or local conditions and are seen as invading foreign forces, into effective military protectors.

The strategy in Afghanistan has an uncanny resemblance to the American strategy in Vietnam. Both Presidents Johnson and Nixon believed that if the Americans showed weakness on the battlefield it would make the Viet Cong believe that they could drive them out. They also were convinced that if they withdrew it would bring a political and military catastrophe to the country. When the Americans finally pulled out and Saigon fell, it did bring great hardship to some people, but nothing like the hardships during the war. Today Vietnam is a country anxious to improve the living conditions of their people and they have been increasingly drawn into the international community through trade and tourism. Peace has been far better than war for the Vietnamese, and that could happen only when the American troops were withdrawn.

The Taliban have said that they will not negotiate unless the western military forces withdraw. At some point soon the hard political decision will have to be made to withdraw the troops and let local people sort out their differences. Perhaps the most that can be achieved by the Americans is a promise from the Taliban that they will not allow terrorist groups to establish training camps in Afghanistan. Osama bin Laden, the leader of al-Quaeda, was tracked down by the Americans and killed. That should be enough. After all, eliminating the al-Qaeda camps was their stated objective at the start of the war.[28]

But one thing is clear; military victory by the Americans and the ISAF will never be achieved in Afghanistan.

War in Iraq

The Americans, British and the small number of troops from other countries in the so called "coalition of the willing" invaded Iraq on March 20, 2003; Baghdad fell on April 9th and members of the Saddam Hussein regime disappeared or were captured. On May 2, 2003 President George W. Bush appeared on the aircraft carrier *USS Abraham Lincoln* which carried the sign "Mission Accomplished." The President's message was that the war in Iraq was over and all that remained were the celebrations. The reality was far more complicated. Americans and their allies now occupied a country of almost 30 million people with a force of 140,000 troops and it was not long before a stubborn insurrection broke out.

Iraq is a much different country than Afghanistan. While Afghanistan is a rural, tribal society, Iraq is mainly urban. Baghdad, the capital, is an ancient city of culture and learning. Three main ethnic and religious groups divide the country. In the north are the Kurds who make up from 15 to 20% of the population. They have ties with Kurdish populations in Turkey and Iran, speak their own language and have their own customs and culture. The rest of the country are Arabs and speak Arabic, but they are divided into two Islamic groups. In the south are the Shiites, making up about 60% of the Arabs in the country, while in the central part of the country are the Sunni with about 40% of the Arab population. Iraq is divided among these three groups, Kurd, Shiite and Sunni, and there is a long history of deep antagonism, hostility and distrust among them. The country has the second largest oil reserves in the world and is potentially very wealthy, but decades of war and political strife have resulted in widespread poverty and economic insecurity.

Saddam Hussein ruled Iraq along with the Ba'ath Party, a non-religious political organization with links across the Arab world. The Ba'ath Party was made up almost exclusively of Sunni Muslims. The Shiites, on the other hand, had links with Shiites in Iran, which has been a traditional enemy of Iraq. Iraq fought an eight year war with Iran from 1980 to 1988 and there have long been hostility and deep suspicion between the two communities. After the Gulf War the Shiites organized a rebellion against the Saddam regime with the encouragement of the Americans. When American support did not materialize, Saddam brutally suppressed the rebellion and executed the leaders. Meanwhile the Kurds in the north were able to use the instability of the period to achieve semi-independence.

After the American and coalition invasion in 2003, the suppressed hatreds of these three groups exploded into violence. The Kurds, feeling they had the support of the Americans, moved south, occupying valuable oil fields that had been controlled by Sunnis. They remained isolated, protecting themselves against attack from the other groups, but Kurd territory remained relatively peaceful. However, major conflict broke out between the Sunnis and the Shiites and the American and coalition troops were caught in the middle.

Iraq is awash in arms. The Sunni had controlled the military during the Saddam Hussein regime, and they secretly hid weapons before the invasion. The Shiites had their own weapons and there are suspicions that they were supplied by supporters in Iran. After the invasion there was no government, and no effective police force that could impose peace and disarm the factions. Shootings of individuals and bombings began to take a deadly toll. The violence was centered in Baghdad and in Sunni and Shiite controlled regions of the county. Some of the violence was directed at the coalition troops, but more often it was conflict between Sunnis and Shiites.

Soon after the invasion, Paul Bremer, who had been given the powers of a governor of Iraq by the American President, announced that no former army members or Ba'ath Party members could be recruited into government or the police force. That decision left Sunni leaders without power, while Shiites were being recruited. The long dominant Sunnis were now subject to the new power of the Shiites. Shiites used their power to seek revenge against their traditional enemies, while the Sunnis tried to protect themselves and their communities. The American Army was the only force that could attempt to impose peace in this rapidly deteriorating situation, but the

Americans were completely unprepared for this role. They did not speak the language, or understand the laws or customs, and they were hated by both the Sunni and Shiites because they were seen as an occupying enemy.

The security situation in Iraq deteriorated quickly as attacks on Americans and other coalition forces increased. Soldiers were killed by roadside bombs. Supply columns were attacked. Patrols were shot at without warning and casualties began to mount. The enemy was elusive, hiding among civilians and striking at unexpected moments. The tension and frustration among the American troops grew and that led some of the soldiers to declare open war on all Iraqis. Soon Americans could only leave the Green Zone fully armed with the most powerful weapons the military could supply.

Everything seemed strange and dangerous to the young GIs. They responded by violence. Doors of ordinary Iraqi homes were kicked in by American soldiers expecting to find armed terrorists inside. There were midnight raids and civilian cars fired upon by nervous troops. It is believed that thousands of innocent Iraqis lost their lives in this campaign to pacify the country. Young men were hauled off to jail simply because they were young and appeared dangerous. Then, making things even worse, it was revealed that some American prison guards abused prisoners by sexually humiliating them. Support for the Americans across the Middle East fell to an all-time low.

The actions of the Americans in Iraq illustrate how the U.S. military has declined. In the Second World War and even Vietnam the American military reflected the American population. In its ranks were men and women from all walks of life. Today the ranks are filled with men from the American south, small towns or impoverished inner city neighbourhoods. Others include foreign born young men, often from Mexico or Central America, who join the U.S. military so they can gain citizenship. In Iraq much of the support work is done by private contractors like the infamous Blackwater Worldwide, a private military company and security firm. Some have called Blackwater a group of mercenary soldiers. William Astore, a retired lieutenant colonel, writes that the U.S. Army has become like the French Foreign

Legion. It has been "transformed into a neocon imperial police force."[29]

Polling data showed that the American people had turned against the war by 2006 and at the same time Iraqis polled said that the U.S. presence had a negative impact on security. One poll result reported 78% of Iraqis said the U.S. army was "provoking more conflict than it is preventing."[30] Even American troops had turned against the war. 72% of those serving in Iraq thought the U.S. should exit the country within a year.[31] A consensus of all of the people involved in the conflict said that the Americans should pull out of Iraq, but still the war continued.

One group who supported the Iraq War was the terrorists themselves. In October 2003 Osama bin Laden announced, "Be glad of the good news. America is mired in the swamps of the Tigris and Euphrates." An al-Qaeda commander commented. "The Americans took the bait and fell into our trap." Another said, "Prolonging the war is in our interests."[32]

But if it was difficult for the American and coalition troops, life was intolerable for the Iraqis after the invasion. Virtual open warfare between the Shiite and Sunni groups broke out in the Sunni and Shiite parts of the country. Massive car bombs tore apart city squares and old neighbourhoods. Whole families were assassinated. Kidnapping became common and roadside bombs were a constant hazard. Shiite militias began to hunt down Sunni leaders, and the Sunnis organized their own militias to carry out assassinations.

The infrastructure had broken down. Electric power and fresh water were only delivered intermittently. The economy barely functioned. Unemployment was high before the invasion and constantly grew worse. Iraq deteriorated from a developing country with high levels of education and women's rights, to a country with one of the lowest standards of living in the world and a high risk of violent death. Some place civilian deaths as high as one million while others set the number at 85,000 civilians.[33]

By the summer of 2007 over four million people in Iraq had been displaced by the war. Two million Iraqis were living in Syria, Jordan and Egypt and another two million were displaced within the country.

Roughly 40% of the Iraqi middle class fled their homes and neighbourhoods. This was the largest forced migration of people in the Middle East since 1948. Social conditions deteriorated. Only a third of Iraqis had access to safe drinking water and only one-fifth had access to a sanitary system. Health care in the country barely functioned and the drug distribution system had collapsed. Of the people displaced, three quarters were either women or children, but 90% of those that died violently were men. Hundreds of thousands of families were supported solely by widows.

Prostitution was on the rise in 2007, because this was one of the few ways that women and girls could contribute to family incomes. Child labor was very common. UNICEF estimated that 4.5 million children in Iraq were under-nourished, and one in five short for their age. In some areas up to 90% of the children were not in school. While the people of Iraq were living a nightmare under the regime of Saddam Hussein, the arrival of the Americans and the other coalition troops made the conditions far worse.[34]

After the invasion the Americans made up the only government that functioned in Iraq. Paul Bremer was anxious to turn power over to Iraqis. In October 2005 an election to accept a new constitution was passed by a 78% margin. It was overwhelmingly accepted by the Shiite and Kurd communities but rejected by the Sunnis. A similar pattern was repeated in December 2005 when a general election was held. Again voting was almost entirely along ethnic lines. The government of Prime Minister Iyad Allawi that was elected was dominated by Shiites and Kurds and the Sunnis were excluded.

The Americans and their coalition allies attempted to enforce a peace but violence between Sunnis and Shiites continued. The Sunnis were outnumbered and they turned to radical factions such as al-Qaeda in Iraq, a violent group that attacked American and Shiites at will. The Shiites were organized into militias such as the Mahdi Army and the Badr Organization, closely linked to powerful Shiite religious leaders and with support from the Iraqi government.

Often the aim of the Iraqi violence was to simply kill members of the other religious group or occupying troops. The American response was to attack anyone who appeared to be an enemy. In November

2004 the Americans struck at Sunni insurgents in the city of Fallujah. The battle, which lasted 46 days, left 95 Americans and 1,350 Iraqis dead, and reduced the city to ruins, but there seemed to be no strategic point to the battle other than trying to intimidate the Sunni population. The insurgency spread and the number of dead increased. But while it appeared to the outside world that the battles and bombings that were going on in Iraq had little purpose, a form of ethnic cleansing was going on. Minority groups of Sunnis or Shiites living in neighbourhoods dominated by the other group were either killed or fled leaving all of their belongings behind. Baghdad was the center of these struggles, but they went on in all parts of the country.

In the United States political opinion polarized around the war. The Bush administration increased the powers of the American police, supposedly to capture and imprison terrorists. The government claimed they had the right to declare people, including U.S. citizens, "enemy combatants" or suspected terrorists and to imprison them without charge or access to lawyers or families until such time as the President declared the war on terror finished. A policy of rendition – sending suspected terrorists to foreign countries to be tortured – was instituted without discussion by Congress. Guantanamo Bay, the U.S. base in Cuba, was used to warehouse suspected terrorists picked up in Afghanistan or Iraq, out of the reach of the American courts. At the same time the United States government had increased spending to $545 per year per household on homeland security, much higher than any other country.[35] Even some forms of torture of prisoners were tolerated by the U.S. government. What shocked many Americans was this entire approach was against their tradition of civil liberties, American law and centuries of British common law.

By the fall of 2007 the American military elite was so disturbed about the course of the war that they turned on the Bush administration. Retired Lieutenant General Ricardo Sanchez, the commander of the coalition forces in Iraq from June 2003 to July 2004, denounced the U.S. political leaders

as incompetent...inept and derelict in the performance of their duty... America is living a nightmare with no

> end in sight.... There has been a glaring and
> unfortunate display of incompetent strategic leadership
> within our national leaders.... After more than four
> years of fighting, America continues its desperate
> struggle in Iraq without any concerted effort to devise a
> strategy that will achieve victory in that war torn
> country or in the greater conflict against extremism.

He concluded that a military-only strategy will simply "stave off
defeat," not achieve victory.[36] These are strong words coming from a
military leader who had spent his entire career in an organization
demanding the respect of authority.

The military situation was hopeless, so the Americans turned to
bribery. Essentially they bought off the leaders of the insurgent groups
by paying them to stop killing American troops. Millions and possibly
billions of dollars flowed to the Shiite and Sunni militia groups. The
payoffs were a type of protection money. This was the first time in
U.S. military history where the enemy was essentially paid to stop
killing American troops.

The other American effort to stop the insurgency was a troop
surge. In January 2007 the President announced an additional 21,500
troops would be sent to Iraq. Most of these troops were sent to the
Baghdad area and in time insurgent attacks began to lessen. George W.
Bush and his supporters claim that this troop surge is the reason for the
drop in violence in 2008, but the critics say it has made no difference.
The Battle for Baghdad, which raged in 2005 and 2006, led to the
ethnic cleansing of the city, and the Sunnis were driven out of mixed
neighbourhoods by the Shiite militias. Today three-quarters of the city
is Shiite controlled. Sunnis who have attempted to go back to their
homes have been assassinated.

The country now is virtually partitioned between the Kurds in the
north, the Shiites in the south and the Sunnis in cities and towns in the
central parts of the country. Baghdad is divided into Shiite and Sunni
enclaves defended by high concrete blast walls often with a
single entrance and exit. By the time the surge began this partition was
largely completed and the insurgency was over. The American troops

have done little more than to confirm and solidify the new ethnic and religious boundaries. This is a description written by Anthony Shadid, a journalist for the *Washington Post:*

> Baghdad is now a city divided from itself. Shiite neighborhoods rarely have Sunnis. Sunni ones, far less numerous today, no longer have Shiites. Christians have all but left. Potentates seek refuge in fortresses, and the poor fend for themselves.... The Americans created none of it, but facilitated all of it, giving space to the region's worst impulses.[37]

Since the invasion of Iraq, the economic situation has worsened. The per capita GNP rank of Iraq relative to other countries sank to 130th, despite Iraq's enormous oil reserves. The Iraqi economy is in ruins as the result of decades of war, political instability and sanctions. Unemployment runs rampant and poverty is widespread.[38] The war has been an economic disaster for the Iraqi people.

Iraq does not exist as a unified state. It is run by gangs, militias, radical clerics and warlords who have carved up the country into ethnic fiefdoms. The government is extremely weak. It has no power or influence in the Sunni dominated regions of the country, and even in the Shiite and Kurd areas the control by local power brokers is much greater than the government. The country is in ruin. Civil war is still a real possibility.

Then in early 2008, as the violence in Iraq was subsiding, it was learned that Exxon Mobil, Chevron, Shell, BP and Total were negotiating agreements to provide technical expertise to assist in the development of the Iraqi oil fields. These were "no bid" contracts. As part of the contracts these major multi-national oil companies insisted on the right of first refusal on the development of the oil fields. One week after the no bid contracts came to light Iraq announced that they were opening six of their major oil fields, totalling about half of the country's reserves. The foreign oil companies would receive 75% of the value of the contracts, leaving the Iraqis with only 25%. This is an unheard-of ratio in the Middle East, where countries or nationals control 100% of the value of oil.[39]

And so it has become clear that the strongest reason for the invasion of Iraq was to gain access to the country's vast oil reserves. Even apologists for the war concede that this was the objective all along. Like the empires of the past, economic plunder was a prime motive for this war. Ironically the Iraq War has also led to higher oil prices. David Kirsch, a former U.S. State Department energy analyst, writes, "Without this disaster, oil prices would be much lower today.... The crippling of Iraq's oil production since the start of the war amounts to one of the biggest disruptions in world oil supply since the end of the Second World War." Other studies estimate the war raised oil prices by between $4 and $5 a barrel.[40] George W. Bush, and the neo-conservatives in his administration, felt they had to attack Iraq to ensure oil supplies, and yet the result has led to a spike in oil prices and a threat to oil supplies.

On November 27, 2008 the Iraqi parliament voted in favour of a security agreement with the United States in which American troops will withdraw from cities and towns by June 30, 2009 and withdraw completely from the country by December 31, 2011. Then there will be no military bases in the country, and it is highly likely that the oil agreements will be abrogated sometime in the near future because they are universally rejected by the Iraqi people. The Americans have attempted to extend their stay but Iraqi politicians have flatly refused. They know the only way that peace can finally come is to have all foreign forces withdraw.

Peace will eventually come to that troubled country, but it will be because the different factions of the Iraqi people establish a political arrangement that is satisfactory to them, not because the Americans have defeated the insurgency. The Iraq War has disappeared from the media, but American attempts to establish imperial control over Iraq with the invasion in 2003 have been a failure.

War and Empire

The consequences of wars in Afghanistan and Iraq and the blunders of the George W. Bush administration have led to a significant reduction in the influence of the United States. Zbigniew Brzezinski, the National Security Advisor to Democrat President Jimmy Carter, writes,

> As America has become more isolated because of Iraq, all major powers have gained more maneuvering room to freely pursue their interests, and as we've seen with China, the greater the power, the more likely the nation is to take advantage of that freedom.... We are going to find ourselves increasingly isolated and powerless.

Brent Scowcroft, the former National Security Advisor to Republican Presidents Gerald Ford, George H. W. Bush and later an advisor to Barack Obama, commented,

> That the international community no longer trusts our motives is a new phenomenon, and I see it as one of the many warning signs of a possible lasting realignment of global power.[41]

Wars in Afghanistan and Iraq were a major contributor to the change of political direction in the United States with the election of Barack Obama and have now led to a new American military strategy. The military approach of the Obama administration is to try and avoid front line military operations where American troops are involved in combat and to focus on covert actions by intelligence groups and special operations groups like the Navy Seals and other elite units. As Nick Turse points out the U.S. is now involved militarily in at least 97 countries in the developing and underdeveloped world. Six of those countries are fighting active wars: Afghanistan, Pakistan, Iraq, Libya, Yemen and Somalia, all Muslim countries. But the U.S. has also deployed special operations and CIA intelligence units in at least 75 other countries where their operations are much less in the public eye. Not only do they supply military support in these countries but the U.S. delivers financial support to their friends and arms to their military.[42]

This is from a *Washington Post* article of June 4, 2010.

> Beneath its commitment to soft spoken diplomacy and beyond the combat zones of Afghanistan and Iraq, the Obama administration has significantly expanded a largely secret U.S. war against al-Quaeda and other radical groups... One advantage of using "secret" forces for such missions is that they rarely discuss their operations in public... They (the administration) are talking publically much less but they are acting more. They are willing to get aggressive much more quickly."[43]

This is the new face of the American Empire. On the surface it may appear that the United States has scaled down its military involvement as they withdraw from Iraq and Afghanistan, but they are expanding their operations in covert ways. But is it working? Is this policy leading to a more peaceful Middle East? Perhaps it is too early to judge but the evidence is not hopeful. The Pew Research reports that across the broader Middle East the U.S. prestige is at an all time low.[44] Even the Arab Spring of 2011 was motivated in part by strong anti-American feelings. The U.S. and many of the authoritarian regimes that it supports are failing to "win the hearts and minds" of the people and that is fundamental if these types of conflicts are ever to be won.

The Americans have failed to put down insurrections and defeat guerrilla wars not because their military has the wrong strategy, or the troops had low morale, or lacked the proper weapons, or did not know the language. The wars have been difficult because the tactics used against them have made it impossible to achieve victory. An asymmetrical war plays to the strengths of the weaker force because they reject sophisticated military hardware and rely on their ability to keep the support of the local people. These wars favour the weaker side and all the counter-insurgency tactics and language training will not change that fact. Asymmetrical wars cannot be won by countries such as the United States because they are perceived as imperial invaders out to exploit and subjugate the local people.

The American political elite – both Democrats and Republicans – have believed that the United States is a country unlike any other, destined to lead the world. The recent wars demonstrate that this is an impossible objective. No single country – no superpower – no empire has the ability to dominate the world community. In the modern world security, peace and the end of war must be a joint responsibility of all people and all nations but peace also must be created and sustained by local people.

Like all empires of the past, the Americans have been arrogant about their political power and overconfident of their military power. They have been guilty of imperial overreach by overestimating their military power and political appeal, a mistake of every empire from Rome to Britain to Nazi Germany and Imperial Japan. The refusal to understand the realities of modern warfare and the limits of power has led to defeat in Vietnam, serious setbacks in Iraq and Afghanistan and continue to be a disaster for the unfortunate people of many countries.

Part III: A Multilateral Future

INTRODUCTION:

We are entering an era fundamentally different than any that has gone before. Wars of empire, that have been the most important events that have shaped the geopolitics of the past, are finished. There are three fundamental reasons for this.

- The advantage that sophisticated weapons and a well organized military gave to empires has now disappeared. Nuclear weapons are unusable because of the enormous loss of innocent lives and the damage they produce and asymmetrical warfare gives the advantage to the weaker force. Iraq and Afghanistan will be remembered as the last imperial wars. There will continue to be insurrections, civil wars, and ethnic and religious wars in the future but they will be less of a threat to the international community than the wars of the past.

- Modernity has created social, economic and political changes such as global trade. the rise of democratic practices and the change in values that stress local autonomy and interdependence. Empires and their *modus operandi* of using war to dominate and exploit others are no longer acceptable by the international community and people in all regions and countries in the world.

- The United States, the last empire, now is in economic and political decline and other countries are rapidly growing in prosperity and power. In attacking and occupying Iraq, the U.S. was condemned by nations and the international court of public opinion. The economic leadership of the United States is in shambles and when the current recession comes to an end, the European Union, along with nations such as China, India, Brazil, Russia and others, will be poised to become world economic leaders along with America. The National Intelligence Council of the United States agrees with this assessment. They recently predicted that by 2025 the U.S. will still be powerful but it will no longer be dominant. The world will be multi-polar and the power of non-state actors will increase.[1]

The age of imperialism and all that entailed is now, finally, at an end. The question remains, then, how are we going to adapt to this new reality? What are the institutions that should be created or strengthened that are appropriate for this new age? How can we make the final step that will eliminate all wars?

Part I of this book explored how empires used war as a tactic for their political and economic advantage. Part II examined how modernity has led to the end of empires and transformed war. Part III examines the wars that continue today and looks towards the future to suggest how we can reorder international relations in fundamental ways to achieve the dream of the end of war.

CHAPTER 8: THE DECLINE OF WAR

A British Ministry of Defence white paper published in 2003 concluded, "There are currently no major conventional military threats to the United Kingdom or NATO... . It is now clear that we no longer need to retain a capability against the re-emergence of a direct conventional threat."[1] A 2006 NATO report summarizes its findings in this way: "Large scale conventional aggression against the alliance will be highly unlikely."[2] China's Defence White Paper of 2004 concludes that Beijing believes that all out confrontations between major countries are avoidable, at least for the foreseeable future, and that peace and development will remain the principle themes of world politics.[3]

War has been constant since1945, but decade by decade the plague of armed conflict, and all of the hardships that are attendant to it, have decreased to the point that today war affects relatively small numbers of people.

Wars from 1945 to 1990

In the late 1940s, at the end of the most destructive war in the world's history, the prospects for peace appeared slim. The world was divided into two hostile geo-political zones. In Eastern Europe and much of Asia the Soviet Union held unchallenged power. There were pockets of resistance to the Soviets, such as in western Ukraine, but they were quickly crushed. In Western Europe, North America and the rest of the Anglo-Saxon world, the United States was the dominant power. Like in the east, there was some resistance to the new order, such as the Greek Civil War (1946-49), but most people were content to accept this arrangement. Rather than war breaking out between the two superpowers, the peace of the Cold War settled in. It was this confrontation that shaped events for the next forty-five years.

In some parts of the world, war continued unabated after 1945. There are similarities in these wars. Virtually all of them were fought in developing or underdeveloped countries. They fall into two general categories. The first group of wars, which roughly extended from 1945 to 1975, were wars of liberation, and the second set that begin about 1975 and extended to about 1990, are surrogate wars of the Cold War

The most destructive war and political conflict of the period was in China. For twenty-five years China was convulsed with internal conflict. The Chinese Civil War (1946-49), which led to the Communist victory, cost 1.2 million lives. After the Communist victory there were a number of internal struggles as they consolidated power: the Chinese-Tibet War (1949-50) with an estimated 1.2 million deaths, the Great Leap Forward (1958-61), 38 million dead, and the Cultural Revolution (1966-69), 11 million.[4] This does not include the Chinese casualties in the Korean War or the millions of political prisoners who died in prison.

China was never conquered by the colonial powers, but large sections of the country had been dominated by Europeans for decades. Japan invaded Manchuria, a Chinese province, in 1931 and ruled it like a colony. The Japanese invasion of China in 1937 was an attempt to conquer China and turn it into a satellite or colony. The Chinese Civil War between the Communists and the Nationalists was a struggle over which political faction should rule China, but it also has the character of a war of liberation. The Communists portrayed themselves as liberators from colonialism and foreign domination, while the Nationalists were seen as the agents of colonial powers and the Americans. In this sense it was a war of liberation, and the internal struggle for the consolidation of political power that followed the war was like many of the other wars in various parts of the world over the next forty-five years.

Wars of liberation from colonial or foreign rule swept the developing and underdeveloped world after the Second World War. The end of colonialism and the partition of India and Pakistan (1947) cost one million lives; the French-Vietnam War (1946-54) 600,000; Kenya's Mau Mau uprising against the British (1952-59) 20,000; the French-Algerian War (1954-62) 368,000; the Mozambique War of Independence (1962-75) an estimated one million deaths; and the USA/Vietnam War (1964-73) three million. All of these wars were struggles for independence against an imperial power. Americans believed that Vietnam was a war to contain communism, but for the Vietnamese it was a war of liberation from the imperial powers of France and the United States. Colonial imperialism has caused more wars in the last 200 years than any other factor. One study found that between 1816 and 2002 there were 81 wars of colonial conquest and subsequent wars of liberation.[5]

By the 1970s wars of liberation came to an end because colonialism was finished. The new generation of European political leaders recognized that they could not hold their colonies by military force any longer, and it was damaging the economic relations that they were trying to establish. The British Conservative Prime Minister Harold Macmillan gave a speech in Cape Town, South Africa in 1960 in which he signalled that the British Empire, the largest and most successful colonial empire the world had seen, was over. He said, "The wind of change is blowing through this continent, and whether we like it or not, this growth of national consciousness is a political fact."[6] The wars of liberation that colonialism had spawned were coming to an end, and the number and frequency of wars dropped significantly.

After these wars of liberation were over there were a number of struggles in the former colonies for political control. In West Africa coups and counter-coups led to the deaths of thousands. Algeria saw a struggle between different communist and socialist factions that resulted in intermittent warfare. In time even these struggles came to an end.

The next set of wars, that stretch from about 1975 to 1990, are surrogate wars sustained and stimulated by the Cold War. In almost all cases these were civil wars fought by political factions trying to impose control over their own countries, but what makes them different is the involvement of the superpowers in providing weapons and other forms of support. The Soviet Union, and sometimes its ally Cuba, would provide support for communists or communist sympathizers while the United States and its allies supported conservative factions sympathetic to the west.

These wars went on in sub-Saharan Africa, South and Central America and the Far East. They include the Indonesian Civil War (1965-66) 250,000 lives lost; Mozambique Civil War (1976-93)

900,000; Ethiopia (1974-91) one million; Rhodesia/Zimbabwe War (1968-79) 30,000; Chile (1973) over 1,000; Argentina (1973-1983) estimated 30,000 "disappearances;" Angolan Civil War (1975-2002) 500,000; Laos (1975-87) 184,000; Cambodia (1975-79) 1.7 million; the Muslim uprising in Philippines (1972) 120,000; Guatemala (1960-96) 200,000; El Salvador Civil War (1977-92) 75,000; Nicaragua (1981-90) 60,000; the Columbia Civil War (1966 and continuing) 31,000; the Arab-Israeli Wars (1947 and continuing) 73,000 and the Soviets in Afghanistan (1979-88) 1.3 million.

None of these wars were actually caused by the Cold War. In only one, the Soviets in Afghanistan, was a superpower involved in the fighting, but the Cold War directly contributed to these wars and prolonged and sustained them by one or more of the superpowers providing weapons and other forms of support. When the Cold War suddenly came to an end in 1989-90, these wars soon came to an end. The ideological justification for the wars disappeared and the sources of weapons dried up. Gradually the hostilities decreased and came to an end, usually with the signing of peace agreements. Again, like the end of the wars of liberation, by 1990 the number of wars and the number of people killed in the wars dramatically diminished.

What is striking about both the wars of liberation and the surrogate wars of the Cold War is the involvement of the two superpowers. Their support for one side or the other prolonged the wars and substantially increased the number of casualties. Empires were the chief cause of these wars, and when this support came to an end the wars stopped.

Humanitarian Intervention

With the end of the Cold War there was optimism that an era of peace was about to emerge, but in the former Soviet Union it led to a new set of conflicts as different groups fought for power. These wars include the Chechnya Civil War (1991- 2009) 200,000 lives lost, Armenia/Azerbaijan War (1991-94) 35,000 and the Tajikistan Civil War (1992-96) 50,000. The Chechnya conflict was a struggle for independence and has all of the characteristics of a war of liberation. It was put down ruthlessly by the Russian military. The other conflicts were struggles between factions for political dominance, and have the characteristics of civil wars.

In the west the end of the Cold War brought a new sense of optimism. There was the belief that the international community could use military force in a humanitarian way to intervene in the internal affairs of countries in times of emergency and crisis. This approach came to be called "humanitarian intervention." There were some successes of this policy. An international force led by the United States drove Iraqi invaders out of Kuwait in 1990-91 in the Gulf War. The NATO led operations in the former Yugoslavia (1991-2001) saved lives and eventually brought peace and political stability in the sensitive south eastern flank of Europe. Altogether 260,000 lives were lost on the battlefield or through systematic genocide in this conflict. But there were also some spectacular failures. In Somalia an international force intervened from 1992 to 1995, but rather than bring peace and stability the effort led to the deaths of several members of the international force. Little was accomplished and after the withdrawal of the international troops the country declined into violence and anarchy. The Somalia experience contributed to the decision not to intervene in the Rwandan genocide, a failure that resulted in the deaths of over 800,000 people.

Despite the failures, by the beginning of the new millennium there was optimism that the international community could work together in an effective way to use their collective military power to stop the most flagrant abuses of human rights and even remove political leaders who were a threat to their people and other countries. 9/11 and the ensuing wars in Afghanistan and Iraq have changed all of that.

The invasion of Iraq in 2003 was justified by the Americans and their allies as an effort to eliminate Iraqi weapons of mass destruction, to drive out al-Qaeda and remove Saddam Hussein. Some saw it as a form of humanitarian intervention, but this proved to be a mere justification. The Americans, British and their allies acted like the imperial powers of the past by using force to access Iraqi oil and to support their ally Israel. That was why there were such widespread protests against the war. To the world community this was Empire

America flexing its muscles in an effort to intimidate and assert its power. It had nothing to do with the policy of humanitarian intervention.

The situation in Afghanistan is more complex. The Americans launched their initial attacks to eliminate the al-Qaida camps where the 9/11 terrorists were trained, but soon the war was transformed into a protracted struggle between the western backed Afghan regime and coalition forces led by the Americans that continues to this day. Presumably the war is being fought to bring peace, encourage economic development, promote education, the rights of women and other humanitarian objectives, but there are concerns that the Afghan government and local officials are corrupt and help protect the opium trade. More Afghan people are killed by American firepower than the Taliban. Now questions are being asked: What are the humanitarian objectives of the mission? Why should the lives of allied soldiers be lost to maintain a corrupt regime?

The war in Afghanistan suggests that to Americans and their allies, humanitarian intervention is military intervention or sanctions against regimes that are out of favour with the international community dominated by the western powers. There are other forms of intervention that are much more humanitarian. "Soft power" it is sometimes called. The use of "hard power," military interventions and sanctions, hurt local people, particularly the poor. The promotion of trade, humanitarian aid, education and democratic practices helps people in the entire population. The policy of humanitarian intervention has not been rejected, but the world community is more cautious now and questions are asked whether the use of military force is ever justified.

Wars Today

Today there are two types of wars going on in the world. One type is the asymmetrical wars fought by the United States and its coalition allies in Afghanistan. Israel also continues to fight asymmetrical conflicts against the Palestinians in Lebanon, the Gaza Strip and the West Bank.[7] The second types of wars are low intensity wars fought by poorly trained, lightly armed civilian populations. There are many wars such as this and they all are found in the poorest and most remote regions of the world.

One observation about the nature of war is particularly striking. Since the end of the Korean conflict, conventional wars between two or more nations have become almost obsolete. The Iran-Iraq War (1980-88) is the major exception. It was fought using conventional weapons and tactics, and it soon became a grim contest of trench warfare and tank assaults that resulted in one million deaths and resolved nothing. The war between Georgia and Russia in 2008 was technically a conventional war between two countries and fought with modern armaments, but Georgia was so badly outclassed and outnumbered by the huge Russian army that they quickly capitulated.

The reasons there are so few conventional wars is that they are far too dangerous and destructive. They are also predictable. The larger military force with the most sophisticated weapons prevails. As Georgia found out, it makes no sense for a weaker power to provoke a war like this. The United States and other countries continue to spend enormous sums of money on armaments and troop training as deterrents to conventional attacks, yet it is increasingly unlikely that wars of this kind will ever be fought again.

One risk is that competition between major powers such as China, India, the European Union and the United States might lead to war. This indeed would be a catastrophe, but it seems to be a remote possibility. China appears to have few imperial ambitions. India has fought three wars with Pakistan but they were limited affairs and although India competes with China for trade they co-operate on most local issues. The European Union has shown little appetite for war since the end of the Second World War and the United States has followed a policy of not confronting other major powers since the end of the Korean War. It seems unlikely at this time that there will be war between the major powers in the world.

War and Underdevelopment

The website "Global Security"[8] listed 42 wars and other low level forms of violent conflicts going on in the world in 2009. With the exception of the Basque independence campaign in Spain, every one of these conflicts was in an underdeveloped or developing society. Global Security concluded: "Africa, to a greater extent than any other continent is afflicted by war. Africa has been marred by more than twenty major civil wars since 1960."[9]

Africa has seen many major conflicts recently. The war in northern Uganda and eastern Congo, carried on by the Lord's Resistance Army, has continued for more than twenty years. It has resulted in the deaths of thousands and the displacement of more than one million people. War in the eastern Congo between various factions has resulted in the deaths of 5.4 million people; it is the world's most deadly conflict since the Second World War. There have been recent wars in Libya, Somalia, Ethiopia, southern Sudan, Darfur (south western Sudan) and Chad and ethnic conflict in Kenya, while Zimbabwe has been perilously close to civil war as the central government imposes its rule with force.

Other impoverished, underdeveloped regions of the world have had similar levels of conflict. There are wars or serious conflicts in Syria, Yemen, Colombia, Nepal, and Tibet. Regions of India, Indonesia, Pakistan, Philippines and Algeria are affected as well. Sri Lanka has just concluded a war that pitted the Tamil population against the central government dominated by Sinhalese. All of these countries have a high level of poverty.

Extreme poverty, war and political instability are inexorably linked. *The Human Security Brief of 2007* summarizes their research in this way: "The most robust finding on the causes of war by researchers is that the higher the per capita income a country enjoys, the lower the risk of armed conflict."[10] Paul Collier, in his book *The Bottom Billion*, a study of the poorest countries in the world, notes, "Seventy-three percent of people in the societies of the bottom billion have recently been through a civil war or are still in one."[11]

There are several reasons why poverty fuels wars in the underdeveloped world. In many areas of Africa traditional authority has broken down, but the new structures designed to take its place, such as police and courts, have little influence. Weak central governments are unable to impose control over regions of their country. With poverty, social agitation in many forms emerges, crime increases and investment vanishes as the country becomes more unstable. Economic stagnation or decline sets in. These are all countries with high birth rates and a "youth bulge" population. With the end of subsistence farming, unemployment reaches levels of 50% or more. Hunger and disease are widespread. Even in developed countries, depression and economic hardship lead to social and political unrest, but these problems are magnified many times in poor societies because these countries have no social safety net to help people weather hard times.

The mass unemployment of young men is a major crisis. A high proportion of young people in impoverished countries are unemployed and not in school. They have no future and only time on their hands. Poverty, unemployment, the lack of educational opportunities and a sense of hopelessness draw young men into gangs and armies, resulting in wars, uprisings and terrorist attacks. "Young men, who are the recruits for rebel armies, come pretty cheap in an environment of hopeless poverty. Life itself is cheap, and joining a rebel movement gives these young men a small chance of riches."[12] War for young men in impoverished countries is an opportunity for plunder, just as it was for the armies of Europe in the Middle Ages and the English pirates in the sixteenth and seventeenth centuries.

Societies plagued with poverty almost inevitably suffer from political instability. Patrick J. McGowan studied political conflict in West Africa covering the years 1955 to 2004. He writes, "From independence through 2004, the sixteen West African states have experience forty-four successful military led coups, forty-three often bloody failed coups, at least eighty-two coup plots, seven civil wars and many other forms of political conflict."[13]

Even idealistic, charismatic leaders with mass followers find it difficult to maintain support when there is widespread poverty. Often the political instability leads to the rise of unscrupulous political leaders supported by a circle of associates who see the state as an opportunity to enrich themselves. Once these "Big Men," as they are called in Africa, gain political power they can plunder the state treasury, or they are put in positions where they can demand bribes from companies or foreign governments. In order to maintain power and control, elites turn to the army or the police to deal with dissenters. This in turn leads to even greater social unrest. Grievances mount. Other political leaders begin to agitate to get rid of the government, and when democratic forms of government do not exist, leaders hatch coups. The more serious conflicts result in civil wars.

Once widespread violence begins, numbers of people are drawn into a life of killings and plunder. Guns and other weapons imported into the region are cheap. The sheer availability of weapons makes the wars difficult to stop. Rebel groups dominate and exploit the people of an area by violence or threats of violence. In regions such as Darfur, Congo, Ethiopia, Somalia and Chad violence turned to organized attacks on traditional enemies. As victims try to defend themselves, war quickly engulfs whole regions and is very difficult to stop.

Some of the rebel armies in places like the eastern Congo are simply forms of organized banditry. It is estimated that there are 23 armed groups in the region who fight each other, try to avoid government troops hunting for them and plunder the mineral riches of the region. In Colombia, FARC is fighting a guerrilla war against a right wing government, but it also provides protection to powerful drug cartels. All of these groups have more of the characteristics of outlaw bandit groups than political movements.

In Africa thousands, some estimate hundreds of thousands, of children have been engaged in rebel armies. They have also been used in Sri Lanka, Colombia, Palestine and Afghanistan. Child soldiers are easy to train and once they are armed with automatic weapons, they can be as deadly as adult soldiers. Many of these child soldiers are abducted from their homes and forced to fight but others join the armies willingly in an attempt to find a way to survive. This is a description by the journalists Stephanie Nolen and Erin Baines:

It is precisely because they are malleable and amenable to indoctrination that children are recruited by armed groups. Hauled into violent conflict before their own moral compass has developed, they become unable to discern right from wrong. Former Lord's Resistance Army (northern Uganda and eastern Congo) fighters describe how, not long after their abduction, they stopped thinking about home and went into 'auto pilot'—some describe, 'going outside their bodies' when forced to kill.[14]

Another characteristic of the tactics of groups in Africa is their use of rape. "Systematic, planned, ordered, collective public rape—rape used as a weapon of war—is a war within a war," reports Mathilde Muhino of the Congo.[15] Rape is used as a tactic of terror and humiliation by these rebel armies, and in regions where HIV/AIDS is rampant, it can be a sentence of death.

There has been no systematic study of the social characteristics of the foot soldiers engaged in the insurrections around the world, but they are not difficult to imagine. From the conflicts in sub-Saharan Africa and the Taliban in Afghanistan to Palestine and Colombia, the armies of insurrection are made up of young males from impoverished families who have little or no education and virtually no employment prospects. If these wars are to come to an end, a meaningful way of life and new hope must be found for them.

Ethnic and Religious Wars

Extreme poverty is the major reason for scores of wars, but conflicts are often shaped by the pre-existing social, ethnic, racial and religious divisions within and between societies. There were clan wars in the highlands of Scotland during the Middle Ages, the Thirty Years War (1618-1648) pitted German Protestants against Catholics and the persecution of the Jews in Nazi Germany was the consequence of extreme prejudice. Today the conflict in Somalia pits Islamic fundamentalists against secular forces organized by the central government. The types of cultural assumptions that groups hold continue to play an important role in many of the wars today.

Europeans during the period of colonial empires assumed that they were superior to aboriginal groups and that justified their domination. The Spanish believed that they were bringing the gift of Christianity to the people of the Americas and that justified their enslavement and exploitation. The French assumed that they were the most civilized of all people, and it was their destiny to rule all of Europe and eventually the world.[16] The British slogan of the "white man's burden" to bring civilization to the black race, illustrates the British belief that they were superior to others in the colonies. All of these were little more than superficial ideological justifications for the European practices of domination and exploitation.

Cultural assumptions of ethnic or racial superiority used to justify war continue today. The people of Afghanistan are portrayed in the daily press as being primitive, uneducated and tribal. They are said to be "medieval" in their religious beliefs and practices, and their rejection of education for girls is proof of their backwardness. The armies of NATO and the United States, on the other hand, are portrayed as forces of modernity and enlightenment. These simple stereotypes are little different than the belief system that built and sustained colonialism.

While empires have been sustained by a belief system of superiority, some conflicts were caused in part by a collective sense of victimization. There are many examples. After the First World War most Germans felt that they had been treated badly by the allies in the Treaty of Versailles. They were forced to give up territory and pay heavy reparations, and they suffered crippling economic hardship. Feelings of victimization contributed to a sense of grievance, which was a major cause for the rise of the Nazis and the Second World War. With the breakup of the former Yugoslavia the Serbs felt that they were denied their rightful glories by the Croatians and Albanians.[17] The Shiites in Iraq felt that they had been victimized by the Sunnis during the Saddam Hussein regime and they sought revenge during the period of anarchy that followed the American invasion. In Sri Lanka the Tamil minority was given special treatment by the British during the colonial times, and when the country gained independence, the majority Sinhalese used their electoral power to remove the Tamils from positions of influence. They suppressed the use of the Tamil language and denied educational opportunities to their young people. The Tamils came to see themselves as victims and in time a violent struggle for Tamil independence emerged. In Rwanda the Hutu majority felt they were victims of Tutsi prejudice which contributed to the violence and genocide of 1994. Jewish feelings of being victims of the holocaust have contributed to the militarization of the State of Israel and the fear of Palestinians. There are many other examples where collective feelings of victimization have contributed to war and violence. Chechnya, Georgia the indigenous people of Central America and Colombia, the Pashtuns of Afghanistan and Pakistan and even African Americans have seen themselves as victims, and this has often contributed to violence and sometimes war.

One of the most important discoveries of psychologists and social scientists is that, although there are individual differences within groups, all racial, ethnic and religious groups have the same abilities. What creates the differences between groups are their differing cultures. Prejudice and discrimination continues in all parts of the world; but things are changing. Modernity and the practices of democracy bring with them the values of equality and equal opportunity. Gradually the cultural assumptions of superiority and feelings of victimization that have contributed so much to war and violence are lessening.

The Decline of War

There was a dramatic drop in the number of wars after the end of colonialism and another drop at the end of the Cold War. Now, even the wars of ethnic and religious divisions and poverty have begun to diminish. Even in sub-Saharan Africa this is beginning to happen. This is a summary by the researchers of The Human Security Centre.

> Between 1999 and 2006 (the most recent year for which
> we have complete data), sub-Saharan Africa's security

landscape was transformed. The number of armed
conflicts being fought in the region fell by more than
half. The number of people being killed dropped even
more steeply—by 2006 the annual battle-death toll was
just 2 percent of that of 1999.[18]

They go on to say that the number of *coups d'état* has dropped
significantly and there were "appreciably more conflicts stopping than
there were conflicts starting."[19] There has been a surge of democratic
governments that have been established in sub-Saharan Africa. By
2007 half of Africa's 48 states were democracies where reasonably
free and fair elections took place and where there was considerable
personal freedom. Between 2000 and 2005 roughly four out of every
five African leaders were replaced democratically. Many African
governments have been able to extend their control over larger regions
of their territory, eliminating rebel armies and bringing peace.

This reduction in war is not limited to Africa. Around the world
the regions controlled by rebel groups have shrunk and the number of
people killed and wounded has been reduced. In Colombia the number
of kidnappings and killings have decreased significantly and the size
of the FARC forces have shrunk to about half in recent years. The civil
wars of Central American countries have come to an end. In Sri Lanka
the Tamil Tigers were finally defeated in May 2009 and the Tigers'
leadership declared that in future they will pursue their aims
democratically.

There are a number of social factors that have led towards a
peaceful resolution of wars, but by far the most important is the
collapse of empires. The First and Second World Wars saw the end of
empires that had used war as a tactic to exploit and dominate others.
The final collapse of colonialism spelled the end of another set of
wars, and the end of the Cold War eliminated yet another type of war.
The imperial war in Afghanistan will soon come to an end and the
Americans will exit Iraq by the end of 2011. This is not because the
insurgencies have been defeated, but because the imperial powers
finally realized that the invasion and occupation of these countries is
stopping the progress towards peace. We are living in the era of the

final chapter of imperialism and when it is over war will be reduced yet again.

There are a number of other reasons for the decline of war. Public attitudes have changed dramatically. In the nineteenth century war was seen as a normal part of relations between nations. Many believed that war was a great adventure and military men were given the highest honours. Today most people understand that war is a horror that brings unparalleled hardship to vulnerable people. Many go further, saying that war is always morally unjustified because war is the use of force to impose the will of the strong onto the weak.

There have been changes in the economics of war. Before the eighteenth century war was seen as an opportunity for plunder and increased wealth for the victorious side. Plunder is still a motivation for war in impoverished countries, but today it is understood that wars do serious harm to economic development by interrupting trade, disrupting local economies and creating desperate poverty for those caught up in the conflicts. Even the United States found that the Iraq War was much more costly than predicted. Many now understand that maintaining the military is costing the Americans and others far more than the benefits.

There is a growing recognition of the limits of war. Despite the enormous costs of maintaining their military, Vietnam, Afghanistan and Iraq taught the Americans that asymmetrical wars make it very difficult to impose their will on other people by military force. The Soviet leadership learned the same lesson in Afghanistan.

Globalization is drawing people together, building greater understanding and increased interdependence. This helps build peaceful relationships and decreases conflicts. This is happening with the spread of mass media but increased trade is even more important. Free trade has its problems, but it has helped to link people in every part of the world into mutually beneficial economic relationships. Co-operation between people is the basis of trade, not competition. It is in the interests of everyone involved in the trading relationship to work together because all participants then can gain economically.

There are new international norms of behaviour that discourage war. An important principle of international law, established after the

Second World War, was that the acquisition of territory through war is illegal. The resort to force is only permissible under international law in self-defence, or with the sanction of the United Nations. The invasion of Iraq by the United States satisfied neither of these criteria, and that is why it is viewed as an illegal war.

The spread of democracy is also reducing the likelihood of war. Democracies have far greater legitimacy than autocratic governments. In most instances democratically elected politicians work to improve the conditions of all people in the country. This helps to bridge the ethnic, class, racial and religious differences that cause divisions and can lead to conflict. Those policies build consensus and support for the political leadership and the national institutions.

Central governments of even the poorest countries have gained greater resources through aid programs, loans or economic development. That has allowed them to extend their control over their territory and stamp out banditry and rebel groups who have been preying on local populations.

There has been a reduction in ethnic and racial discrimination and a strengthening of minority rights in many countries. This is far from perfect. Discrimination is still rampant in many parts of the world and is one of the major causes of a number of conflicts. All efforts to eliminate discrimination lessen the grievances that lead to war.

Social change is coming to even the most remote parts of the world. Extreme poverty has not been eliminated but strides have been made in mass education in almost every part of the underdeveloped world. Public health programs have helped to eliminate disease, improve nutrition and lengthen life expectancy. Grassroots programs such as local co-operatives and non-profit organizations have been particularly successful. In sub-Saharan Africa today co-operatives are the second largest employers after government. Often Non-Governmental Agencies in the developed world are much more adept than governments in providing programs that reach the poorest people. These programs and economic development have begun to affect even the poorest parts of Africa.

With the end of the Cold War the United Nations has been liberated from superpower politics, and has become much more effective in ending wars and preventing conflicts from escalating into wars. Between 1988 and 2004 the number of U.N. peacekeeping operations has increased from 7 to 16 and these operations have been much more ambitious. U.N. peacekeeping intervention has become the new form of "humanitarian intervention," and one that has much greater support and legitimacy than the intervention by a single power like the Americans. While the restricted U.N. mandate kept the peacekeepers on the sidelines during the Rwandan genocide in 1994, today the 17,000 peacekeepers in the Congo have been given a mandate to use force if necessary to impose peace and protect non-combatants. There has even been criticism that they have not used enough force to ensure peace.

If there has been one social factor that has led to the decline in war it has been the gradual spread of prosperity. With the easing of desperate poverty comes the rise of hope for millions of people and the reduction of fear, suspicion, anger and hopelessness. It is that change that reduces the likelihood of war. The opposite is also true. If there is one factor that threatens peace more than any other, it is the spread of economic hardships through recession or depression.

Finally, many believe that it is deterrence that stops wars. The United States has invested trillions of dollars in the military in the belief that if they are strong militarily no other nation will dare attack. The American policy of MAD, Mutually Assured Destruction, is based on this principle. If another nation was mad enough to attack the United States with nuclear weapons then they would be annihilated.

A policy of deterrence seems incompatible with the other reasons for the decline of war, but the lessons of the Cold War suggest that deterrence did help to stop war between the two superpowers. Peace between the major powers of the world has prevailed since 1945. But now even the policy of deterrence is being reconsidered and ideas for disarmament are once again being discussed. New proposals are coming from the most unusual sources.

Disarmament and Nuclear Weapons

In the period between the two world wars the League of Nations spent much of its time debating disarmament. The reason was that the political leaders of that day had grown up in the time of the arms race prior to the First World War, and it was widely believed that the proliferation of weapons was a major cause of the war. Efforts were made to control the spread of weapons in the belief that, if only the arms race could be controlled, then peace would prevail. When those efforts failed many concluded that the League itself was a failure and it ultimately collapsed.

Nuclear weapons were first developed in the dying days of the Second World War, and they have totally changed the disarmament issue. Once the full horrors of the bombings of Hiroshima and Nagasaki became known, many around the world grew alarmed. Now war could not only kill millions of people; it could result in the virtual elimination of the human race and possibly the destruction of the planet. For some it became a moral question. The argument was, what gives political leaders the right to kill millions of ordinary people and endanger the lives of everyone on the globe so they can prevail in war?

But this disturbing question was ignored. With the onset of the Cold War the United States and the Soviet Union engaged in an unprecedented arms race that dwarfed all arms races of the past and resulted in the production and installation of thousands of nuclear weapons, each with a destructive power many times that of the Hiroshima and Nagasaki bombs. A decade after the end of the Second World War the so called "nuclear club," those countries that had nuclear weapons, included the United States, the Soviet Union, Britain and France.

Disarmament was not a major issue in the west after the beginning of the Cold War.[20] The main reason was that the United States, the leader of the western alliance, believed in deterrence and poured resources into keeping a significant edge in both conventional weapons and nuclear weapons over the Soviets. Other political leaders either agreed with that policy or did not want to challenge it, and the issue of disarmament disappeared from the political agenda.

Beginning in 1969 there was a significant break-through in the nuclear arms race when discussions for the Strategic Arms Limitation Treaties (SALT) began. Ultimately there were two rounds of SALT talks between the United States and the Soviet Union. SALT I was concluded successfully in 1972, but SALT II was not ratified by the U.S. Congress. Other international agreements put a cap on the size and number of nuclear weapons and testing,[21] but the arms race continued. In 1983 President Ronald Reagan announced that the United States would build a "star wars" defence system designed to intercept incoming weapons and destroy them. This was a serious escalation of the arms race.

With the end of the Cold War in 1990 it seemed for a time that there were new opportunities for disarmament. Politicians and opinion leaders talked about the "peace dividend," and many countries reduced their military budgets, but there was little change in the United States. In 2007 the United States had enough active nuclear warheads to obliterate the world,[22] and under President George W. Bush the U.S. prepared to design and implement a new generation of nuclear ICBMs (Intercontinental Ballistic Missiles).

But although there were some restrictions on the nuclear arms race between the superpowers, a more disturbing development was the expansion of the nuclear club. By 1998 the countries with nuclear weapons included the United States, Russia, Britain, France, China, India, Pakistan and Israel.[23] Nuclear proliferation became a real concern. At least another thirteen countries have the ability to "go nuclear" in the next decade. The danger is that some of these countries like Iran, North Korea and Algeria, are considered politically unstable and a threat to world peace. To add to these worries there is increasing concern that nuclear weapons may fall into the hands of terrorist groups.

These concerns have led to new efforts for nuclear disarmament, and surprisingly the people advocating this radical departure are coming from influential conservative political circles in the United States. On January 15, 2008 an opinion piece was published in the *Wall Street Journal* entitled "Towards a Nuclear-Free World." The article was co-authored by George P. Shultz, U.S. Secretary of State

1982-89, William J. Perry, Secretary of Defence 1994-97, Henry Kissinger, Secretary of State 1973-77 and Sam Nunn, Chairman of the Senate Armed Services Committee. The opinion piece begins:

> The accelerating spread of nuclear weapons, nuclear know-how and nuclear material has brought us to a nuclear tipping point. We face a very real possibility that the deadliest weapons ever invented could fall into dangerous hands.... One year ago, in an essay in this paper, we called for a global effort to reduce reliance on nuclear weapons, to prevent their spread into potentially dangerous hands, and ultimately to end them as a threat to the world. The interest, momentum and growing political space that has been created to address these issues over the past year has been extraordinary, with strong positive responses from people all over the world.[24]

The article goes on to name prominent people who support this position in Russia and Britain and then describes how a system of controls can be put in place to reduce and ultimately eliminate nuclear weapons from the arsenals of all countries.

This new effort to eliminate nuclear weapons has been prompted by concerns about the proliferation of weapons of mass destruction and the threat of terrorism. The United States has attempted to block countries like Iran from developing nuclear weapons, but it is difficult to make the argument that Iran should not be allowed to have these weapons as long as the U.S. has a huge arsenal themselves. People are coming to understand that these weapons are more of a liability than an asset. History since the end of the Second World War has shown that politicians are not willing to use nuclear weapons in time of war. They promote fear and hostility from other countries rather than respect. These weapons and their delivery systems are expensive to create and maintain. Why have nuclear weapons if they create more political problems than advantages?

With the election of Barack Obama the issue of nuclear weapons has become even more central. On March 26, 2010 the U.S. and Russia announced a new nuclear arms treaty that limited each side to 1550 deployed warheads.[25] Obama made clear that he wants missiles off "hair trigger" alert, and is opposed to new systems that would "weaponize" space. The President has been very critical of the star wars missile defence technology and points out that, despite the $120 billion cost, this weapon system has achieved only a "lacklustre performance."[26]

The effort to stop war has now come full circle, and once again disarmament has become a major issue. There are new concerns about the spread of conventional weapons and the amount of money squandered on weapons by the poorest countries.[27] The initiative "towards a nuclear-free world," is another indication that there is a growing understanding that weapons hinder rather than enhance the chances of peace.

Is there a case for Humanitarian Military Intervention?

In April 2009 a group of local women in Kabul, Afghanistan gathered on the street to protest a law the Afghan government had passed that made women the property of men and legalized a husband's right to rape his wife. As the women gathered they were surrounded by angry men with raised fists and contorted faces. "Whores!" they shouted, "Dogs!" "Death to the slaves of Christians!"

This scene, captured by television cameras and broadcast around the world, created a firestorm of debate. Everywhere in the west men and women were appalled at the blatant violation of the rights of Afghan women and the obvious insensitivity and inhumanity shown by the Afghan men. For Canadians, who had already lost a number of military personnel in the conflict, two of them young women, the debate was particularly intense. Two radically different conclusions were drawn.

Margaret MacMillan, a historian best known for her influential book *Paris 1919: Six Months that Changed the World*,[28] commented that feminists on the left have had trouble trying to separate their distaste for Western imperialist intervention and the way in which women were treated. Pulling out is not an option for her.

> This is a regime that depends very heavily on Western backing and the Canadian government and others should bloody well use their influence over President Karzai. They have been too timid and they don't want to appear like they are telling him what to do, but I think they jolly well should.

Judy Rebick is a Canadian feminist, writer and political activist.[29] She points out that life is much worse for women since the military occupation of Afghanistan by the United States and ISAF countries began.

> How has the war helped women in Afghanistan? It hasn't ...Never have women achieved equality by somebody coming in and giving it to them. We can't bomb our way into equality.... We should never have gone into Afghanistan in the first place and we should leave.[30]

Rebick believes that we should support women's groups who are struggling to establish women's rights.

This is the question that will come to dominate future political debates. Should the international community intervene militarily when minorities are repressed, when there is systemic discrimination of an entire gender, as in Afghanistan, or when a regime uses its military power to attack its citizens as happened in Libya and Syria? Should we intervene when genocide is threatened in countries like Rwanda or the Darfur region of Sudan? Should the international community launch military interventions on humanitarian grounds? And who has the right to make such decisions?

But military intervention is only a part of the question. The discussion has to be broadened to ask how the international community can work collectively to solve the problems of poverty and discrimination. Empires are fading into history. No longer will the United States dictate the international political agenda. The time has come to build a new multilateral, democratic political system where decisions can be made collectively. That is the way to address problems of poverty, discrimination and it is the way that we can take that final step towards ending war.

CHAPTER 9: WAR AND RECONCILIATION

Pacifism has been a powerful force in all religions. Non-violence is a theme in Buddhism. Mahatma Gandhi, one of the great pacifists of our age, was a devout Hindu and several protestant denominations from the Anabaptists to the Quakers have advocated pacifism. During the nineteenth century many socialists and anarchists were opposed to war. They argued that violence was inherent in capitalism and would disappear once the capitalist state was overthrown. The beginning of the First World War ended that belief when socialists on both sides joined their national armies and died in the trenches along with their capitalist comrades.

The disillusionment that emerged from the experience of the First World War revitalized the pacifist movement in Europe and North America, but the rise of fascism in the 1930s again turned people away from the belief that war was morally wrong. Bertrand Russell, a leading British philosopher and pacifist during the First World War, changed his views and spoke publicly about the need to defeat Hitler militarily. Albert Einstein, commenting about nuclear weapons, said, "I loathe all armies and any kind of violence; yet I'm firmly convinced that at present these weapons offer the only effective protection."[1] Belief in the "just war" goes back at least as far as the Roman Empire and remains the dominant position of intellectuals and politicians to this day.

Pacifism was a strategy to end war. If, when the call to arms went out and no one responded, then wars would have to end. But even though pacifism has been rejected, the movement has an important message. In the past the motto of war has been "to the victor go the spoils." Pacifists teach that we must treat our enemies with compassion, humanity and understanding. That is an important lesson. If we are to end war, we must reject the warriors' creed and adopt the humanitarian approach of the pacifists.

Lessons from Four Wars

Students study the causes of wars, examining the social, economic and political roots of the conflict, but how wars are concluded tell us whether the conflict will continue or if people can live in peace and harmony. This it true of all wars but the following four examples are instructive because each war was concluded in a different way with different outcomes.

Case 1: The Indian Wars

As Europeans arrived in North America they learned the necessary skills to survive in this strange and hostile environment from native people. In Canada, settlement by the French and later the British was motivated by the profits of the fur trade. The trappers were native people who provided the merchants with the furs and soon the trappers and their families became dependent on them for European goods. The Cree, Ojibwa and Dene became an important part of the mercantile empires that prospered until the late nineteenth century. Relationships between the different groups remained cordial because each group had an important role to play in the fur trade and conflict rarely broke out.

In the territory that is today the United States, the relationships between Europeans and native groups were quite different than in Canada. Most of the Europeans were farmers and they needed land to grow their crops and pasture their animals. Settlers cleared and fenced the land keeping out all intruders, and native people found themselves excluded from their own territory. Disputes arose and then violence, and war sometimes broke out across the frontier. A pattern was established. European settlers would occupy a piece of land, the native groups who claimed the territory would resist, skirmishes would break out and then war. In a short time the settlers would prevail in the war because they had superior weapons and numbers, and the native groups would either move west or settle on reserves set aside for them. This pattern continued from the first settlements of the Plymouth Colony in the 1620s[2] to the massacre at Wounded Knee in 1890.[3]

The European occupation of North America was shattering to the native people and had an impact on natives in Canada as well as the United States. With the end of the fur trade in the north and the nomadic way of life in the south, the economic basis of traditional society came to an end and native people could not support themselves or their families. [4] Across the continent native people had lost their land and traditional way of life as a result of war. Herded onto reserves, most native groups were forced to rely on meagre government rations that kept them in desperate poverty. At the same time they faced prejudice and racism and their culture was systematically attacked through a policy of cultural assimilation by residential schools and other institutions and practices.

The Indian Wars came to an end not because the issues were resolved, or because the warring groups came to a mutual understanding and established just conditions for the peace. They ended because native people understood that they had been defeated and there was no point in continuing the resistance. The defeat and the harsh conditions of peace imposed by governments affected native people in profound ways and continue to do so to this day. Native people suffer the highest rates of poverty in North America. The loss has led to crippling levels of alcoholism, drug abuse and suicide.[5] Only now, 120 years after the last outbreak of violence in the Indian Wars, are communities and individuals healing themselves and regaining their sense of pride and self-confidence.

Case 2: The Indian and Pakistan Wars

The roots of the Indian and Pakistan Wars lie in the conflict between Hindus and Muslims. The Indian sub-continent was dominated by the British from the middle of the eighteenth century and was a colony from 1858 to 1947. India is an incredibly diverse country with many different religions, castes, languages and ethnic groups, but the dominant groups were Muslims and Hindu. During this time they lived together in an uneasy peace. Muslim-dominated areas were in the north and Hindus dominated the rest of the country.

Although there was antagonism between the religious groups, they also had a history of co-existence that went back centuries.

After the First World War momentum began to build for independence. The Congress Party led these demands. The Congress Party leaders were primarily of Hindu origin, but most were secular and believed all groups could live in peace in an independent country. As proposals for independence became more serious, the Muslim minority grew concerned that their interests would be ignored, and they would not have the same rights as the majority Hindu in an independent India. The Muslim League became prominent and its leaders began to demand a separate Muslim country. Mahatma Gandhi believed that Hindus and Muslims could live together in peace and preached reconciliation. He was opposed to the partition of India, but by the 1940s feelings became inflamed and Gandhi was increasingly ignored,

After the Second World War India was in turmoil as demands for independence grew more and more strident. The British Labour government led by Clement Attlee knew they could not contain these demands and agreed to grant independence. In August 1946 riots broke out between Muslims and Hindu in Calcutta and across Northern India, killing 5,000 people and injuring thousands more. India was at the point of civil war and in the midst of this crisis the Hindu and Muslim politicians agreed that the only way to avoid complete chaos was to partition the country.

The partition of India in August 1947, and the creation of East and West Pakistan and India, was a momentous event that had huge repercussions across the developing and underdeveloped world as well as the Indian sub-continent. A commission was established to settle the boundaries. Territories where the majority was Muslim became part of Pakistan, and Hindu majority areas became part of India. This sparked the mass movement of millions of people. It is estimated that over 7 million Muslims and an additional 7 million Hindus left their homes and moved across the border, creating millions of homeless refugees. Between 250,000 and one million people were killed in the riots and upheavals that resulted from partition.

That was the beginning of the conflict and wars that have plagued relations between India and Pakistan from partition to the present day. The two countries have fought three wars in Kashmir, in 1947, 1965 and 1999, and in 1971 India played the decisive role in the war of liberation waged by East Pakistan, which resulted in the creation of the state of Bangladesh.

In Kashmir, where most of the wars were fought, the conflict goes back to the terms of settlement of partition. Kashmir was a semi-independent state ruled by a Hindu Maharaja but the majority of the population was Muslim. Under the terms of the partition the Maharaja could decide whether the territory would become part of India or Pakistan. This Maharaja decided he wanted Kashmir to remain independent. In 1947 Muslims from Pakistan invaded Kashmir intending to liberate it and have it join Pakistan. The Maharaja did not have the military force to repel the invaders so he made a deal with the Indian government that Kashmir would join India if the Indian army repelled the Pakistanis, and that is what happened. Today India stations 500,000 troops in the Kashmir Valley, making it the most militarized zone in the world. The war has claimed 70,000 lives, tens of thousands have been tortured, thousands more "disappeared," women raped, and others left to live in poverty.[6]

There are many reasons why peace should prevail between India and Pakistan. People on both sides of the border share a history and a common language; trade would benefit both countries; 138 million Muslims continue to live in India – thirteen percent of the entire population. And yet leaders continue to let this conflict poison relationships. It could get much worse; today right wing Hindu nationalists and fundamentalist Muslims inflame emotions by blaming the other side for real and imagined transgressions. The tradition of Gandhi has been overwhelmed by those preaching intolerance, and the result has been decades of war and conflict.

Case 3: Germany after World War Two

The Treaty of Versailles of 1919 did much to create the conditions that led to the Second World War, and the same political blunder almost happened at the end of the Second World War. As the war drew to an end the allied leaders met to discuss the terms of the peace. Foremost on the agenda was the desire to strip Germany of its power for all time. By 1945 Germany was at the point of collapse. Seven and a half million Germans had died in the conflict. Their cities were in ruin from sustained bombing raids, industrial production was at the point of collapse and distribution was at a standstill, but this was not punishment enough for the allies.

Stalin wanted summary executions of between 50,000 and 100,000 German staff officers. The American Morgenthau Plan called for the deindustrialization of Germany to turn it into an agricultural nation. These two proposals were not carried out, but other punitive policies were put in place. A large section of eastern Prussia, roughly 25% of the German territory before the war, was permanently ceded to Poland and the Soviet Union. Millions of people of German origin were expelled from these lands and forcibly moved to East Germany. Thousands lost their lives. Factories in East Germany were dismantled and sent to the Soviet Union. Hundreds of thousands of German prisoners of war were used as forced labour or held in camps with little food. The pattern had been set to repeat Versailles and extract the maximum revenge on Germany and the German people.

Despite these plans history did not repeat itself. By 1947 the Cold War had begun and Germany became the front line in the conflict between the Soviet Union and the United States. The Americans quickly understood that it was very important to maintain the loyalty of the German people. Their policy changed from exacting revenge and ensuring Germany would never become a power again to active support of the redevelopment of the country based on humanitarian principles. Prisoners were released. Loans and grants were made available through the Marshall Plan. A new democratically elected government was set up in West Germany with the support of the Americans. By the 1950s the "economic miracle" – the reindustrialization of Germany – was well underway and Germans regained their economic strength and self-confidence. West Germany became the economic powerhouse of Europe. In 1955 Germany was allowed to join NATO and in 1957 it became a founding member of the European Union.

In time Germans struggled to face the horrors of the history of the Nazi regime. The Nuremburg Trials were conducted by the victorious allies after the war to punish the top Nazi leaders. These trials were largely discounted by the German people because they were seen as show trials imposed by the victors, but in the 1950s and 60s the Germans held their own trials of prison guards and officers who had been involved in atrocities and programs of extermination during the war. This brought a new awareness of how the Nazis had operated and helped people understand the level of inhumanity that the regime had imposed on others.

It was the Cold War, and the need to bring West Germany into the American orbit that led to more humanitarian policies. In time those policies fundamentally changed the outlook of the German people, and it is no exaggeration to say that they resulted in a much different and more peaceful Europe. West Germany became a democratic state and once Germany was reunited, after the Cold War in 1991, Germany became a full-fledged member of the international community and the central core of a democratic Europe. Treating those defeated in war with justice and humanity changed everything.

Case 4: Chile

The South American country of Chile has had a long history of parliamentary democracy going back to 1891. In 1970 Salvador Allende, a Marxist medical doctor and member of the socialist party was elected president in a "Popular Unity" coalition of socialists, communists, radicals and social-democrats. Allende came to power in the midst of a recession. Soon the economic crisis led to a flight of capital, high levels of unemployment and falling production. The government responded by nationalizing banks, mines and some factories. Opposition to Allende's government grew and finally on September 11, 1973 the Chilean military, under the leadership of General Augusto Pinochet seized power, with the support and help of the CIA. Allende was killed or committed suicide and in December 1974 Pinochet was appointed President by the military junta.

The early years of the Pinochet government witnessed major human rights violations. Over 80,000 people, mainly young men and women of the left, were rounded up by the military and held without trial for months. It is estimated that 200,000 went into exile, 30,000 were tortured and over 3,000 killed. By 1980 most of these human rights violations had come to an end and Pinochet became President for an eight year term. In 1988 the government lost a referendum, new elections were called and a Christian Democrat, Patricio Aylwin, was elected president.

Aylwin had been elected on a platform that promised truth and justice for the political prisoners, exiles and families of the disappeared. Within a month after his election he appointed a Truth and Reconciliation Commission, called the Rettig Commission after its chairman. There were many problems with the commission. It was composed of an equal number of Pinochet supporters and opponents. Pinochet continued to have considerable support in the country and there were fears that if the commission were overly critical it would lead to major disturbances. As a result the commission did not have the right to prosecute those who had broken the law – even serious laws like homicide. In spite of this provision, the military still refused to co-operate. But the biggest criticism came from those who said that its terms of reference were too narrow. The commission could investigate only the disappearances, not the human rights violations of those who survived. Despite all of these problems and the mounting political controversy, the commission investigated 3,400 cases of death and was able to come to conclusions about the circumstances of the deaths in all but 641 cases. The findings attributed the cause of death to the military in 95% of the cases.

Leaders on both extreme left and right rejected the conclusions but the majority did accept the findings. The families of the disappeared had some closure and sense that justice had been done. Almost 5,000 receive a monthly pension to compensate them for their loss. The military never accepted responsibility for the deaths, but both conservative and moderate political leaders expressed contrition for their actions. At the end of the process a number of laws protecting human rights were passed by the legislature.

Although the process was incomplete and unsatisfactory, for many it remains a turning point for Chile because it restored the public trust in democracy and the political culture of the country. The high point of this emotional process came when President Aylwin introduced the report with an impassioned televised speech, apologizing on behalf of the state to the victims and pleading with the people for reconciliation.[7] The process has helped people in the country to move on. Today Chile has a vibrant democracy and the memory of those terrible days when thousands of people were detained, tortured and killed is fading.

Ending War

Every war is different, and these four case studies are hardly representative of all wars or even all of the wars since 1945, but they tell us something about how conflicts can be resolved. It is not easy to reconcile differences that were so strongly felt that they resulted in war and all the inhuman acts that go with this level of conflict, but if wars are not resolved with humanity and justice then they will set in motion the causes for the next war. New ways have to be found to resolve conflicts, and lessons have to be drawn from the failures and successes of the past.

The tragedy of the Indian Wars was not just the native people's loss of their territory and culture; it was that their feelings of defeat were allowed to fester to the point where whole generations of native people were consumed by a sense of anger, hopelessness and victimization. It is a tragedy that that was allowed to happen by the so-called "civilized" people of European heritage.

The prolonged conflict between India and Pakistan illustrates how war can lead to a level of violence that can poison the relationship of millions of people. Hindus and Muslims lived together in peace on the Indian sub-continent for centuries, but the partition of India and the violence that came with it have driven a wedge between the two communities that will take decades to heal. This is a failure of political leadership of a most fundamental kind.

The way forward is illustrated in what happened in Germany after the Second World War. Peace and reconciliation finally emerged out of the most devastating war the world has witnessed, not because the victorious nations decided to treat the defeated with humanity but because in view of the Cold War it was in their interest to gain the support and respect of the German people. Regardless of the motivation, what is instructive is that by treating the Germans with justice and humanity, hostility came to an end and peace finally returned.

But the most interesting case of all is the Truth and Reconciliation Commission in Chile. It took political courage to set this process in motion. It was risky. Friends, comrades, brothers and sisters had died in brutal ways. How can political acts so premeditated and murderous be resolved and forgiven? The Chileans chose the simplest and most direct way of all – speaking the truth – and in a cathartic, emotional way, most were able to put the horrible memories to rest. It was not entirely satisfactory, but it began the reconciliation process and in time people have been able to live in peace again. This was inspired leadership that drew people together and helped them heal the perceived injustices of the past.

In the past wars were settled when the powerful dominated the weak and exacted what they deemed as appropriate compensation and revenge, but too often this did not bring peace. In the future the international community must end wars and work for peace based on principles of justice and humanity.

Tools for Peacemakers

It was during the 19th century that practical steps to limit war were taken, and organizations were created to promote peace. Henri Dunant wrote on the horrors of war, and this led to the creation of the Red Cross and the First Geneva Convention on the treatment of prisoners and non-combatants during war. Today there are five Geneva Conventions on war that have the status of international treaties and are still in force. At the end of the First World War there was broad agreement that efforts must be made to end war, leading to the formation of The League of Nations. The League is thought to have been a failure but it was the first international body created specifically to try to stop war and resolve international conflicts. The United Nations was created after the end of the Second World War with a mandate to promote peace, but soon it too was caught in the conflict between the two major empires of the day, the United States and the Soviet Union.

During the Cold War the prospects for peace were dim. The two superpowers wanted to maintain maximum flexibility with no interference from other countries or the United Nations. The Americans in Vietnam, the Soviets in Afghanistan, and the many surrogate wars in the developing and underdeveloped world – in each case the superpowers or their closest allies used war as the means to try to attain their political objectives. At the same time, the Cold War relationship between the two superpowers – the most important threat to world peace – was dealt with not by the international community, but by direct negotiations. The Cuban Missile Crisis was resolved in talks between the leaders of the United States and the Soviet Union as were the negotiations around the SALT I and II disarmament agreements.

All this has now changed. The end of the Cold War and the relative decline of the United States have ushered in a new era with much greater scope for peacemakers. The United States is still involved in two wars, Iraq and Afghanistan, that are out of bounds for international peacemakers, at least for the moment, but peacemakers are focusing on other conflicts. There are successes and failures. Making peace is not for the impatient or faint of heart, but now it is almost universally understood that it is in everyone's interest to reduce wars in the world.

While new prospects for peace have emerged, a broader and more comprehensive set of tools for peacemakers has become available. Some of these tools have existed for a long time; others are being modified and adapted in the face of criticism, while still others are new innovations that hold promise. The following summarizes the tools that now exist in the peacemaker's kit.

A Clear Definition of a Legitimate War

For centuries philosophers have tried to define just wars, but most do little more than provide a convenient justification for one war or another. The Nuremburg Trials determined that wars of aggression that seized territory are illegal. This is an important distinction. In the past many wars were waged in an attempt to take over territory. That now is defined as illegal.

The clearest definition of a just war comes from the Charter of the United Nations. Essentially it says that the only legitimate wars are those fought in self-defence or for the enforcement of the U.N. Charter.[8] Under this definition the U.S. invasion of Iraq was an illegal act of aggression. The involvement of the U.S. and the coalition forces in Afghanistan is more difficult to judge. Al-Qaeda admitted that the planning and training for the 9/11 attack and other acts of terrorism happened in Afghan camps. The U.S. justified the war as self-defence, but the war has gone well beyond clearing out the camps. The U.S. and coalition forces are helping the Afghan government defend the country against attacks by the Taliban. Is this a war of self-defence or intervention in the internal affairs of a foreign country? Even the simple definition of a legitimate war used by the United Nations is open to interpretation. In the final analysis, a legitimate war is what the United Nations Security Council deems legitimate.

The real difficulty with the U.N. definition is that it does little to define when a civil war is legitimate, and civil wars are some of the most destructive, protracted conflicts that are going on today. From the point of view of a national government a civil war violates a host of laws, from homicide and rape to intimidation and kidnapping, but when is it legitimate for people to take up arms against a corrupt government that flouts the human rights of its citizens? No simple definition can help here.

Human Rights

Concern for human rights in times of peace as well as war goes back to the Enlightenment, but this concern finally turned into action after the Second World War when the atrocities of both the Germans and Japanese became known to the general public. There is reference to human rights in the U.N. Charter, but it was the Universal Declaration of Human Rights of 1948[9] that clarified the issue. This document describes human rights in detail. They include freedom of speech, assembly and association, security of the person and equality before the law as well as atrocities such as murder, torture and slavery.

The Universal Declaration of Human Rights document was published in dozens of languages and was widely discussed around the world but the difficulty has been that it was a recommendation and had no force of law. This was corrected in 1976 when the U.N. adopted the International Covenant on Civil and Political Rights.[10] The Covenant included virtually all of the provisions of the Declaration on Human Rights and gave them the force of international law. In 1993 the Office of the United Nations High Commissioner for Human Rights[11] was established. It is a U.N. agency with headquarters in Geneva, working to promote and protect human rights. In 2006 the U.N Human Rights Council[12] was established to "strengthen the promotion and protection of human rights around the globe."

But even with this multi-pronged effort, designed to protect human rights, violations continue. The problem is enforcement. Grand statements are fine, United Nations High Commissioners and Human Rights Councils are important symbols, but if they cannot affect the behaviour of governments, military forces or police then they have done little to deal with the real human rights violations in the world. To respond to these criticisms the International Criminal Court has been set up to move beyond words to action.

International Criminal Court

In the 1990s acts of genocide took place in the former Yugoslavia and Rwanda that shocked people around the world. In response to these atrocities the United Nations Security Council established special criminal tribunals to bring the leaders of these genocides to justice. These efforts were not entirely satisfactory but they helped in forming a consensus that some type of permanent judicial procedure was necessary so that individuals who had committed serious human rights violations could be prosecuted.

In July 1998 representatives of 120 countries met in Rome and adopted the Rome Statute, an agreement that became the legal basis for the International Criminal Court[13] (ICC). It came into force on July 1, 2002. Courts such as this had been established at the end of the Second World War, but this was the first time a permanent court with jurisdiction over international criminal acts had been established.

The ICC is an independent court "with jurisdiction to prosecute individuals responsible for the most serious crimes of international concern: genocide, crimes against humanity and war crimes."[14] It is a court of last resort. It cannot act if a national judicial system is undertaking proceedings against accused individuals unless those proceedings are not genuine. The court operates under rules of evidence, such as the presumption of innocence until proven guilty, much like other courts around the world. To date the ICC has pursued cases in the following countries: Uganda, the Democratic Republic of the Congo, Darfur, Sudan, the Central African Republic, Kenya and Libya.

The ICC remains controversial both with legal experts and practical peacemakers trying to bring an end to war. In effect a judicial system has been put in place that grants the ICC the power to deal with criminal behaviour in a way that supersedes national laws. Legally this is a very significant precedent that many lawyers feel uncomfortable with because it challenges the principle of national sovereignty that has existed for centuries.

But there is another criticism of the ICC that is more practical. Peacemakers who are working in wartime conditions, or in volatile situations where war could erupt at any moment, often need immediate solutions to calm the situation and end the violence. One solution often used in the past has been the exile of a leader. For example, Idi Amin, the so-called "Butcher of Uganda," was allowed to go into exile in

Saudi Arabia when his regime collapsed in 1979. This brought calm to the country and helped to return peace. Recently the ICC has launched criminal proceedings against the President of Sudan, Omar Hassan Ahmad al-Bashir, and there is concern that this may make it more difficult to bring the war in Darfur and southern Sudan to an end because it denies al-Bashir an exit strategy. Justice under the law is satisfying to people who have been persecuted, but what if it prolongs suffering and continues the war?

Truth and Reconciliation Commissions

Criminal proceedings against political leaders can create more problems than they resolve, especially if those leaders continue to have a following among the population. Another approach that is equally controversial is Truth and Reconciliation Commissions. Commissions such as this have been set up in a number of countries, including Chile, but the most successful was in South Africa.

With the collapse of the white apartheid South African regime in the early 1990s, and the election of the African National Congress in 1994, led by Nelson Mandela, a political problem faced by the new government was dealing with the atrocities that had been carried out by the apartheid regime and laying the groundwork for a multi-racial, democratic country. In an attempt to deal with these twin problems the South African government set up the Truth and Reconciliation Commission.

The success of this effort was in part due to the prestige of the leaders of the commission. Archbishop Desmond Tutu, the chairman, was highly respected in both the black and white communities and other commissioners had equal prestige in their own communities. Their mandate was to bear witness to the atrocities of the past. They had the power to grant amnesty but only if, first, the acts committed were politically motivated and, second, those who had committed the abuses gave full disclosure of the crime. The commission held hearings in every part of the country. Thousands of people from all races came forward with their stories. Amnesty was granted in a number of cases but in others it was denied. The South African media followed the proceedings closely; they also attracted considerable world attention because of the unique quality of the hearings and the sincerity of the efforts to resolve the crimes of the past. The final report tabled in October 1998 detailed many of the atrocities committed by agents of the apartheid regime, but it also criticized the ANC for violence that was committed in their struggle to overthrow the government.[15]

In the judgement of many South Africans the Truth and Reconciliation Commission was a difficult but important effort to resolve the injustices of the past. The white community tended to be more critical than the black.[16] Many of the victims of the violence felt that the process had robbed them of justice but the consensus was that it was more important to seek reconciliation than to seek retribution.

Others have tried to use the process of Truth and Reconciliation Commissions but have not had the same success; still it is a very important new tactic in the efforts to achieve peace. The approach seems to be most appropriate as a conflict winds down and people are sincerely attempting to resolve differences and past atrocities. The process is particularly suitable for trying to deal with the events and issues that come as a result of civil wars. Speaking the truth – bearing witness – honestly revealing what has happened – seeking forgiveness: the experience of Truth and Reconciliation Commissions demonstrates that these are powerful ways to try to resolve the violence and conflict of the past.

International Sanctions

One of the oldest and most commonly used strategies of dealing with so-called rogue states, or countries involved in wars, is to level sanctions against them. Single countries can initiate sanctions, or the United Nations Security Council can declare sanctions against a country and ask all the member states to comply. The United States has been much more prone to use sanctions than others. The Europeans prefer to cut off aid. Sanctions used by one state often have little impact because the target can find ways to avoid the restriction. Still, the size and power of the American economy has meant U.S.

sanctions can be very effective. The U.S. embargo against Cuba has not resulted in a change of the leadership of the regime, but it has led to real hardships for Cubans. During the Cold War the Security Council rarely applied sanctions because one or the other super powers would use their veto, but since 1990 the council has increasingly used sanctions to attempt to bring compliance in time of war or when there have been humanitarian violations.[17]

Some sanctions are relatively mild. Countries can demand the expulsion of diplomats or sever diplomatic relations with a country. There can be travel bans against leaders or a ban on the travel of all citizens of a country by refusing to grant visas. There can even be sanctions against a country to stop their citizens from participating in cultural, scientific or sporting events. The boycott of the Moscow Olympics in 1980 was in response to the Soviet invasion of Afghanistan. This infuriated the Kremlin leaders who had hoped the Olympics would help to repair their international prestige.

These are all relatively minor forms of sanctions but there are another set that are designed to deal with more serious conflicts. Arms embargos are often imposed either against rebel groups or countries. These are difficult to enforce. There has been a U.N. arms embargo against Somalia since 1992 but the country is awash in weapons, and more arrive on a regular basis.[18] The freezing of overseas assets of key individuals in target states is felt to be more effective, but again, there are many ways to avoid these sanctions by using "middle men" or tax havens.

Trade embargos are one of the most effective ways of dealing with rogue states. There can be restrictions on the export of strategic materials or specific types of goods. For example, the U.N. banned the export of diamonds from rebel held territories in Angola and Sierra Leone, and there have been restrictions on timber exports from Liberia. These embargos were put in place to try to deny rebel groups or governments the funds needed to carry on war.

Comprehensive sanctions that include the trade in virtually all goods can be devastating for a country. The Security Council imposed a total ban on trade with Iraq on August 6, 1990, just four days after the Iraqi invasion of Kuwait, and kept the ban in force until May 22,

2003, after the fall of the Saddam Hussein regime. These economic sanctions created a humanitarian crisis for the Iraqi people. There was widespread hunger and malnutrition, a lack of medical supplies and a ban on chlorine leading to contaminated water. Sanctions led to an 80% per capita drop in income for Iraqis, the increase of child labour and a rise in illiteracy. It is estimated sanctions led directly to 100,000 deaths of children, while other estimates put the figure at 227,000; an article in the British Medical journal, *The Lancet,* claimed that sanctions were responsible for 567,000 Iraqi children's deaths.[19]

A similar situation soon developed when comprehensive economic sanctions were imposed on Haiti, the poorest country in the Western Hemisphere, between 1991 and 1994. The purpose of the sanctions was to rid the county of a dictator who had seized power illegally, but it soon created a humanitarian crisis with worsening health conditions and a drop in living standards. Over 60% of all private sector jobs were lost and scores of desperate Haitians lost their lives trying to flee the country in makeshift boats.[20]

The experiences in Iraq and Haiti have sparked a debate about international sanctions and their usefulness. Jeffrey Sachs and others have argued that sanctions have failed almost everywhere they have been tried. They failed to bring down the Saddam regime in Iraq and may have strengthened it. In Myanmar economic sanctions have been in effect for over 15 years. They have weakened the economy and brought hardships and a humanitarian crisis to the people but have not weakened the military regime.[21]

This criticism of sanctions has led to a new set of policies but not a total rejection of the tactic. Comprehensive sanctions are out of favour and what are called "targeted sanctions" are now advocated. For example, in 2001 the U.N placed a trade embargo against Liberia in an attempt to stop a civil war that was raging. It included an arms embargo, a ban on the importation of Liberian rough diamonds, a travel ban and a ban on all Liberian registered aircraft.[22] The tactic was to target just those areas that would impede the leaders of Liberia from continuing with a civil war.

But although some claim that sanctions have never stopped war, and there is not one case of a dictator or military leader being ousted because they have been applied, it is likely that sanctions will continue to be used by countries and the United Nations for some time to come. The great benefit is they are inexpensive, easy to administer and do not risk the lives of citizens in the countries applying them. Sanctions give the appearance that something is being done to stop wars and solve humanitarian crises, but they are more show than substance. The most optimistic thing that can be said is that targeted sanctions may be a useful tactic to stop wars or deal with rogue states in some cases, but only if they are used in conjunction with other efforts.

United Nations Peacekeeping

United Nations peacekeeping has been the most important peace initiative that the international community has been involved in since the end of the Second World War. The first U.N. peacekeeping effort was in 1948 when the Security Council agreed to monitor the armistice between Israel and its Arab neighbours. Since then peacekeepers have been involved in 68 peacekeeping operations around the world. Fifty-two have been successfully completed and there are current deployments in 16 countries. The successes of these operations were recognized when U.N. peacekeeping efforts won the Nobel Peace Prize in 1988.

During the Cold War U.N. peacekeeping was limited to monitoring conflicts between states, inter-state conflicts as they are called. The peacekeepers acted as observers monitoring ceasefires or stabilizing the situation on the ground so that peace agreements could be negotiated and implemented. The U.N. peacekeepers were strictly neutral and instructed not to use force of any kind. During the 1956 Suez Crisis the Canadian Minister of External Affairs, Lester Pearson, proposed an extension of peacekeeping to create a military force that could supervise the withdrawal of British and French forces and monitor the peace. At that time it was agreed that the peacekeeping force could be lightly armed, but they were only to use their weapons in self defence.

With the end of the Cold War U.N. peacekeeping efforts expanded. The superpower confrontation at the Security Council had disappeared and greater effort was made to work for peace, but the initial peacekeeping missions soon ran into serious problems. The U.N. peacekeepers found themselves in the midst of war without a mandate to use force even to protect civilians. In the former Yugoslavia and Rwanda peacekeeping efforts did not stop the genocides that took the lives of hundreds of thousands of people, and the U.N. peacekeeping mission in Somalia ended in disaster when soldiers were killed, the peacekeeping force was pulled out and anarchy returned to the country. An analysis of these missions led to the conclusion that they "proved to be impossible to implement with the resources and the manpower provided,"[23] because they were in highly volatile situations where war and violence raged. Peace agreements and even cease fires had not been negotiated and the parties were not willing to stop fighting.

Rather than abandoning peacekeeping after these failures the U.N. Security Council decided that the efforts had to be strengthened. It was recognized that some missions, like those where war continued, were beyond the capability of U.N. peacekeepers. Special U.N. mandates have been given in those countries. In the former Yugoslavia the European Union and NATO were given a mandate, and in Afghanistan the International Security Assistance Force (ISAF) led by the United States has been given a mandate by the Security Council. In other conflict zones, where a cease fire or a negotiated peace were in effect, but help was still needed to enforce the peace, the U.N. peacekeepers were asked to play a role. The other major change was that the mandate given to the U.N. peacekeepers was strengthened. The term "robust peacekeeping" is now used to describe the new, more "muscular" military presence of peacekeepers. The mandates allow troops to use force to protect the mission and to protect the civilian population, but they are not to take sides in the conflict.

Military force is still at the core of peacekeeping but the missions now use what they call a "multidimensional" effort that includes police officers, economists, legal experts, electoral observers, human rights monitors, humanitarian workers, and communications officers, and work with non-governmental agencies in the field. The work includes tasks such as monitoring peace agreements, observation and intelligence, policing, demobilization of rebel armies, disarmament, reintegration programs, building justice systems including correctional facilities and the removal of landmines. This is a description of the work a U.N. peacekeeping mission did in Sierra Leone:

> The UN helped disarm and demobilize some 75,000 combatants. U.N. peacekeepers reconstructed roads; renovated and built schools, houses of worship and clinics; and initiated agricultural projects and welfare programmes. [They] also helped Sierra Leone to ensure that the rights of its citizens are fully protected; to bring to justice those who bear the greatest responsibility for serious violations of international humanitarian law through the UN-backed Special Court for Sierra Leone; and to develop a professional and democratic police force.[24]

All U.N. peacekeeping missions operate under a mandate of the United Nations Security Council. The mandates are different depending on the needs of the local situation. Before they are put into effect they are agreed to by the host country and usually the U.N. will only send in troops if it has the support of the major parties in the conflict. During the Cold War U.N. peacekeepers dealt primarily with inter-state conflict but now most of the missions deal with civil wars. This is a U.N. description.

> Internal armed conflicts constitute the vast majority of today's wars. Many of these conflicts take place in the world's poorest countries where state capacity may be weak and where belligerents may be motivated by economic gain, as much as ideology or past grievances.[25]

Today the largest missions are in eastern Congo, Liberia, Côte d'Ivoire, Sudan, Darfur and Chad, all impoverished African countries or regions bordering on anarchy, where well armed militias and criminal gangs operate. These are difficult places with little infrastructure, deep ethnic and religious differences and human rights abuses which make reconciliation very difficult. In these areas civil government is virtually non-existent and peacekeepers play an important role in protecting the civilian population.

Today U.N. peacekeepers have a mandate in 16 missions around the world. The force has 130,000 personnel in the field involving 117 member nations. Most of the troops come from the developing world. Even China now has stopped criticizing peacekeeping and contributes troops to U.N. peacekeeping efforts. Although not all missions have been successful, U.N. peacekeepers have been responsible for peace and security in many parts of the world. The U.N. credits their success with the fact that their operations are perceived as legitimate by the leaders and people that they are working with.

> The fact that multi-dimensional United Nations peacekeeping operations enjoy a high degree of international legitimacy and represent the collective will of the international community gives them considerable leverage over the parties. This leverage can be used to build and sustain a political consensus around the peace process, promote good governance and maintain pressure on the parties to implement key institutional reforms.[26]

Despite the praise, a number of criticisms of the U.N. peacekeeping efforts remain. In some cases the troops lack discipline. In both the former Yugoslavia and eastern Congo some U.N. troops committed serious human rights violations and it took time to rebuild the confidence of local people in the mission. The eastern Congo, the most volatile region on the planet, has a strong and well armed U.N. peacekeeping force whose task it is to establish and maintain peace and protect the civilian population, but the peacekeepers have been criticized because they have avoided confrontation with the armed militias that operate in the region, and local people continue to be preyed upon by criminal gangs. The greatest criticism is that the

United Nations Security Council avoids the most difficult areas of conflict in the world such as Somalia, Myanmar and Zimbabwe. The counter argument to this is that there has been no request for assistance from these countries; there are no wars and no cease fire agreements to monitor. In the meantime, people in these countries are dying from political violence. U.N. peacekeeping efforts have achieved success in many war torn countries but that alone will not solve the crisis of war.

Responsibility to Protect

U.N. peacekeeping efforts continue to have support from the international community but it is limited in what they can do to avoid conflict and war. What if the leaders of a country violate human rights principles by turning the power of the military against their people? This has happened again and again and the United Nations has stood by and done nothing. Surely, some argued, it is important to protect innocent people from the human rights violations of their own governments.

In 2001 the Canadian government released a paper arguing that the international community had the responsibility to protect the citizens of a country if their government committed genocide, war crimes, ethnic cleansing or crimes against humanity. In 2006 the U.N. Security Council voted in favour of this policy and in 2009 it was accepted by the U.N. General Assembly.

The U.N. policy called "Responsibility to Protect" (R2P) introduces a new era in which the United Nations Security Council has the power to act proactively to protect innocent people during conflict. In effect this means that under special circumstances the international community has the right to intervene directly in the internal affairs of countries, if innocent people are at risk. Martin Gilbert, a historian, called R2P the most significant adjustment to national sovereignty in 360 years because, for the first time this policy broke the international agreement that prohibited international involvement in the domestic affairs of a country.[27] This challenge to the principle of sovereignty is the major objection to the new policy, but it is not the only one.

In 2011 the Muammar Gaddafi regime of Libya attempted to put down a rebellion of its citizens by force of arms. Innocent civilians were killed in a reign of terror by the Gaddafi military. In the debate that this created it was argued that this was a crime against humanity and the U.N. voted to authorize military action on the basis of the policy of the Responsibility to Protect. A "no fly zone" was authorized; a coalition of countries led by France, Italy, Canada and the United States began a bombing campaign and attacked the forces loyal to Gaddafi.

Soon criticisms arose. It was argued by some that the U.N. had intervened to support one side in a civil war. But that was not the major criticism. At the same time of the insurrection in Libya, other uprisings arose in Syria and Yemen and those governments killed demonstrators in much the same way as the Gaddafi forces. The question was asked, why does the U.N. act against the government of Libya and not against Syria or Yemen? The answer seems to be political expediency. Gaddafi and his government were unpopular in the west while Syria and Yemen have large populations and it would be much more difficult to intervene.

With the successful overthrow of the Gaddafi regime in August 2011 many felt that the R2P policy and the bombing campaign was a great success. The actual fighting on the ground was done by the Libyan rebel army so they could claim victory when the authoritarian regime was overthrown, but that would not have happened without the bombing campaign.

With the implementation of R2P the international community has a powerful new method to deal with regimes that violate the human rights of their own people, but questions remain. What is the appropriate level of military action? Is it ever justified to intervene in a civil war? What nation or coalition of nations will take on the task of launching military action and risk the lives of their own soldiers in order to enforce the policy? And the most important question, what justifies taking action in one situation and not in a similar situation? Inconsistencies in the implementation of policies like this are difficult to justify.

The policy of R2P is a real departure from U.N. peacekeeping. It is the use of offensive military action by the international community to stop the violation of human rights. It seems likely that the principle of R2P will survive as U.N. policy, but it will not be easy to determine when and how the policy should be implemented

Making Peace

Making war is easy. Imagine the meetings in the White House prior to the invasion of Iraq in 2003. The military men were assembled by the politicians and asked how difficult it would be to defeat the Iraqis? The response was predictable. By that time there was no Iraqi air force or navy. The army had virtually no modern equipment and was demoralized. It will be a "cake walk," the politicians would have been told. Was there any discussion about the deep divisions in Iraqi society that would make insurrection a problem? Perhaps a little, but ask a military man his opinion about the possibility of defeating an enemy and he will give a military answer.

Making peace is much more difficult. A lasting peace must be based on what the major combatants feel is a just solution, but above all history teaches that the defeated must be treated in a humanitarian way. Fundamental grievances must be addressed and reconciled or they will fester and become a major cause of the next war.

The key thing about ending war is that the peace agreements must be negotiated and agreed to by the parties of the conflict. They cannot be imposed by other countries or even the United Nations. Outside groups can help facilitate discussions and can help supervise the terms of the agreement once it is in place, but the agreement must be agreed to and have the support of the people affected or it will fail.

Every conflict is different, but we have developed enough insight to understand what elements are necessary for a lasting peace and, equally important, the international community has the resources to help make a difference. Still a major problem remains: how can we get people to choose peace over war? These are four of the most difficult conflicts facing us and some thoughts on how they can be resolved.

Iraq:

The effects of the divisive Saddam Hussein regime and the American and British invasion will take decades to heal in Iraq. It will be best to allow Iraqis to sort out the many difficulties themselves now that the invaders are about to leave. However, there are some major problems that may benefit from international help.

The American neo-conservatives imposed an economic solution on Iraq that is totally unacceptable to many Iraqis. Oil is the chief resource of the country and the hope for economic recovery, but the Americans arranged sweetheart deals with international oil companies that granted concessions that will allow them to reap most of the profits from the oil for decades to come. The Iraqis will need the help of the international community to rewrite those contracts and counter the political influence of the oil companies.

A much more serious problem is the poisoned relationships between the three major communities in the country: Kurds, Sunni and Shiites. To leave this problem unaddressed is to invite serious conflict in the future. The three Iraqi groups now live in their own enclaves and violence has decreased because neighbourhoods and regions have been ethnically cleansed. The danger is that fears in one community could lead to the build up of arms. That in turn can trigger a response by the other community and they begin building a storehouse of arms. An arms race settles in until it leads to the outbreak of violence.

The international community has experience in dealing with these problems. Would a Truth and Reconciliation Commission help to reduce tensions? Should the International Criminal Court be given the task to bring those responsible for the violence of the past to justice? Only the Iraqis can make this judgment, and only they can put a process in place that will help to resolve the underlying grievances that so badly divides their society. The United Nations has the prestige, experience and resources to help make a process like this work, but the Iraqis must put the process in place that can relieve these tensions.

Bill Freeman

Sri Lanka:

By the summer of 2009 calm had finally returned to Sri Lanka. The national army had defeated the Tamil Tigers and occupied the entire northeast region of the country where the Tamils live. The Tiger leadership had been killed or fled in disarray and the remnant leaders called for peace and the reintegration of Tamils into Sri Lankan society.

This is the crucial time in the peace process. The war was the consequence of the Tamil belief that they were being discriminated against by being denied government positions and not allowed to use their language in schools and government institutions. If the government, dominated by the majority Sinhalese, refuses to recognize the grievances of the Tamil and work to accommodate them, then they could well be recreating the conditions that lead to terrorist attacks and growing insurrection.[28]

If ever there was a situation that called for reconciliation between communities, this is it. The United Nations is poised to make a meaningful contribution here. They have the respect of both parties and the capability to move peacekeepers into the conflict zone quickly to help with serious problems such as the resettlement of refugees, the distribution of food and the provision of shelter. They can help to negotiate a peace agreement and enforce it. The decision remains with the Sri Lankan government. Will they follow the warrior's creed and try and gain maximum advantage from their military victory, or will they choose the humanitarian course and reconcile with the Tamils?

Afghanistan:

Like Iraq, the greatest blunder of the Americans in the Afghan War was that they thought they had the ability to impose a military solution on the country and dictate the terms of the peace. They have learned, or should have learned by now, that this is impossible. The best time to have negotiated peace with the Taliban was in 2001, after the Muslim fundamentalists fled the country and when they were at their weakest. Now, as the Taliban grow in strength, it is getting increasingly difficult, yet it is essential that the ISAF and the Americans work to achieve a lasting peace.

The Americans, and their coalition partners in the ISAF, cannot win the war and even NATO commanders now recognize that there is no military solution.[29] The Obama strategy to escalate the war, along with the help of the Pakistan military in the "tribal areas" on their side of the boarder, in an attempt to punish the Taliban and force them to the peace table, is unlikely to work. In guerilla wars, when insurgent groups are attacked, they retreat, regroup and wait for the right moment to strike again. The Americans appear to be determined to play out the military strategy to the end, but it is unlikely that the offensive will force the Taliban to negotiate.

The first rule of peacekeeping is that the major parties involved in a conflict have to agree to the terms of a peace settlement. The Soviets failed to impose peace by force of arms and now the Americans and their allies have failed. Only the Afghan government has the ability to negotiate the peace with the Taliban. The one precondition that the Taliban have put on peace talks is that before they come to the table all foreign troops must leave Afghanistan. Up until now this has never been taken seriously because it would be seen as a retreat, or recognition of defeat by the Americans, but all options must be considered. If the only way to bring the Taliban to the table is to have the ISAF and the American forces leave the country, then that will have to happen.

The Americans have already achieved their military objectives by cleaning out the al-Qaeda camps where the 9/11 terrorist attacks were planned. They have provided training to the Afghan army and given them weapons. Now they have to step out of the way to let the local people decide the outcome of the conflict. Admittedly that is a risky military strategy. The Afghan army could lose, but clearly the Americans and the ISAF cannot win. There is one other advantage to this approach. By leaving and turning the military responsibility over to the Afghan government the Americans can deliver on their promise of aid to deal with humanitarian issues and economic development that is needed to solve the desperate poverty of the country. This does not mean that the Afghan government should give in to the Taliban and adopt their intolerant, inhuman views and practices. Now is the time for the Afghan people to struggle for the type of country that they want, not what is wanted for them by western governments.

The Israeli/Palestinian Conflict:

No other conflict has been more difficult to resolve than the one between the Israelis and the Palestinians. Since 1948, when the State of Israel was recognized, there have been three major wars between Israel and its Arab neighbours (1956, 1967, 1973), several incursions and occupations of Lebanon by the Israeli army, intifada uprisings by Palestinians, suicide bombings, Israeli bombing raids on Iraq and Syria and daily harassment of the Palestinian population by the Israeli army. The violence has been unrelenting.

For over sixty years this unresolved conflict has caused major problems in the relations between nations. It has been a significant reason for anti-western and particularly anti-American feelings in Muslim countries from Morocco to Pakistan and was a main contributing factor in the rise of al-Qaeda and the 9/11 terrorist attacks. For the last thirty years or more the United States and major Arab nations have made concerted attempts to try and resolve the conflict without success.

To add to the frustration, the outline of a peace agreement acceptable to both sides has existed since the negotiations of the Oslo Accords in 1993. A majority of both Israelis and Palestinians agree that a two-state solution is a fair resolution to the conflict but what stands in the way is a political accommodation between the parties.[30] According to the Oslo Accords the territory of Israel would be defined by the pre-1967 boundaries and the territory of the State of Palestine would be the West Bank and the Gaza Strip, but there would be some adjustments of the boarders to accommodate some Israeli settlements. There are still serious issues to be resolved such as the governance of the City of Jerusalem, the "right to return" of Palestinians displaced in 1948, Israeli West Bank settlements, water rights, Palestinian access between the West Bank and Gaza and so on, but the important territorial issues have been settled.

So how can the Israelis and Palestinians take the next step to make a comprehensive peace settlement? The answer, in part, can be found in the negotiations of the Oslo Accords. Before 1993 there was no discussion between the two major protagonists in the conflict: the State of Israel and the Palestinian Liberation Organization (PLO). The Israeli parliament, the Knessat, had even passed a law in 1986 making it illegal for any Israeli citizen to have contact with members of the PLO.[31] There were clandestine discussions but nothing that either side would admit.

A group of Norwegians had been in touch with the PLO. They were acquainted with the Norwegian Deputy Foreign Minister who in turn had a relationship with his Israeli counterpart. With the approval of the Israeli Foreign Minister Shimon Peres and the Americans, secret talks began in Oslo between two Israeli academics and three PLO officials.[32] The talks were prepared very carefully by the Norwegians. They insisted that the delegates eat their meals together and socialize as much as possible. They were applying the peacemaking techniques of the Quakers and others. (It is no accident that Quaker fellowships are called "Friends.") Soon the Israeli and PLO delegates began to enjoy each other's company, something that would have been impossible before this process started. The Norwegians also suggested, and the delegates agreed, that they not talk about the injustice of past decisions and actions. The focus was on present circumstances and how differences could be resolved. It took months but a comprehensive peace agreement that provided solutions to the major contentious issues emerged. A key moment came when Yasir Arafat recognized the right of Israel to exist. In return for this concession the Palestinians would gain the State of Palestine and the Israelis get security for its people and peace. Finally, the agreement was signed in a public ceremony on August 20, 1993 in the rose garden of the White House and sealed with a hard shake between Yasir Arafat and Yitzhak Rabin with U.S. President Bill Clinton watching.

The Oslo Accords, of course, failed in spectacular fashion. The Israelis blame Arafat and the Palestinians blame the Israelis. The rejection by the Israeli right wing sealed its fate. Binyamin Netanyahu, leader of the Likud Party, speaking at a large political rally, said that

Oslo was "an act of surrender" and constituted a "danger to the existence of the State of Israel."[33] The end came with the 1995 assassination of Rabin by a right wing Israeli. Despite the failure, the Oslo Accords live on because it is the basis – the starting point – of further negotiations between the Palestinians and the Israelis.

The real reason the Oslo Accords failed is because the delegates who negotiated the agreement had gone well beyond the conflict and the emotional feelings of people in both communities to reconcile their differences in the friendship and trust that they established in Oslo. To say that the only way that this conflict can be resolved is to make a similar reconciliation between the Palestinians and Israelis is unrealistic, but it is important to recognize that the wars and constant violence between these two peoples has destroyed the trust between them. The continuing violence plays into the hands of the radicals: Likud, who promises to be tough but whose real objective is to oppose any reconciliation, and Hamas, the Palestinian party who promise to drive the Israelis out of Palestine. It will take moderates on both sides, who sincerely want to make a deal, to finally bring peace.

Reconciliation between people who have been at war is difficult, as South Africans, Chileans and others who have been down that road will attest, but the rewards are worth the sacrifice. For the Israelis it will allow them to live with security – the ability to live their lives without fear of violence. For the Palestinians the reward will be the right for self-determination with their own state apparatus and the chance for economic development that will allow them to rise above the poverty that the violence has spawned. Above all it will let people live in harmony with their neighbours. Peace in the Middle East is worth the sacrifice and effort.

The Rise of the United Nations:

The belief that war is inevitable – that it has always been with us and will always plague the human race – is simply not true. We have learned a great deal about how to make peace and have developed strategies and tools to end even the most stubborn conflicts. Empires have come to an end and we have strengthened our ability to end wars but who is going to provide the leadership for the new world that is emerging?

It is in the interests of everyone to develop a balanced, multilateral world where no single power is able to dominate. The way to do that is to put in place organizations where nations can work co-operatively to bring prosperity to their people, and establish humanitarian principles and practices that maintain peace. There is only one organization that can do that, the United Nations. It is the only world body that has no vested interests, is guided by humanitarian principles and has sufficient prestige that it commands respect. But the United Nations has to change as well if it is going to become an instrument of world leadership. It must become democratic, responsible and responsive to the needs of every state and every person on the globe.

In the last few years the U.N. has grown in stature and capability until today it is the preeminent international institution of the world, and it has at its command a wide range of strategies that can be used to enforce compliance to U.N. decisions. Until now its greatest achievements has been in helping to resolve wars, but it can do much more than that by heading off wars before they start, mediating differences between states, confronting practices that violate humanitarian principles, establishing fair trade policies and helping to solve the desperate poverty that afflicts the underdeveloped world. How to achieve that agenda is the tough task ahead.

CHAPTER 10: DEVELOPMENT, DEMOCRACY AND PEACE

In a speech to the United Nations on September 23, 2009 President Barack Obama spoke of a "new era of engagement," and exhorted other nations to shoulder more of the burden to ensure world peace, prosperity and security. He made it clear that he wanted to repair the scepticism and distrust of America that was the legacy of his predecessors.

> "Those who used to chastise America for acting alone in the world cannot now stand by and wait for America to solve the world's problems alone. We have sought – in word and deed – a new era of engagement with the world. Now is the time for all of us to take our share of responsibility for a global response to global challenges."

This is a call for multilateralism. It is saying that the United States has established a new policy and will no longer act unilaterally. It is also saying indirectly that the U.S. no longer has the resources to play the role of world policeman. Peace must be a collective effort of all nations. This is as clear a statement as we will ever hear coming from a U.S. President that the era of the American Empire is over and they welcome multilateralism.

But this announcement is only the first step in the creation of a multilateral world. Empires are finished and in their place we must reform international organizations that reflect our democratic values and practices and can meet the challenges that lie ahead. We also must create sustainable economic development so people have the promise of prosperity and security. Building world peace is an enormous task, and that task is the responsibility of all of us.

Promoting Modernity

We forget that the world has been transformed since the dark days of the Second World War. Our parents and grandparents defeated the most tyrannical regimes of modern times that used murder as the means to cleanse the nation of minorities, and war as the way to dominate and exploit others. Those autocratic dictatorships were seen as legitimate by the supporters of those regimes, and democracy was rejected in favour of the cult of the strong leader. Not only were Nazi Germany and Imperial Japan defeated, but so were the fascist values that supported those regimes. That was no small achievement.

Roosevelt laid the foundations for a more secure and democratic world with new economic policies and the establishment of the United Nations. Unfortunately that world was still-born by the competition between the Soviet Union and the United States. Not only has the Cold War now come to an end, but even empires and the imperial tactic of using war to impose the will of the empire on others is now considered illegitimate. Empires and the ideology and baggage that they brought with it are dead. New political values of interdependence, the self determination of nations, democracy and economic development are in ascendency. Those who see only chaos, destruction and destitution in our world – and there are many – miss the positive changes that have been accomplished. In recent years the lives of billions of people in the developing world have been improved immeasurably by economic development and more open, participatory governments. As those changes have happened, conflict and war have receded because people believe that they now have the ability to improve their lives, the lives of their families and others in their society.

But still, far too many people are caught in the grinding poverty that all too frequently leads to violence and war. It is no accident that the wars of today are located overwhelmingly in the poorest countries ruled by the most autocratic political leaders. If that is to change then those parts of the world will have to embrace modernity and the values and practices that go with it. The twin pillars of modernity are economic development and participatory democracy, but it also means human rights and toleration of minorities and others different than ourselves.

Establishing modern, progressive societies everywhere in the world is an ambitious undertaking, but no more ambitious than the defeat of fascism achieved by our parents and grandparents. There can be little doubt that modernity will reach every part of the globe sometime in the future – the forces of modernity provide the trajectory of our history – but there are ways that it can be encouraged. It will take some sacrifice to get there, but we will all benefit when it is achieved.

What follows is a discussion of the two pillars of modernity: economic development and democratic institutions. These ideas are offered to stimulate discussion. It will take much more participation and debate before decisions can be made on how to move forward.

Development: Aid and Trade

If we are to live in a world without war, then economic development that eliminates poverty and provides hope to millions of people is absolutely essential. This is a partial list of problems.

- 1.3 billion people live on less than one dollar a day.

- Half the human race, or 3.3 billion people, live on less than two dollars a day.

- 790 million people are chronically under nourished, harming their physical and intellectual development.

- 30,000 children die each day due to poverty and malnutrition.

- Nearly half a billion people cannot read or write.

- Women are discriminated against in much of the underdeveloped and developing world, and girls often receive little or no education.

- 1.1 billion people have inadequate access to water

- 2.6 billion lack basic sanitation.

- 20% of the world's population consumes 86% of the world's goods.

- In 2004 about 0.13% of the world's population controlled 25% of the world's assets.

- The income gap between the developed and the underdeveloped world grows wider every day.[1]

And yet this is only part of the story. Kofi Annan, the former U.N. General Secretary, made the point that statistics, "fail to capture the humiliation, powerlessness, and brutal hardship that is the daily lot of the world's poor."[2] Is it any wonder that the poor in poverty stricken countries often turn to violence and war?

Nations, non-governmental agencies (NGOs) and individuals have been attempting to improve the lot of the poor in the developing world since the late nineteenth century. This effort gained momentum after the Second World War. In 1970 the U.N. General Assembly, with the leadership of the Canadian Prime Minister, Lester Pearson, passed a resolution that recommended that the developed countries should commit 0.7% of their GNP in aid to developing countries. By 2006 only Sweden, Norway, the Netherlands and some other very small countries reached or exceeded the goal of 0.7%, but the large, wealthy nations did not come close. These are the figures: Britain, 0.52%; France, 0.47%; Germany, 0.36%; Canada, 0.30%; and the United States, the wealthiest country in the world, 0.17%. In 2004 it is estimated that in total $79.17 billion dollars in aid flowed from the developed to the underdeveloped world,[3] but this overestimates the amount of money flowing from the developed to the underdeveloped world. Roughly half of the total amount of aid, $37 billion, (2004) is "phantom aid" that is not available to help fight poverty. Some of it is in the form of military hardware, or products such as earth moving equipment that are manufactured in the developed country donating the aid. At least $19 billion is in the form of consultants, research and training that pays people in the donor country, and only indirectly benefits developing countries. Much of this technical assistance and research is overpriced and useless because the consultants often know little about conditions in the countries that are to receive the help and their work cannot be adapted to meet local needs. In the worst cases the studies destroy rather than build capacity.

One of the problems is that aid programs are often designed to meet political rather than humanitarian objectives. The United States directs its aid to regions where it has national security concerns: the Middle East, Central America and the Caribbean. Seventy percent of American aid is spent on U.S. goods and services, and more than half is spent in middle income countries in the Middle East such as Israel.[4] Only $3 billion a year of American aid goes to South Asia and sub-Saharan Africa, the regions of the world that have the most desperate poverty.[5] France spreads its aid to countries in its sphere of influence such as Lebanon and its former colonies in Africa. Britain gives most of its aid to its former colonies. Japan gives aid to counties in East Asia where it has close trading relationships.

As well as aid, a system of loans administered through the World Bank and other national banks has existed since the Second World War. Brazil is a good example of what happened in some of these loan programs. The World Bank lent billions of dollars to the military governments of Brazil beginning in the 1950s. The money was used to buy military hardware and to fund infrastructure programs such as dams and roads. By the 1980s the country was so indebted Brazil had to borrow heavily just to pay the interest on past borrowings. By 1991 it was estimated that 55% of the infrastructure projects had failed. Then the IMF insisted on "structural adjustments" and privatization. Industries were deregulated and government enterprises were sold off. By 1999 inflation soared, more money had to be borrowed and the incomes of working people plummeted. Ultimately Brazilians grew extremely critical of these types of programs because they did little or nothing to deal with the chronic poverty of the country.

What some call the "debt habit" is the most destructive of all the programs. Lenders push loans onto borrowers, ignoring the fact that substantial amounts of the money is spent on the military or simply disappears in different corruption scams. Many of these loans serve the interests of the lenders rather than the borrowers. As the loans mount, the interest on the debt grows. Many developing countries have found that they are spending virtually all of the foreign currency that they earn on paying the interest on the debt.[6] The most shocking statistic of all is that today the poor countries pay some $200 billion to the rich each year in the form of payments on debt. This is about three times the amount of money given in aid.[7]

Aid is both a blessing and a curse. It is necessary, but it is so badly managed, and the motivations of the donor countries so pervert the programs and objectives, that the aid often becomes useless. This is the assessment of William Easterly, an American professor of economics with broad experience in Africa. He speaks with passion as well as experience.

> "A tragedy of the world's poor has been that the West spent $2.3 trillion on foreign aid over the last five decades and still had not managed to get twelve-cent medicines to children to prevent half of all malaria deaths. The West spent $2.3 trillion and still had not managed to get four-dollar bed nets to poor families. The West spent $2.3 trillion and still had not managed to get three dollars to each new mother to prevent five million child deaths. It is heart-breaking that global society has evolved a highly efficient way to get entertainment to rich adults and children, while it can't get twelve-cent medicine to dying poor children."[8]

For many, aid has proven to be a complete failure in the efforts to improve the living standards of people in the developing world. Africa has received $600 billion in foreign aid since 1960 and yet most African nations are poorer today than they were before the programs started. Peter Bauer, a British academic who studied development, commented, "Government to government transfers…are an excellent method of transferring money from poor people in rich countries, to rich people in poor countries." Dambisa Mayo, the author of *Dead Aid: Why Aid is Not Working and How There is a Better Way for Africa*,[9] argues that economic aid, aimed at development, has been harmful for Africa. Paul Collier, who has made an in depth study of the economic impact of aid, calculates that it has added about 1% to the annual growth rate to the bottom billion, not much but the growth rate of most of these countries is below 1%. He concluded that, "Aid alone is really unlikely, in my view, to be able to address the problems of the bottom billion." [10]

What most of these studies say is that economic aid has been driven by the needs of the donor country and do not help people in the poorest countries. Humanitarian aid, on the other hand, has led to improvements in education in almost every part of the underdeveloped world. Public health programs have helped to eliminate disease, improve nutrition and lengthen life expectancy. Grass roots programs, such as local co-operatives and non-profit organizations, have been particularly successful. Often private foundations in the developed world are much more adept than governments in providing programs that reach the poorest people.

One of the most successful programs has been micro lending, that provides small loans to the poorest people with no credit. Muhammad Yunus, a Bangladeshi economist, and the Grameen Bank that he founded received the 2006 Nobel Peace prize for their contribution in improving the economic circumstances of the poorest people. Micro loan programs now exist in almost every part of the developing world and they have been a huge success at improving the lot of the poorest people, particularly poor women. What is interesting about this program is that it is not aid at all. It is a form of private enterprise that is self-funding because it provided the funds for new loans when the debts plus interest are repaid.

A number of countries have adopted a new model of aid called "sustainable development." These programs are based on the belief that local people know best how to improve their economic circumstances, not experts. A sustainable development approach is founded on the belief that it is small enterprises that are the major economic engines in the developing world, not large multinational corporations.[11] This grassroots model stimulates economic activity at the local level and the wealth quickly multiplies among the poor. These types of projects may not be spectacular, but the approach empowers local people because the poor involved in these projects come to see that their actions can change their economic prospects. They have the power, not remote bureaucrats, politicians or experts in a foreign country half a world away. But though aid has helped some countries and pockets of people, generally this major international undertaking has produced disappointing results.

Many claim that the answer to underdevelopment is trade not aid. Trade stimulates economic activity not only of people and countries in the underdeveloped world, but in the developed world as well. It is a mutually beneficial arrangement. Low wage countries can produce products less expensively than high wage countries, and developed countries have the capital to establish factories and the markets for the products. All parties in the trade benefit. These economic relations are said to bring a more efficient allocation of resources, lower prices, more employment and a higher standard of living. It is trade that has helped the developing countries, and the promise is that, although it will take time to develop, trade will help the poorest countries as well. Over time wages will improve, child labour will be reduced, living standards will be raised, opportunities for young people will multiply and the wars that ravage the impoverished nations will come to an end.

Free trade is not a new idea, although those who have recently adopted it seem to think so. In 1776 Adam Smith, in his book *An Enquiry into the Nature and Causes of the Wealth of Nations*, advocated free trade. The Bretton Woods agreements of 1944 are based on the belief that freer trade is ultimately better than protectionism. Today, the advocates of free trade have become the orthodox economists and those who differ are viewed as protectionist dinosaurs.

There is little doubt that free trade has done much more to increase the prosperity of people in the developing world than economic aid and there is much to be optimistic about. A World Bank study published in 2007 found that countries that were more open to trade also performed better on growth.[12] Life expectancy in the developing world has increased dramatically and infant mortality has fallen.[13] These are two of the best indicators of improving living conditions. Economic growth in Asia in the last forty years has been remarkable and the growth is continuing. South America now is joining this economic growth, and India has joined the group of countries that are experiencing high growth. China and India in recent years have had high rates of economic growth of between 7% and 10%. Developed countries like the United States and Western Europe have modest growth in the range of 2% to 4%, even many countries in sub-Saharan Africa are experiencing growth. Significant problems remain. Poverty is widespread in city slums and rural areas of India, China, much of Southeast Asia, South America and the Middle East; Russia and Eastern Europe have high rates of poverty in rural areas and stubborn pockets of poverty remain in even the richest countries.

Free trade has helped the developing countries but the poorest countries remain trapped in poverty. Multi-national companies avoid these countries because of the social problems, wars and other conflicts. They prefer to invest in China, India and other countries in the Far East because these countries are more politically and socially stable and have a highly motivated workforce. As a result the poorest countries are actually falling further and further behind. Nelson Mandela sketched out the problem in this way:

> "We welcome the process of globalization. It is inescapable and irreversible.... However, if globalization is to create real peace and stability across the world, it must be a process benefiting all. It must not allow the most economically and politically powerful countries to dominate and submerge the countries of the weaker and peripheral regions. It should not be allowed to drain the wealth of smaller countries towards the larger ones, or to increase inequality between richer and poorer regions."[14]

If we are to develop programs that "create real peace and stability across the world," and if we hope to lessen the burden of social problems and end war, much more has to be done. We must develop new programs that bring hope and prosperity to people at the grassroots level.

A New Kind of Development Program:

People around the globe are willing to make sacrifices to eliminate poverty and help to stop the terrible destructiveness of war but there are unrealistic expectations and conflicting objectives. Part of the problem is that people in the developed world believe that the underdeveloped world should follow the Western model. We expect Africa to become like Europe, or India to develop a North American life style. This is impossible; the environment of the planet cannot sustain that level of development. People in developing countries are much more practical. They know how to solve their own social and economic problems. We must focus on helping them to achieve their goals, not impose economic models based on our history.

We have to begin with the question, what do people in the underdeveloped world want? This is how the IBON Foundation, an independent research group based in the Philippines, expresses it: "The most basic capabilities for human development are to lead long and healthy lives, to be knowledgeable, to have access to the resources needed for a decent standard of living and to be able to participate in the life of the community."[15] These are the aims of people everywhere.

It is impossible to fund every need but as IBON suggests, funding should be provided in three general areas: health care, education and infrastructure. In developed countries programs such as this are considered the responsibility of governments and paid for out of tax dollars. If the costs of these programs were shared, it would relieve a huge burden from the governments of the poorest countries in the world and leave them with funds to provide other types of programs for their people. More important, it would guarantee the funds in vital areas to improve the quality of these programs over a long period of time.

Priority 1: Education

Education holds the greatest promise for change. There is a great hunger for learning across the underdeveloped world. Teachers who spend time in the classrooms of sub-Saharan Africa report an eagerness of the students that they describe as almost overwhelming. In recent decades there has been an enormous growth of the numbers of children attending schools in the developing world. The U.N. millennium goal of universal primary education by the year 2015 will not be achieved everywhere, but many of even the poorest African countries have already achieved it and others are determined to get there.

And yet today the problems of education in the developing world are so difficult that the goal of a good education for every child is beyond the reach of these societies with their present resources. Few children go beyond the primary grades and secondary schooling does not exist in many rural areas. There are few teachers and they are so poorly paid that many are forced to take other jobs or leave education altogether. Teachers are poorly trained; many are isolated in rural communities and have no support from colleagues or the school system. The numbers of children in the average classroom are often so huge the children get little individual attention. Some countries require parents to provide uniforms and pay fees to send their children to school. The poorest families do not have the money and their children are unable to attend. In some countries girls are rarely sent to school. Most schools have virtually no classroom materials. Books are scarce and often non-existent. And perhaps worse of all, some schools are little more than places to indoctrinate the young in intolerant values and dogmatic religion.

The recent history of western societies demonstrated the importance of education for economic development. In the one hundred and fifty years since universal, compulsory education was introduced, developed countries have been transformed. Education is not the only thing that brought this social change, but it played a major role. There is no reason to believe it will be any different in the developing world. How then can a high quality, universal education system be delivered to underdeveloped countries?

Fortunately a new type of education is on the horizon that holds enormous promise. That, of course, is education delivered by computer technology. A group of computer experts from the Massachusetts Institute of Technology (MIT) in the United States and other parts of the world have developed the $100 computer. These computers have been designed to be used in the underdeveloped world. They can be powered by conventional electricity, batteries, alternative sources of power such as solar or wind power, or each computer will come with a hand crank that can provide power. These computers are already in some schools in Peru, Uruguay, India, Ghana, Mongolia, Papua, New Guinea and other countries.[16]

The developers of these computers, coming from the world of information technology, imagine that they will be used by children to source out their own information through the Internet, but the real promise is that these computers will transform teaching methods. Educators, filmmakers, software developers, writers and performers are working on educational programs that can be delivered either by DVD or over the Internet. These programs will contain rich packages of learning materials on every imaginable subject such as reading, nature study, arithmetic, science, history, advanced mathematics, second language study, literature, geography and social studies. Programs can be designed for children in any age group from primary school to college and university. Not only can these programs deliver organized, curriculum based units of study, but they can provide supplementary texts and access to whole libraries of books. Programs can be designed to teach specialized subjects such as local agricultural practices, regional history or tribal customs. This is a technology that can deliver full course curriculums to students in a country or region, and it can also deliver individual study where students can learn at their own pace. If these educational programs are to be truly effective they must be developed by local educators who are attuned to the cultural needs of the children.

Perhaps this is an overly optimistic way of seeing the computer as an educational tool; technology rarely delivers on its full promise. But if the computers only provided enriched teaching materials to the children of the developing world it would be worth the investment. Children who are eager to learn can teach themselves if they have the proper materials, but packaged course curriculum that teaches skills in an incremental way, appropriate to the age of the child, is the way to get the maximum out of this technology.

If the opportunity of using education to help transform underdeveloped societies is fully developed even more can be accomplished. Good nutrition programs for children have been adopted in some school systems with great results. Many educators believe that school programs delivering balanced, nutritious food is necessary the world over, not just the parts of the world suffering from poverty. Physical fitness and health education programs are also essential. If education is to be the major tool for transforming societies then school must be open twelve months a year and the facilities of schools must be available not just to children but to everyone in the community.

Good education feeds the mind as well as the body. It addresses the issue that Kofi Annan spoke of: the feelings of humiliation and powerlessness of people in the underdeveloped world that contribute to crime, violence, social instability and war. Billions of people in the underdeveloped and developing world can be helped in this way and in the process it can reduce the risk of war.

Priority 2: Health Care

In May 2009 a group of researchers published a report on AIDS transmission that condemned the international community for failing the women and children of the underdeveloped world. If mothers with HIV or AIDS were given a simple treatment of anti-viral drugs during pregnancy, they would not transmit the virus to their babies. Despite promises by world leaders in 2001 that an effective program would be put in place, it has been a failure. Each day 900 babies are born with HIV in the underdeveloped and developing world and face a life of misery and early death.[17]

This is not a failure of medicine. The blame has to be put on the political leaders of the developed world. What is necessary is to put in place a medical delivery system that can effectively provide anti-viral drugs in the underdeveloped world. This is an organizational problem, not a medical problem, and in order to meet the needs of the people in the developing and underdeveloped world, the health care delivery system must be reorganized.

Medical services in the developed countries are delivered on an individual basis through the doctor/patient health care system. Trying to export this system to the underdeveloped world makes no sense. There are simply not enough doctors and health care practitioners to go around. It is preventative health care programs that are needed. Bed netting soaked in insecticide is a proven, low cost way of reducing malaria. Vitamin A deficiency is one of the leading causes of childhood death in the underdeveloped world and a risk to pregnant women. Water borne bacterial infections kill thousands of children every year and this can be easily remedied by adding low cost chemicals to water. Tuberculosis diagnosis and treatment saves lives and stops the spread of this infectious disease. HIV/AIDS has reached epidemic proportions in some parts of Africa, but effective ABC (abstinence, be faithful and condomize) education programs can make a real difference in the spread of the virus. Anti-viral drugs to pregnant women who have HIV or AIDS are essential to stop the spread of the disease to the next generation. The problem in every one of these cases is not the costs of the medicine; it is developing effective health care delivery programs.

An excellent system of health care delivery has already been developed in some places in the underdeveloped world. Bangladesh, for example, has a system based on training local health care practitioners to provide basic care at the village or neighbourhood level. Women are used in this work because they traditionally provide care and nurturing in that culture. These health care providers speak the local language, understand the culture, have connections in the community and know how to relate to people in intimate, non-threatening ways. The women are paid, and the money stays in the local community. People such as this are more effective in delivering basic health care programs than the well trained medical specialists who have the knowledge, but do not understand the language or culture of the local people.

A necessary part of programs such as this will be an increase in regional health clinics. More highly trained professionals like doctors and nurses can work out of these centers and provide the more complicated treatments to individual patients. There can even be a few hospital beds available at the clinic along with diagnostic equipment and a pharmacy, but the major responsibility of the group working out of these centers will be to provide back up and training for the neighbourhood health care practitioners and to design public health programs appropriate to the needs of people living in the region. Programs delivered in this way are affordable and can quickly improve the health care of even the most impoverished people.

Priority 3: Infrastructure

Most would say that economic development tops the list of needs in the underdeveloped world. The very term underdevelopment means a lack of economic development, but there is confusion and controversy around what type of economic development is needed. The idea of economic development to people in the developed world usually means multinational corporations coming into an area and exploiting the resources. This helps a few people, but it does little to raise the wealth of the entire society or region. In Nigeria the oil industry has made a few people wealthy, but has brought terrible environmental destruction and has left much of the population as poor as ever. Even the gold and diamond mines of South Africa, that have been operating for almost one hundred years, have done little to improve the economic well being of the poor in South Africa.

Infrastructure development is the best use of international economic development funds. Water is a special problem. In some areas in the Middle East and Africa there is not enough water or it only comes in the rainy season. In many places the water is badly polluted and can cause serious health problems. Sewage systems in city slums are non-existent. There are solutions to all of these problems but they are expensive, and to tackle these problems in an organized way will take co-ordination, political will and money. Funds will be needed for research and planning, pipelines must be laid, sewage systems built and in some cases desalination plants will have to be constructed.

The generation of electricity and the building of adequate electricity grids is another area that is prohibitively expensive for the developing world. Dreams of nuclear power stations and dams to generate electricity are unrealistic because of their costs. But new technology has emerged that is appropriate to underdeveloped countries. The cost of solar panels and small scale wind turbines is now within the reach of many people and communities. Individuals can put up their own electric generating plants. Villages and people in city neighbourhoods can work together to build communal facilities that everyone can draw from.

It would take decades for most underdeveloped countries to afford the capital for this type of investment but the projects need to begin now. The developed world has the expertise and money to make this possible. It is an investment that must be made.

The Peace Levy:

It is all well and good to dream up new development programs, but how are they to be paid for? One thing we know. The present system of aid and loans is not doing much to reduce poverty or bring peace in the underdeveloped world. What is essential is a new way to fund impoverished nations that is not dependent on the politics of developed countries and will not be withdrawn whenever there is a recession or political upheaval. The answer lies in the way developed countries pay for their own education, health care and social programs. All of these countries levy taxes against citizens and spend the money on these programs. Few seriously question the notion that if we want services, we have to pay for them through our taxes.[18] What we need is a system of taxation that raises money on an international basis and provides the funds to underdeveloped countries. Let's call it a "peace levy" because the intent is to create an equitable tax system that will help to reduce poverty and promote peace. It is not so difficult to design.

Perhaps the easiest system would be a small tax of about 1% of global trade. In 2008 1% of global trade was $185 billion in U.S. dollars.[19] This is almost three times the amount of money that is currently provided in aid, and it would all be in cash, not phantom aid.

Another proposal goes by the name of the "Tobin Tax," after James Tobin, an American economist who first proposed it. This is a tax on short-term currency speculation. It is estimated that every day over $3,200 billion is traded on international money markets. This can lead to harmful volatility of currencies of small countries. The South East Asian economic crisis of the late 1990s was caused by speculators abandoning the currencies of these countries. That led to the collapse of the value of these currencies and the near economic collapse of several countries. Millions of people lost their jobs and poverty increased quickly. Tobin proposed a tax to deal with exactly this situation. Even a 0.25% tax would calm the speculation and decrease the hardships that happen as a result of the collapse of currencies. But the Tobin tax would also raise a tremendous amount of money that could be used for development. One estimate is between $300 billion and $1 trillion could be raised every year.

The advantage of tax systems based on international trade or currency speculation is that the taxes would be equitable, fair and transparent. All goods that are traded across national boarders or all transactions of currency would be taxed at the agreed upon rate. The money then would be distributed to those countries most in need. That is similar to the way that taxes are raised in the developed world. Some regions of a country pay more taxes than others because they are wealthier, while other regions receive more services. The peace levy would work in the same way. Countries would receive a portion of the peace levy based on their relative poverty.[20] Perhaps the greatest advantage of these types of taxes is that they would not encroach on the taxing ability of national governments.

Getting an international consensus to implement a program to help the desperately poor of the world will take political commitment and inspired leadership. An even more complicated task will be the administration of such an international program. That raises another core issue. How can the international community develop democratic institutions to administer these types of programs?

The People's Assembly:

A popular slogan during the American Revolution was, "No taxation without representation." The British system of government was founded on the tradition that only the representatives of the people have the right to levy taxes on the people. The British Parliament had levied a tax on tea and other goods imported into what was then British North America, but the people of the American colonies had no representation in the British Parliament, and they refused to pay.

That principle of, "no taxation without representation," is now imbedded not only in the British and American political systems, but it exists in virtually every other democratic country. Only the people's representatives have the right to levy taxes. Following this logic, if it is decided to introduce a system to tax international trade or financial transactions, then the only legitimate way that this can be done is to have the people's representatives set the level of the tax and administer it. The United Nations cannot do that. It is an organization of nation states. Only a "People's Assembly" elected by the citizens of the world should have that right.

A People's Assembly is not a new idea. Since the end of the Second World War there have been several proposals for a United Nations Parliamentary Assembly.[21] In the Cold War the Americans attacked this idea as communist inspired, but now that the Soviet Union has disappeared and China has been transformed into a capitalist state, it will be difficult to use that argument again.

Like all democracies, the principle determining the electoral system must be proportional representation based on population, or "rep-by-pop" as it is called. For simplicity sake lets assume that a People's Assembly is created made up of 1,000 representatives. Today the world's population stands at approximately 6.684 billion people. This is the regional distribution of the population and a snapshot of where the 1,000 members would come from.

REGION	POPULATION	ONE REP FOR 6.684M.OF POP
United States	303,825,000	45
Western Europe (29 countries)	398,563,000	60
Eastern Europe (14 countries)	160,891,000	24
Russian Federation	287,447,000	43
Canada, Australia, New Zealand	58,434,000	9
Japan	127,426,000	19
China	1,326,856,000	199
India	1,125,368,000	168
Other East Asian (43 countries)	902,865,000	135
Middle East	466,707,000	70
North Africa	155,823,000	23
Latin American & Caribbean	575,376,000	86
Sub-Saharan Africa	794,719,000	119
World	6,684,300,000	1,000

The People's Assembly would be given the sole responsibility for administering the international aid programs of education, health care and infrastructure projects. They would determine the budgets of these programs, set the levy that would be required to pay and implement the programs along with local people. That is a huge responsibility and a difficult one, but if these programs are to be successful they must be promoted and defended by democratically elected representatives who have a mandate from the people and are seen as legitimate decision makers.

There is another benefit to the People's Assembly. Approximately 40% of the world's population live in countries without democratic institutions and even more live in very fragile democracies. It would be invaluable to have a functioning democratic organization, such as the People's Assembly, that provides and administers fundamental services like education, health care and infrastructure, as a model of how people can democratically govern themselves.

Reforming the United Nations:

The People's Assembly would have the legitimacy to collect levies and administer programs to combat poverty and promote development, but it would not have the power to deal with issues of war. Only nation states have military forces and the ability to intervene at times of crisis. The Security Council of the United Nations has played that role since it was created and is ideally positioned to continue that role because it is an organization of nation states, but to be effective the U.N. must be reformed root and branch.

There have been controversies about the U.N. almost since its inception. The Americans led the criticisms because many members of the U.N. attacked their foreign policy. The chief defenders of the U.N. were developing countries because it was the only international institution where they could promote and gain recognition for their views. The basic complaint continues to be that the U.N. is unrepresentative of the people, and that is certainly true. The General Assembly is currently made up of 193 member states whose delegates represent the views of the governing party or clique in power in those countries. Debates in the General Assembly often have no coherence and resolutions frequently represent ideological positions of member countries rather than wrestling with substantive problems. Another complaint is that the U.N. bureaucracy is filled with failed politicians from member states who have little interest in promoting change. Individuals who have worked for the U.N. describe the operations of the organization as "byzantine" or "labyrinthal."[22] But these complaints are minor compared with the criticism of the Security Council, the major decision making body of the U.N.

The Security Council has the primary responsibility of promoting peace, human rights, justice and social progress.[23] It is dominated by the five victorious nations of the Second World War over sixty years ago: the United States, Britain, France, Russia and China. Each of these countries has a veto, and the veto has often rendered the U.N into impotence on the most serious and dangerous issues threatening world peace.[24] Three of the five members of the Security Council are members of the western alliance and only one comes from a developing country. The council does not reflect the world's population, and it does not even reflect the powerful nations of the world at the present time.

The American invasion of Iraq in 2003 finally spelled the end of the effectiveness of the United Nations as it is presently constituted. According to the U.N. charter only the Security Council can sanction the military intervention of one country into the affairs of another. In the run up to the Iraq War the United States brought a motion to the Security Council to sanction the invasion. It was withdrawn because it would have been vetoed by France, Russia and possibly other permanent members. The Americans invaded anyway. In effect the U.S. launched an illegal war against Iraq that violated international law. The United Nations had failed in its most important role, preventing war.

The United Nations is now in the same position as the League of Nations in 1935. Italy invaded Ethiopia contrary to the charter of the League and that spelled the end of the League of Nations. In a similar way the American invasion of Iraq should have led to the end of the United Nations, but no one wants to deal with this reality because the world desperately needs an international body where issues can be discussed. The international community can carry on, bumbling through, pretending that the United Nations is effective, or begin to discuss substantive reforms.

The only way to head off a crisis such as Iraq in the future is to restructure the Security Council to make it more inclusive and to eliminate the veto. Currently, along with the five permanent members, ten member countries are elected to the Security Council every two years who do not have a veto. Of the ten elected members, three come from countries in Africa, and two members each from Asia, Western Europe. Eastern Europe chooses one member and the others come from smaller counties included Canada, Latin America and the Caribbean. It is unlikely that any permanent member of the Security Council would willingly withdraw. The sensible thing is to expand the council to reflect the political power and social make up of the world and keep the current permanent members.

The new Security Council must have permanent representatives from all regions, major religions and cultures. With the expansion of the permanent members of the Security Council from five to ten members, this is what it might look like.

COUNTRY	POPULATION SIZE IN MILLIONS
Brazil	183.8
China	1,326.8
Egypt	80.3
France	64.4
Great Britain	58.8
India	1,097.2
Indonesia	234.7
South Africa	47.9
Russia	145.2
United States	303.8
TOTAL	3,532.0

In addition to these ten permanent members of the Security Council, the practice of having another ten countries elected every two years should continue. That would give the council 20 members.

There are a number of advantages to structuring the council in this way. The permanent members would represent over 50% of the world's population and there would be representatives from every continent, every major religion and cultural group. This would give the Security Council much greater legitimacy and at times of crisis and war the decisions of the council would carry much greater weight. This list presents problems. The Security Council would exclude Japan and Germany, the third and fourth largest economies in the world. That may be a mistake but if the council is to be expanded there would be intense lobbying by nations and the powerful politicians will have to strike a deal as to which countries are included and which excluded. The important thing will be to keep to the principle that every continent and major religious and cultural group be included on the council.

The veto has proven to be a serious problem, and if the Security Council is to be reformed it will have to be abandoned. With ten permanent and ten elected members of the council, a system could be established where each resolution must pass two tests. It must be supported by the majority of the votes of the twenty members of the council and two-thirds or more of the permanent members. This second test would mean that a resolution would have to have the support of at least seven of the ten permanent members.

With these reforms the U.N. Security Council would have the ability, legitimacy and prestige to exercise its mandate to maintain peace and security in the world. It could also create a set of laws or norms of conduct that would be acceptable to the international community. The system would be flexible and not present impossible roadblocks. The council would have a clear mandate to act in times of emergency and head off conflicts that are developing. It would also put in place the means by which the international community could enforce its will on countries or groups that operate outside the rules and conventions of the United Nations. The most important impact of this restructuring is that it would encourage the most powerful nations to be leaders of this new multilateral world and to act in concert in the best interests of all nations and people, not just themselves. In effect, the United Nations would then have the ability to enforce the peace, just as the Roman Empire imposed *Pax Romana* in the ancient world and the British Empire imposed *Pax Britannica* in the nineteenth century. The peaceful era in the future may come to be called *Pax United Nations* because only the United Nations could sanction the use of military force.

A new international system based on the objectives of peace, security and prosperity will not happen because a few people wish it. When the Security Council is restructured, and policies are fully implemented so that the council can act to resolve conflicts, suppress wars and protect innocent people, then a powerful institution has been created that has legitimacy and support around the world and the new multilateral world will have an organization where decisions can be made. A stronger United Nations, willing to act in times of emergencies, is the best deterrence to war.

The End of War:

There is no going back. To eliminate war we have to establish and strengthen the multilateral world. The days of empire are finished and multilateralism is the natural outcome of our economic, political and social development. No single country has the political or military power to impose its imperial will on the people or nations of the world. We need strong international institutions willing to act for the collective good of all people on the globe. The risk of war is lessening, but it remains a major problem for millions of the poorest people of the world. War will not disappear by accident or miraculously wither away. It will end when we eliminate poverty, discrimination and domination and build new organizations and practices that support political rights, sustainable economic development and the toleration of minorities.

One thing is certain. A new international order will only happen with the support of the United States. America's power may be diminished, but it is still far too important to be ignored. If the U.S. does not put its political muscle behind proposals for change, they will not happen. And yet there is every reason to believe the Americans are ready for change. The vibrant tradition of liberalism in the United States which produced Abraham Lincoln, Woodrow Wilson and Franklin Delano Roosevelt lives on in America. Barack Obama and others like him are ideally positioned to carry on that liberal tradition and convince the people of the world of the necessity to make a new set of international institutions and practices a reality.

But if a multilateral world is to emerge, other countries must also step forward to assume responsibilities for peace and security. Multilateralism means responsibilities as well as shared power. A new consensus is emerging that we need greater co-operation between nations and greater efforts to bring peace. The European Union, along with their member countries, has become a strong force, ready to play a more important international role. India and China are much poorer countries, but they are making trading links around the world and are ambitious to be leading actors on the international stage. It would be foolish and risky to deny them a role. Russia, Japan, Brazil, Indonesia, Canada and many other countries have much to offer if peace is to be achieved.

All this is well and good, but there is one problem that must be addressed by all citizens no matter where they live. As Tom Engelhardt reminds us, "History is, in a sense, a history of state terror."[25] Empires and the wars they have perpetrated on innocent people is state terror writ large, and there are the terrors of the hidden wars perpetrated by secret state organizations like the CIA or Britain's MI5. Why then, do we argue that it must be nation states that must bring about reforms that lead to a more peaceful world? The reality is only states and international organizations like the U.N. have the power and ability to bring about fundamental changes such as this. It is our responsibility – the responsibility of citizens – to point the way, to insist, to demand, that fundamental changes must be made in our international system if we are to live in a peaceful world.[26]

Changing the way we govern ourselves in the international arena and providing poor countries the means they need to develop and prosper will not be easy. Real and effective leadership will be required if we hope to build a better world. The end of empires and the growth of multilateralism marks a new era – a new beginning – where world peace has become a possibility. It is time for brave thoughts and noble actions.

REFERENCES

Author's Note

[1] Bill Freeman and Richard Neilson, *Far From Home: Canadians in the First World War*, (Toronto: McGraw-Hill Ryerson Ltd., 1999)

Intoduction

[1] *The Human Security Report, 2005: War and Peace in the 21st Century*, "Part III Assault on the Vulnerable," pp. 101-103 http://www.humansecurityreport.info/HSR2005_PDF/Part3.pdf
[2] *Ibid.*, p. 102
[3] Stephanie Nolen, *The Globe and Mail*, October 18, 2008, "Rape again rampant in Congo"

Introduction to Part 1

[1] Dostoyevsky, *Brothers Karamazov*, ii, V.4, "Rebellion"
[2] http://en.wikipedia.org/wiki/Death_drive
[3] Ledeen made this statement in a speech on March 25, 2003 to explain why he did not think that American casualties in the Iraq War would turn the American public against the war. http://www.historycommons.org/context.jsp?item=complete_timeline_of_the_2003_invasion_of_iraq_3167
[4] Hannah Arendt makes the point that war can convert ordinary people, who have lived normal lives, into killing machines. Her books and essays are some of the most disturbing and thoughtful writings on the psychological impact of war that exists in our literature.

Chapter 1

[1] Quoted in Harper's Magazine, November 26, 2007, "Tacitus on the costs of war," http://www.harpers.org/archive/2007/11/hbc-90001699
[2] Historians consider the period of the Empire as lasting from 31 BC, when Octavian Caesar was proclaimed Emperor, to 476 when the last Emperor was deposed and not replaced. In fact Rome operated as an empire much longer than this. The end of the Punic Wars in 146 BC marks the time when Rome became the dominant power in the Mediterranean region. The Eastern Roman Empire continued until the fall of

Constantinople to the Turks in 1453. If those dates are used the Roman Empire can be said to have lasted 1699 years.

[3] The people of Tibet would not agree with this statement. They have been dominated by the Chinese for centuries but have never lost their identity. Many Tibetans do not recognize the legitimacy of Chinese rule.

[4] Silver was the real source of wealth of the Spanish.

[5] Charles C. Mann, *1491: New Revelations of the Americas Before Columbus*, (New York: Vintage Books, 2005). Pp 29-30

[6] There are many studies of the Spanish Empire. The classic study is Clarence Henry Haring, *The Spanish Empire in America*, (New York: Harbinger Books, 1947)

[7] http://www.ucalgary.ca/applied_history/tutor/eurvoya/columbus.html pp. 82-90

[8] Charles C. Mann, *op. cit.* Mann provides a detailed description of the decimation of indigenous cultures by the Europeans through war and disease.

[9] The term "British" is used in this section, although it was not in use until the Act of Union in 1707.

[10] Arthur Herman's *To Rule the Waves* focuses on the role of the British navy in the creation of the empire. Not only is the book comprehensive and well documented but it is well written and enjoyable to read.

[11] The French retained the islands of St. Pierre and Miquelon on the Grand Banks to be used as fishing stations. They remain French possessions.

[12] The term *Pax Britannia* is adapted from the term *Pax Roma*, the Roman peace.

[13] The parallels between the British economic policies of the 1840s and the American policy of today are striking.

[14] Daniel R. Headrick, *The Tools of Empire*, (New York: Oxford University Press, 1981) p. 3

[15] Karl Marx was involved in these troubles. In 1849 he fled to London, England where he spent the rest of his life analyzing the "capitalist system," as he coined it.

[16] This was the height of the romantic period and Kaiser Frederick William III was influenced by romantic ideas such as noble spirit and leadership of kings.

[17] http://www.tacitus.nu/historical-atlas/population/westeurope.htm

[18] Prior to the First World War many socialists believed that war could never happen because the working class of different countries would not fight each other. This proved naïve in the extreme. German, French and British young men joined their national armies in the First World War regardless of their class or whether their politics were socialist, liberal or conservative.

[19] http://www.firstworldwar.com/features/germanyduringww1.htm

[20] Bill Freeman and Richard Nielsen, *Far From Home: Canadians in the First World War*, (Toronto, McGraw-Hill Ryerson, 1999)

[21] *Ibid.*, p. 102

[22] Many accounts of the First World War discuss the significance of the mutiny. A short overview is found at: http://www.crf-usa.org/bria/bria17_3.htm

---

[23] Russians call this the "October Revolution" because they used the Julian calendar which placed the event in October 1917.

[24] The information in this section has been gathered from a wide number of sources. There are shelf loads of books about the First World War.

[25] Margaret Macmillan, *Paris 1919, Six Months that Changed the World*, (New York: Random House, 2002)

[26] I have explored this theme in my earlier work, *Far From Home*. Freeman and Nielsen, *op. cit.*, p. 231

[27] Historians usually date the Battle of Britain as lasting from July 9 to October 31, 1940. This was the period of the most intense German air attacks. The battle continued until May of 1941 when the Germans withdrew the *Luftwaffe* to attack the Soviet Union. German bombing raids and rocket attacks on British cities continued until the end of the war.

Chapter 2

[1] The full text can be found at: http.//www.constitution.org/kant/perpeace.htm

[2] The International Labour Organization and the World Health Organization both originated with mandates of the League of Nations.

[3] Churchill was a strong supporter of the British Empire. He once said, "I was not elected to preside over the dismemberment of the British Empire."

[4] As a young man Roosevelt was a member of the Wilson government and was deeply impressed and influenced by Wilson's efforts to create a new international order during the negotiations for the Treaty of Versailles

[5] Many of the Bretton Woods agreements were not implemented until 1959. Some economists believe that a great opportunity was lost at the Bretton Woods Conference, and that the agreement has led to an international economic system that allowed the United States to dominate the world economy, trade and monetary systems. In recent years there has been mounting criticism by developing countries about the World Bank and the IMF. Those issues will be discussed in greater length in later chapters.

[6] Today the U.N. has 192 members.

[7] Michael Shank, "Chomsky on World Ownership," *FPIS Commentary*, January 23, 2008, http://www.fpif.org>www.fpif.org There continues to be debate as to whether the United States violated the Nuremburg Conventions with the invasion of Iraq.

[8] This was called the Oder-Neisse Line.

[9] Some researchers claim that the allies purposely starved the German soldiers held in prisoner of war camps after WWII. This is vehemently denied by the allies and has never been proven.

[10] http://www.fordham.edu/halsall/mod/churchill-iron.html

[11] The dismantling of the British Empire had an impact on hundreds of millions of people in almost every corner of the globe. The first wave of independence was of

the so called "settler" nations in the late nineteenth century and early twentieth. This included Canada, Australia, New Zealand and South Africa. The second wave after the Second World War included India, Burma, Sri Lanka and Pakistan. The third wave in the 1950s and 60s included colonies in Africa and the Caribbean. Today Britain has only one or two small dependencies like the Falkland Islands. Even Scotland, whose union with England and Wales led to the creation of the United Kingdom, is discussing independence.

[12] Palestine was a British Protectorate mandated by the League of Nations after the First World War. Civil unrest in Palestine grew in intensity as Jewish refugees came into the country after the Second World War. At first the British tried to suppress the violence but without success. The British government told the United Nations that they wanted to terminate their mandate, and it was ended on May 15, 1948. The State of Israel was proclaimed the day before and the 1948 Arab-Israeli War began almost immediately.

[13] http://www.americanrhetoric.com/speeches/harrystrumantrumandoctrine.html

[14] Yugoslavia led by Marshall Tito was the only communist country that accepted aid from the United States. It was the only eastern bloc country that was independent of Soviet domination.

[15] Today the twenty-seven member states of the European Union are a single market with a common trade policy. The EU has 494 million people and a combined nominal GDP of €11.6 (US$14.5) trillion in 2006.

Chapter 3

[1] E.N. Luttwak, *The Grand Strategy of the Roman Empire from the First Century to the Third*, (Baltimore: John Hopkins University Press, 1976)

[2] It is strange that scholars and journalists have still have not evaluated the Soviet and American archives to answer this question.

[3] Tim Weiner, *Legacy of Ashes: The History of the CIA*, (New York: Doubleday, 2007) p. 158 and p. 191.

[4] *Ibid.*, p. 73

[5] The classic arms race in modern times was between Germany on the one side and Britain and France on the other in the first decade and a half of the Twentieth Century. The arms race was a contributing cause of the First World War.

[6] The real purpose of the space program was to develop rocket technology to accurately deliver nuclear warheads to their targets. NASA turned this weapons program into one of the great public relations triumphs of the American government.

[7] Ronald Reagan's Strategic Defense Initiative, or "Star Wars" as it came to be called, was a proposal to develop a defence system that could shoot down incoming missiles before they reached the United States. From the moment it was proposed critics said that it would never work and would lead to a false sense of security. After Reagan left the White House Star Wars was quietly dropped, but the military and

various contractors continue to work on it. George H. Bush proposed a similar system early in his presidency but little more has been heard about it.

[8] The Eisenhower administration placed great reliance on nuclear deterrence. Kennedy and subsequent Presidents have built up the American conventional forces but continued to expand American nuclear capabilities.

[9] Chalmers Johnson, *The Sorrows of Empire*, (New York: Henry Holt and Company, 2004) p. 21

[10] Chalmers Johnson, *Blowback*, (New York: Henry Holt and Company, 2000)

[11] http://www.cassiopaea.org/cass/uswars.htm

[12] http://coursesa.matrix.msu.edu/~hst306/documents/indust.html

[13] Chalmers Johnson, *The Sorrows of Empire*, (New York: Henry Holt and Company, 2004)

[14] C. Wright Mills, *The Power Elite*, (New York: Oxford University Press, 1956) *The Power Elite* is the classic work that describes the emergence of an interlocking elite that controls the United States.

[15] http://www.sourcewatch.org/index.php?title=Military-industrial_complex

[16] Paul Koistinen, "Towards a Warfare State," in *The Militarization of the Western World*, edited by John R. Gillis, (New Brunswick and London: Rutgers University Press, 1989) p. 64

[17] William Ashtore, "Going Rogue in Combat Boots," http://www.tomdispatch.com/post/175193/tomgram:_william_astore,_going_rogue_in_combat_boots__/

[18] The same could be said for the British Empire. The cost of maintaining the military was borne by the British government which was paid for out of taxes that everyone paid. The military, particularly the British Navy, maintained and supported the empire but the benefits of that empire went to the merchants and industrialists.

[19] Jeffry A. Frieden, *Global Capitalism: Its Fall and Rise in the Twentieth Century*, (New York: W.W. Norton and Co., 2006) see Part II, pages 127 to 250

[20] United Nations Department for International Development, http://www.odi.org.uk/PPPG/politics_and_governance/publications/Trade_template_1_1.pdf

[21] This is a term used by Federal Reserve Board chairman Alan Greenspan.

[22] Henry C.K. Liu, "US Dollar Hegemony Has Got to Go," *On Line Asia Times*, April 11, 2002

[23] Some writers like Chalmers Johnson use the term globalization to indicate the economic policies of neo-liberalism that were introduced by the Reagan-Thatcher governments. I am using the term in a much broader context because in popular usage the term has come to mean the economic and social changes that have resulted from the liberalization of trade.

[24] Thomas L. Friedman, "A Manifesto for the Fast World," *The New York Times*, March 28, 1999

25 Lester R. Brown, "Is World Oil Production Peaking?" Earth Policy Institute, November 15, 2007, http://www.earthpolicy.org/Updates/2007/Update67.htm

26 The stereotype of the evil communist was so persuasive in American culture that it was difficult for Nixon and Kissinger to pursue the policy of détente. It has often been pointed out that only a president like Richard Nixon, with a strong right-wing, anti-communist record could have visited China in 1972 and changed the direction of American foreign policy.

27 There are many books and articles about the American media but the classic analysis is the Herman, Chomsky book *Manufacturing Consent*. Edward S. Herman and Noam Chomsky, *Manufacturing Consent: a Propaganda Model*, (New York: Pantheon Books, 1988)

28 General Westmoreland used this phrase in 1968 to describe the American situation in the war in Vietnam. Almost immediately afterwards the Viet Cong attacked and inflicted heavy damages to the American and South Vietnamese troops.

29 *The New York Times*, May 28, 2004

Chapter 4

1 http://www.nam.gov.za/background/history.htm The Non-Aligned Movement has flourished in some periods and languished in others. This website discusses some of the issues and background of the movement.

2 After talks the 38th parallel was accepted as the border between North and South Korea and the demilitarized zone (DMZ) was established with the North Korean troops on one side and South Korean and American troops on the other. No peace treaty has been signed to date to formally end the conflict.

3 http://www.historycommons.org/context.jsp?item=vietnam_631 This anti-democratic policy decision was only one of many the Americans committed in Vietnam.

4 Tim Weiner, *Legacy of Ashes: The History of the CIA*, (New York: Doubleday, 2007). Weiner's exhaustive history of the CIA is instructive. Everyone interested in American politics and foreign policy must read his account.

5 Graham Greene's novel, *The Ugly American*, and the later movie by the same name, is based loosely on Vietnam. In the novel and movie the American Ambassador completely misunderstands the local political situation. A nationalist movement is thought to be a Communist uprising which the Americans attack because they see the movement as a threat to their interests. As a result the nationalists turn to the Communists for support and the movement is transformed into a Communist insurrection which is a threat to American interests.

6 Later it was confirmed that Kim Philby, the British agent, was giving information to the KGB.

[7] At the time of the Cuban Revolution Eisenhower was president and he first directed the anti-Castro efforts. Kennedy was elected soon after and he continued and intensified the operation.

[8] As late as 1987 the CIA learned that every Cuban agent they had recruited was a double agent. Weiner, *Op. Cit.*, p. 417

[9] *Ibid.*, p. 142-154

[10] *Ibid.*, p. 258-262

[11] *Ibid.*, p. 316

[12] *The Globe and Mail*, August 18, 2011

[13] *Ibid.*, p. 337

[14] The end of the Cold War is marked with the collapse of the Soviet Union. On December 25, 1991 Mikkhail Gorbachev resigned as president of the USSR. On December 31 Russia became the successor state and the USSR ceased to exist. The Cold War was over.

[15] Michael T. Klare, "Is Energo-fascism in your Future?" http://www.tomdispatch.com/post/157241/klare_the_pentagon_as_an_energy_protection_racket

[16] http://www.pbs.org/wgbh/amex/bush41/more/gulfwar.html

[17] http://www.historycommons.org/context.jsp?item=us_international_relations_41

[18] "The National Security Strategy of the United States of America," September 20, 2002

[19] *Ibid.*

[20] Noam Chomsky, *Hegemony or Survival: America's Quest for Global Dominance*, (New York: Henry Holt and Company, 2004) p. 12

[21] http://www.nato.int/isaf/topics/mandate/unscr/resolution_1386.pdf

[22] Only future research will determine whether President Bush and his close advisors believed that Iraq possessed weapons of mass destruction. As of this writing it appears that the administration chose to believe and promote this view in order to justify the invasion of Iraq. Others, however, have concluded that the Bush administration simply lied. George W. Bush has never apologized for misinforming the American people.

[23] http://news.bbc.co.uk/2/hi/middle_east/3661134.stm

[24] On September 16, 2004 Kofi Annan, the Secretary General of the United Nations at the time, said of the invasion, "I have indicated it was not in conformity with the UN charter. From our point of view, from the charter point of view, it was illegal." Richard Pearl, a neo-conservative and close advisor to George W. Bush, has also admitted that the war was illegal under international law.

[25] Compiled from Edward S. Herman, "U.S. Now Poses Greatest Threat of any Country in History, " in *The CCPA Monitor*, July/August 2007, p. 44

[26] Peter Gillespie, "Rich prosper, society suffers," *Toronto Star*, April 28, 2008

[27] Richard Du Boff, "If You Still Don't See the U.S. as a Rogue Nation, read this," *The CCPA Monitor*, May 2007, p. 30

Chapter 5

[1] The struggle between the governor and the legislative councils was central to gaining independence of almost every British colony from the time of the American Revolution to the independence of the African colonies in the 1960s. The slogan of the American Revolution – "no taxation without representation" – was a demand for the end of the arbitrary rule of the governor, the representative of the crown, and the institution of democratic rule of the people.

[2] Marcus Gee, "Military's influence stifling democracy," *The Globe and Mail*, December 29, 2007

[3] Gerald Caplan, *The Betrayal of Africa*, (Toronto: Groundwood Books, 2008)

[4] Milton Friedman, *Capitalism and Freedom*, (New York: Phoenix Books, 1962)

[5] Francis Fukuyama, *The End of History and the Last Man*, (New York, N.Y.: Free Press, 1992)

[6] The model of modernity that is developed in these pages is what sociologists call an "ideal type." Ideal types are limited because historical reality rarely follows the model, but they are useful as a heuristic device to help understand social reality at a macro level.

[7] These figures are suggested by Paul Collier's work but the estimates are my own.

[8] There are many different interpretations and explanations for the rise of modernity but most point to the changes in the mode of production from small scale agricultural and craft production to factory production. That is why this analysis begins at this point. However, the roots of modernity go back in Europe at least to the late Middle Ages if not before. The mercantile economic system that emerged during the period of colonialism played an important role in stimulating economic activity and contributed to the growth of industrialization. I have glossed over this complex historical development but there are many books that describe it in detail.

[9] UN, "The World at Six Billion," November 23, 2005

[10] Demographers call this the Theory of Demographic Transition.

[11] In fact undeveloped societies often have great swings in population as epidemics wipe out large numbers of people. Much of sub-Saharan Africa is in Stage 2 with high birth rates and low death rates.

[12] "Mayday 23: World Population Becomes more Urban than Rural," http://mews.ncsu.edu/release/2007/may/104.html

[13] http://pewglobal.org/commentary/display.php?AnalysisID=1051

[14] Mark E. Pietrzyk and other political scientists have put forward a theory that relates societal stages of development and democracy. This theory holds that so called "primitive societies" are characterized by free discussion and popular assembly where decisions are made either by consensus or popular vote. As populations grew and war became a threat, permanent hierarchical structures emerged. Authoritarian leaders backed by military power were established and

governed the dominated territory often in a despotic way. In the modern era a number of social factors combined to strengthen democracy. These include the growth of wealth, a large middle class, national unity, the establishment of bureaucratic practices and a vibrant political culture. See: Mark E. Pietrzyk, *International Order and Individual Liberty*, (University Press of America, 2002)

[15] This is from a speech given by Churchill on November 11, 1947. "Many forms of government have been tried, and will be tried in this world of sin and woe. No one pretends that democracy is perfect or all-wise. Indeed it has been said that democracy is the worst form of Government except all those other forms that have been tried from time to time." The statement has been expressed by many over the years but credit is usually given to Churchill. I have provided my own précis.

[16] Bill Clinton's second inaugural address, January 27, 1997

[17] *New York Times*, January 21, 1997

[18] Democracy House, "Democracy and the rise of global capitalism," www.business.uconn.edu/redirect/CIBER/sitefiles/resourceguides/vol3/3-2.5.pdf

[19] Both Zimbabwe and Kenya have a form of representative democracy because citizens are allowed to vote, but the entrenched elites do not recognize the results of these elections. They can hardly be considered democratic countries.

[20] Many have become concerned that democracy in Russia under Vladimir Putin has become seriously eroded.

[21] Mildred Amer, Membership of the 110th Congress: A Profile," Congressional Research Service, November 28, 2008, http://www.senate.gov/CRSReports/crs-publish.cfm?pid='0DP%2BP%2CO%3E%23%40%20%20%0A

[22] Pew Global Attitudes Project, "America's image slips, but allies share U.S. concerns over Iran, Hamas," http://pewglobal.org/reports/display.php?ReportID=252

[23] Chalmers Johnson, *Blowback: The Costs and Consequences of American Empire*, (New York: Henry Holt and Company, 2004)

[24] Vincent Ferraro, http://www.mtholyoke.edu/acad/intrel/kant/kant1.htm

[25] BBC news, November 17, 2004, http://news.bbc.co.uk/1/hi/magazine/4017305.stm

[26] George W. Bush, September 17, 2002

Chapter 6

[1] Social-Democracy is the term used in Germany and the Scandinavian countries. In Southern Europe they usually call themselves Socialists. The British Labour Party had social-democratic policies but under Tony Blair the party has swung to the center. Liberal is the term used for people with these beliefs in the United States.

[2] Will Hutton, *A Declaration of Interdependence,* (New York: W.W. Norton and Company Inc., 2003) p. 9

[3] *Laissez-faire* as a political philosophy has its roots in mid nineteenth century liberalism.

[4] http://economics.about.com/cs/keynesianism/

[5] The "invisible hand" was a metaphor used by Adam Smith in his book *The Wealth of Nations,* published in 1776. The metaphor is still widely used by economists to describe market forces beyond the control of individuals and corporations.

[6] Milton Friedman, *Capitalism and Freedom*, (New York: Phoenix Books, 1962)

[7] Ronald Reagan, First Inaugural Address, January 20, 1981

[8] Margaret Thatcher, interviewed by the *Women's Own* magazine, October 31, 1987.

[9] Jonathan Chait, *The Big Con: The True Story of How Washington Got Hoodwinked and Hijacked by Crackpot Economics*, (New York: Houghton Mifflin, 2007)

[10] The debate among economists on the impact of monetarism on the U.S. economy remains heated and highly politicized. I would not pretend to be an objective observer, but it seems obvious from a 2008 perspective that monetarism has created enormous damage to the U.S. economy.

[11] Wikipedia has perhaps the most accurate summary of the Washington Consensus. http://en.wikipedia.org/wiki/Washington_Consensus See also, Frieden, *op. cit.*, p. 385

[12] This group was active in the right wing think tank called the "American Enterprise Institute." The AEI website consistently supported their views and approach to foreign and domestic policy. http://www.aei.org/

[13] The biggest lobbying scandal came to light in 2004 when it was revealed that Jack Abramoff and others charged an estimated $85 million in fees for lobbying on behalf of Indian casinos. Illegal gifts and campaign donations were made in return for votes in congress in support of legislation benefiting the casinos.

[14] http://money.cnn.com/magazines/fortune/global500/2008/countries/US.html

[15] "List of countries by size of armed forces," http://en.wikipedia.org/wiki/List_of_countries_by_size_of_armed_forces

[16] Vladimir Putin, "Unilateral force has nothing to do with global democracy," *The Guardian*, February 13, 2007

[17] http://findarticles.com/p/articles/mi_m2519/is_n5_v14/ai_14558170

[18] Quoted in, David Harvey, "Why the U.S. Stimulus Package is Bound to Fail," Socialist Project E-Bulletin No. 184, February 12, 2009, http://www.socialistproject.ca/bullet/bullet184.html#continue

[19] The nearest rivals to U.S. military spending are China and Russia. Each of them spends less than $100 billion on the military. See http://www.globalsecurity.org/military/world/spending.htm

[20] http://wallstcheatsheet.com/stocks/us-per-capita-debt-reaches-this-scary-level.html/

[21] *Toronto Star*, "Obama sees years of $1 trillion deficits," January 7, 2009

[22] http://www.heritage.org/research/socialsecurity/wm2458.cfm

[23] Joseph Stiglitz, "The Myth of the War Economy," the *Guardian*, February 12, 2007

[24] *The Globe and Mail*, February 29, 2008

[25] http://pewglobal.org/

[26] Alan S. Binder, "Free Trade's Great, but offshoring Rattles Me," *The Washington Post*, May 6, 2007

[27] I have taken the year 2005 as the moment of "peak oil" from the website: http://www.lifeaftertheoilcrash.net/

[28] *The Globe and Mail*, September 22, 2007

[29] http://www.tradingeconomics.com/united-states/balance-of-trade

[30] Tavia Grant, *The Globe and Mail*, September 21, 2007

[31] http://www.washingtontimes.com/news/2010/mar/02/chinas-debt-to-us-treasury-more-than-indicated/

[32] In 2009 China began purchasing major commodities companies around the world. China has also loaned money to Brazil and Russia and in return has received concessions for future oil. China is doing this to protect its access to raw materials.

[33] Thomas Walkom, "Loonie's rise signals end of American era," *The Toronto Star*, November 8, 2007

[34] Barrie McKenna, "$1,230,000,000,000," *The Globe and Mail*, October 13, 2007

[35] Thomas Walkom, "If the greenback wobbles, all bets are off," *Toronto Star*, February 28, 2009

[36] Barry McKenna, "Farm bill shows U.S. forgets free trade starts at home," *The Globe and Mail,* June 26, 2007

[37] Johnson, *op. cit.*, *The Sorrows of Empire*, p. 270

[38] The food crisis that suddenly developed in the world in the early months of 2008 has led to food shortages and a dramatic rise in the prices of staples. Economists who have studied the crisis maintain that if the subsidies given to farmers in the developed world were eliminated it would stimulate food production in the developing world and head off the crisis. In the short term, however, the rising food prices are bringing real hardships to millions of people. This problem must be addressed by the international community by establishing policies that do more than increase the wealth of farmers in the developed world.

[39] Stephanie Nolen, "U.S. cotton subsidies are a part fabric of Malian life," *The Globe and Mail*, February 13, 2008.

[40] The role of poverty in war is explored in Chapters 8 and 9 of this book.

[41] *Ibid.*

[42] Treasury Secretary Henry Paulson was the greatest of these evangelists. He was also the George W. Bush appointment who brought in the government package to rescue the financial industry in 2008. See: *The Globe and Mail*, "The End of the American Order," October 4, 2008

[43] Uwe E. Reinhardt, "An Economist's Mea Culpa," http://economix.blogs.nytimes.com/2009/01/09/an-economists-mea-culpa/

[44] *The Globe and Mail*, "The End of the American Order," October 4, 2008

[45] Robert Reich, "America's Middle Class Are No Longer Coping," *The Financial Times*, 29 January 2008. http://www.truthout.org/docs_2006/013108B.shtml

[46] http://business.timesonline.co.uk/tol/business/markets/china/article775117.ece

[47] Timothy Garton Ash, "New World Disorder," *The Globe and Mail*, September 11, 2008

[48] *New York Times*, December 12, 2004

[49] *Ibid.*

Bill Freeman

---

[50] Jeremy Rifkin, *The European Dream: How Europe's Vision of the Future is Quietly Eclipsing the American Dream*, (New York: Polity Press, 2004) p. 70
[51] http://aparc.stanford.edu/news/745/
[52] *Ibid.*, pp.79-80
[53] *The New York Times*, January 12, 2005
[54] Rifkin, *op. cit.*, p.81
[55] David Olive, "A country divided by compassion gap," *Toronto Star*, May 2, 2008
[56] Konrad Yakabuski, "When wealth became a character flaw," *The Globe and Mail*, March 21, 2009
[57] The Gini Index is an indicator of the inequality of income of a country. A score of 0 would be perfect equality; everyone would have the same income. A score of 100 is perfect inequality; one person has all of the income. The higher the Gini Index score, the greater the inequality.
These are the Gini Index scores of selected countries. The reason underdeveloped countries have high Gini Index scores is because they have a large number of impoverished people with very low incomes, and a few people, like government and corporate employees, with incomes comparable to employees in the developed countries.

USA	47.0 (2006)
Canada	32.1 (2005)
Britain	34.0 (2005)
France	26.7 (2002)
Germany	28.3 (2000)
Sweden	23.0 (2005)
Russia	40.5 (2005)
China	47.0 (2001)
India	36.8 (2004)
Egypt	34.5 (2000)
South Africa	57.8 (2000)
Brazil	56.6 (2005)

[58] *New York Times*, January 12, 2005
[59] *New York Times*, January 12, 2005
[60] Rifkin, *op. cit.*, p. 28
[61] CNN, December 10, 2004
[62] *U.S. News and World Report*, March 19, 2001
[63] *USA Today*, October 4, 2004
[64] http://www.nationmaster.com/graph/cri_pri_per_cap-crime-prisoners-per-capita

Chapter 7

[1] Afghan President Hamid Karzai, *The Globe and Mail,* "Karzai demands timeline for victory," November 26, 2008

284

[2] *New York Times*, October 30, 2007

[3] British ships used the press gangs to force thousands of American seamen into the British navy in their war efforts against Napoleon. This was a major cause of the War of 1812.

[4] There are many books on the conduct of war during this period. Those who would like an overview of warfare from ancient times to the present should read: John Keegan, *A History of Warfare*, (Toronto: Vintage Books Canada, 1994)

[5] Despite the harsh conditions of the British regular soldier, they were forged into a very effective army. In the War of 1812, British regular troops in Upper Canada numbering about one thousand held off American forces at least six times their number. The Americans were volunteer militiamen who elected their officers. Not only did they lack discipline, most were farmers and in planting and harvest seasons many would desert and go back home to tend their crops. It was not until the last year of the war that the Americans were any match to the British regular troops.

[6] It is inaccurate to say that guerrilla war as it is practiced today was first used in Spain in the Napoleonic Wars. It has been used many times in the past. The early skirmishes in the American War of Independence had the characteristics of guerrilla struggles, particularly the battles of Concord, Bennington and Saratoga.

[7] Bill Freeman and Richard Nielsen, *Far From Home: Canadians in the First World War*, (Toronto: McGraw, Hill Ryerson, 1999) p. 228

[8] http://www.secondworldwar.co.uk/casualty.html

[9] Conn Hallinan, "The Algebra of Occupation," *Foreign Policy in Focus*, November 28, 2007

[10] David Halberstam, "The History Boys," *Vanity Fair*, August 2007

[11] Chalmers Johnson, *The Sorrows of Empire*, (New York: Henry Holt and Company, 2004) p. 289

[12] *Toronto Star*, September 9, 2007

[13] The issue of terrorism brings out very polarized views and it is difficult to discuss it in most political circles. A suicide bomber kills innocent people, but so do bombs dropped out of planes from 30,000 feet. Some call both acts of terrorism. "One man's terrorist is another man's freedom fighter," is an apt phrase. I suspect that my discussion of terrorism will offend some, but I believe it is time to attempt a balanced discussion.

[14] Israeli actions have been criticized around the world. Former U.S. President Jimmy Carter has said "Israel's apartheid policies are worse than South Africa." http://www.haaretz.com/hasen/spages/799476.html Even more interesting is the furious debate in Israel about what is the proper response to terrorism. At the moment those who support military action have dominated the debate and hold political power but there are many who support the "Peace Now" movement.

[15] Robert Parry, "Does Chaney validate al-Qaeda?" http://www.consortiumnews.com/Print/2007/030107.html

[16] General Stanley A. McChrystal, Commander U.S. Forces, Afghanistan, "Commander's Initial Assessment," 30 August 2009, p 2-6. http://media.washingtonpost.com/wp-srv/politics/documents/Assessment_Redacted_092109.pdf?sid=ST2009092003140

[17] Anand Gopal, "Who are the Taliban?" http://www.tomdispatch.com/post/175010/anand_gopal_making_sense_of_the_taliban

[18] Over 50% of Canadian casualties have been from IEDs.

[19] Gloria Galloway, "Largest mission since Korea turns deadly," *The Globe and Mail*, March 21, 2009

[20] Doug Saunders, "Pain aside, by our own rules, the Afghanistan war should be over," *The Globe and Mail*, December 6, 2008

[21] Transparency International, "2008 Corruptions Perceptions Index," http://www.transparency.org/news_room/in_focus/2008/cpi2008/cpi_2008_table

[22] Robert Dreyfuss, "Obama's Great Afghanistan Gamble," *Mother Jones*, May/June 2009, http://www.motherjones.com/politics/2009/05/obamas-great-afghanistan-gamble

[23] John F. Conway, "Canada's combat role in Afghanistan can't be glorified," *The CCPA Monitor*, Volume 18, No. 4, September 2011

[24] "British envoy says mission to Afghanistan is doomed, according to leaked memo," *The Times*, October 2, 2008

[25] CNN interview with Stephen Harper by Fareed Zakaria, March 1, 2009

[26] Eric Margolis, *Toronto Sun*, February 10, 2008, http://www.torontosun.com/News/Columnists/Margolis_Eric/2008/02/10/pf-4838323.html

[27] McChrystal, *op. cit.* General McChrystal's words are recommended reading for anyone interested in insurrection and modern warfare.

[28] The Americans and their allies justify their occupation of Afghanistan by claiming that it is part of the War on Terrorism. Al-Qaeda was driven out of the country in 2001. The Taliban are not part of the al-Qaeda terrorist network and recent accounts suggest that the two groups do not co-operate.

[29] William Astore, "An American Foreign Legion: Is the U.S. Military now an Imperial Police Force?" *TomDispatch.com*, February 15, 2009, http://www.tomdispatch.com/post/175034/william_astore_whose_military_is_it_anyway

[30] "The Iraqi Public on the U.S. Presence and the Future of Iraq," *Program on International Policy Attitudes*, September 27, 2006

[31] http://www.zogby.com/news/ReadNews.dbm?ID=1075/

[32] http://en.wikipedia.org/wiki/War_in_Iraq

[33] http://en.wikipedia.org/wiki/Iraq_War#2004:_The_insurgency_expands

[34] Haroon Siddiqui, "Iraq's little-known humanitarian crisis," *Toronto Star*, November 1, 2007

[35] Naomi Klein, *The Shock Doctrine: The Rise of Disaster Capitalism* (Alfred A. Knopf, Canada, 2007) p. 15

[36] Retired Lieutenant General Ricardo Sanchez, October 13, 2007

[37]   Quoted   in   TomDispatch.com   July   14,   2009
https://app.e2ma.net/app/view:CampaignPublic/id:25612.2204951016/rid:621af411
6819ffcc1fc6651ad738bcac
[38] http://en.wikipedia.org/wiki/Iraq#Saddam_Hussein
[39] Naomi Klein, "Big oil's Iraq deals are the greatest stick up in history," *The Guardian*, July 4, 2008
[40] *Washington Post* and *Dallas Morning News*, November 11, 2007
[41] These two quotes, and others reflecting on the deterioration of American power, may be found at the Tribune's Washington Bureau blog called *The Swamp*, "Has Bush led to decline of 'American era?'" posted by Frank James, May 18, 2007 http://www.swamppolitics.com/news/politics/blog/2007/05/has_bush_led_to_decline_of_ame.html
[42] Nick Turse, "Obama's Arc of Instability," TomDispatch.com, September 18, 2011
[43] Karen De Young and Greg Jaffe, "U.S. Secret War expands globally as Special Operations forces take a larger role," *Washington Post*, June 4, 2010
[44] Pew Research Center, "Support for campaign against extremists wanes," June 21, 2011 http://www.pewglobal.org/2011/06/21/u-s-image-in-pakistan-falls-no-further-following-bin-laden-killing/

Introduction to Part III

[1] http://www.dni.gov/nic/NIC_home.html

Chapter 8

[1] Ministry of Defence, December 2003, "Delivering Security in a Changing World: Defence White Paper."
[2] Richard Norton-Taylor, "Military alliance battles to reinvent itself as it struggles for credibility in first real test," *The Guardian*, November 25, 2006
[3] "White Paper on National Defense," published December 27, 2004, The State Council Information Office
[4] All of the estimates of war dead in this chapter come from Piro Scaruffi's "Wars and Genocides of the 20th Century," http://www.scaruffi.com/politics/massacre.html
[5] Kristian Gleditsch, "A Revised List of Wars Between and Within Independent States, 1816-2002," http://www.prio.no/CSCW/Research-and-Publications/Publication/?oid=58396
[6] Harold Macmillan, speech made to the South African Parliament, 3 February, 1960, http://africanhistory.about.com/od/eraindependence/p/wind_of_change2.htm
[7] I have called the Israeli/Palestinian wars both surrogate wars and asymmetrical wars because they have the characteristics of both. Israel receives significant support from the United States, its closest ally, and its powerful military is fighting an asymmetrical war against poorly armed and supplied Palestinians.

[8] http://www.globalsecurity.org/military/world/war/index.html Global Security lists 42 wars as of January 2008.
[9] *Ibid.*
[10] Human Security Brief 2007, p. 6 http://www.humansecuritybrief.info/hsb07_overview.pdf
[11] Paul Collier, *The Bottom Billion*, (New York, Oxford University Press, 2007) p. 17.
[12] *Op. Cit.*, Collier, p. 20.
[13] Patrick J. McGowan, "Coups and Conflicts in West Africa, 1955 – 2004," *Armed Forces and Society*, 2005; 32, 5-23
[14] Stephanie Nolen and Erin Baines, "The Making of a Monster," *The Globe and Mail*, October 25, 2008
[15] Stephanie Nolen, "Rape again rampant in Congo," *The Globe and Mail*, October 18, 2008
[16] This belief in French superiority permeates the Napoleonic era but has deep roots in French society. The settlers in New France in the seventeenth and eighteenth centuries called all aboriginal people *"les sauvages"* – the savages – which suggests their regard for aboriginal culture.
[17] In his book, *The Warrior's Honour*, Michael Ignatieff discusses how a feeling of being victims contributed to the sense of insecurity felt by the Serbs and led to the wars in the former Yugoslavia.
[18] Human Security Report Project, "Human Security Brief 2007," p.5 http://www.humansecuritybrief.info/hsb07_overview.pdf
[19] *Ibid.*, p. 5
[20] The exception was the Campaign for Nuclear Disarmament which came to prominence in the late 1950s.
[21] http://www.state.gov/www/global/arms/treaties/salt1.html and http://www.state.gov/www/global/arms/treaties/salt2.html For a useful summary of the various SALT talks and other treaties to limit nuclear weapons see: http://en.wikipedia.org/wiki/Strategic_Arms_Limitation_Talks
[22] http://nuclearweaponarchive.org/Usa/Weapons/Wpngall.html The U.S. has 5,736 active nuclear weapons.
[23] Pakistan tested its first nuclear weapon in 1998. Israel continues to deny that they have nuclear weapons, but no independent analysts believe them.
[24] Shultz, Perry, Kissenger, Nunn, "Toward a Nuclear-Free World," *The Wall Street Journal*, January 15, 2008
[25] *The Washington Post*, March 27, 2010, Mary Beth Sheridan and Michael D. Shear, "U.S., Russia agree to nuclear arms control treaty."
[26] This paragraph summarizes points made in "Rethinking Star Wars," *Toronto Star*, March 7, 2009
[27] This article prepared by members of the New America Foundation critically examines the international sales of conventional weapons. http://www.newamerica.net/publications/policy/u_s_weapons_war_2008_0
[28] Margaret MacMillan, *Paris 1919: Six Months that Changed the World*, (Toronto: Random House 2002)

[29] Judy Rebick's most recent book is an interesting discussion on recent forms of political participation. Judy Rebick, *Transforming Power*, (Toronto: Penguin Canada, 2009)
[30] Sandra Martin, *The Globe and Mail*, April 18, 2009

Chapter 9

[1]   Quoted   in   "Learn   Peace,   A   Peace   Pledge   Union   Project,"
http://www.ppu.org.uk/learn/infodocs/people/pp-einstein2.html
[2] Nathaniel Philbrick, *Mayflower*, (New York: Penguin Books, 2006)
[3] Dee Brown, *Bury My Heart at Wounded Knee*, (New York: Henry Holt, 1971)
[4] Canadians are taught that their history is different than the United States because native people were full partners with Europeans in the fur trade, and therefore, were treated as equals. This is far from reality. Trappers received a fraction of the true value of the furs and were often plied with liquor by the merchants to get a better price for the furs. By the 1870s the fur trade was isolated in the far north and the native people in the south faced the same problems as groups in the United States. By then the pattern was clearly established, and they knew there was little point in armed resistance. Groups like the Plains Cree, Assiniboine, Blackfoot and Dene settled on reserves without resorting to war.
[5] http://www.ccsd.ca/pr/2003/aboriginal.htm
[6]   Arundhati   Roy,   "What   have   we   done   to   democracy?"
http://www.tomdispatch.com/post/175119/arundhati_roy_is_democracy_melting
[7] Eric Brahm, "The Chilean Truth and Reconciliation Commission," July 2005 http://www.beyondintractability.org/case_studies/Chilean_Truth_Commission.jsp?nid=522
1. See also http://origin.usip.org/library/tc/doc/reports/chile/chile_1993_toc.html and Abrams, Jason S., and Priscilla B. Hayner. "Documenting, Acknowledging and Publicizing the Truth." In *Post-conflict Justice*, edited by M. C. Bassiouni. (Ardsley, N.Y.: Transnational Publishers, 2002)
[8] Articles 2-4 of the U.N. Charter state: "All Members shall refrain in their international relations from the threat or use of force against the territorial integrity or political independence of any state, or in any other manner inconsistent with the Purposes of the United Nations. "
Article 2-5: "All Members shall give the United Nations every assistance in any action it takes in accordance with the present Charter, and shall refrain from giving assistance to any state against which the United Nations is taking preventive or enforcement action." http://www.un.org/en/documents/charter/chapter1.shtml

This is Article 1-1 of the U.N. Charter "To maintain international peace and security, and to that end: to take effective collective measures for the prevention and removal of threats to the peace, and for the suppression of acts of aggression or other breaches of the peace, and to bring about by peaceful means, and in conformity with the principles of justice and international law, adjustment or settlement of international disputes or situations which might lead to a breach of the peace." http://www.un.org/en/documents/charter/preamble.shtml

[9] http://www.un.org/en/documents/udhr/

[10] http://www1.umn.edu/humanrts/instree/b3ccpr.htm

[11] http://www.ohchr.org/EN/Pages/WelcomePage.aspx

[12] http://www2.ohchr.org/english/bodies/hrcouncil/

[13] http://www.icc-cpi.int/Menus/ICC/About+the+Court/

[14] "Frequently asked questions: What are the key features of the ICC?" http://www.icc-cpi.int/Menus/ICC/About+the+Court/

[15] The Report of the Truth and Reconciliation Commission: http://www.doj.gov.za/trc/report/execsum.htm

[16] Vora, Jay A. and Erika Vora. 2004. "The Effectiveness of South Africa's Truth and Reconciliation Commission: Perceptions of Xhosa, Afrikaner, and English South Africans." *Journal of Black Studies* 34.3: 301-322.

[17] Kimberly Ann Elliott, "Trends in Economic Sanctions Policy: Challenges to Conventional Wisdom," *International Sanctions: Between words and wars in the global system*, eds. Peter Wallensteen and Carina Staibano, http://books.google.com/books?id=BmOohwSlwfAC&pg=PA3&lpg=PA3&dq=international+sanctions&source=bl&ots=WROJS8wM0W&sig=rvqObkZaoVW9Fpgv9MYn3RWzt_8&hl=en&ei=HxtBSpnQA5GYMt2n4cwI&sa=X&oi=book_result&ct=result&resnum=12

[18] Herve Couturier, "UN: Arms Embargo on Somalia Constantly Broken," *Mail & Guardian Online*, December 20, 2008, http://www.mg.co.za/article/2008-12-20-un-arms-embargo-on-somalia-constantly-broken

[19] http://www.globalpolicy.org/component/content/article/202/41759.html

[20] http://www.ndu.edu/inss/books/Books%20-%201997/Imposing%20International%20Sanctions%20-%20March%2097/chapter2.html

[21] Jeffrey Sachs, Myanmar: "Sanctions Won't Work," *The Financial Times*, 27 July, 2004

[22] Carina Staibano, "Trends in U.N. Sanctions," *International Sanctions: Between words and wars in the global system*, eds. Peter Wallensteen and Carina Staibano, p. 46 http://books.google.com/books?id=BmOohwSlwfAC&pg=PA3&lpg=PA3&dq=international+sanctions&source=bl&ots=WROJS8wM0W&sig=rvqObkZaoVW9Fpgv9MYn3RWzt_8&hl=en&ei=HxtBSpnQA5GYMt2n4cwI&sa=X&oi=book_result&ct=result&resnum=12

[23] "United Nations Peacekeeping, Meeting New Challenges," http://www.un.org/Depts/dpko/dpko/faq/q3.htm

[24] *Ibid.*

[25] "United Nations Peacekeeping Operations, Principles and Guidelines," http://pbpu.unlb.org/pbps/Library/Capstone_Doctrine_ENG.pdf

[26] "United Nations Peacekeeping, Meeting new Challenges," *op. cit.*, P. 24

[27] Lloyd Axworthy and Allan Rock, "Breathe new life into R2P," *The Globe and Mail*, January 29, 2008

[28] Before the collapse of the Tigers, government officials and military leaders predicted that there was a good chance that the defeat of the Tamil Tigers could lead to a prolonged insurrection.

[29] Peggy Mason, "Back to the 'Peace' in Peacebuilding: An Old/New Role for Canada," *Afghanistan and Canada*, eds. Lucia Kowaluk and Steven Staples, editors, (Montreal: Black Rose Books, 2009) This is an excellent review of the peace process that is in use by the United Nations and the difficulties of establishing peace in Afghanistan.

[30] Ephraim Yaar and Tamar Hermann, "Just another forgotten peace summit," Haaretz.com, http://www.haaretz.com/hasen/spages/933214.html

[31] Michael Rubner, "Review Essay: The Oslo Peace Process Through Three Lenses," *Middle East Policy Journal*, Vol. VI, October 1998

[32] *Ibid.*, Rubner's discusses the process and the issues of the Oslo Accords in depth.

[33] *Ibid.*

Chapter 10

[1] These statistics can be found in a number of U.N. and international publications. A good survey is provided on the website, "Global Issues," created by Anup Shah, http://www.globalissues.org/

[2] Kofi Annan, "Message of the United Nations General Secretary, Kofi Annan, on the International Day for the Eradication of poverty," October 17, 2000. http://www.un.org/events/poverty2000/messages.htm

[3] International Development Statistics Online. www.oecd.org/dac/stats/idsonline See also., Anup Shah, http://www.globalissues.org/

[4] "In 1995, the director of the US aid agency defended his agency by testifying to congress that 84 cents of every dollar of aid goes back into the US economy in goods and services purchased. For every dollar the United States puts into the World Bank, an estimated $2 actually goes into the US economy in goods and services. Meanwhile, in 1995, severely indebted low-income countries paid one billion dollars more in debt and interest to the International Monetary Fund (IMF) than they received from it. For the 46 countries of sub-Saharan Africa, foreign debt service was four times their combined governmental health and education budgets in 1996. So, we find that aid does not aid." Jean-Bertrand Aristide, *Eyes of the Heart: Seeking a Path for the Poor in the Age of Globalization*, (Common Courage Press, 2000) p. 13.

[5] The World Bank, March 21, 2002, http://go.worldbank.org/9AWCZDYY40

[6] Joseph Hanlon and Ann Pettifor, "Kicking the Habit: Finding a lasting solution to addictive lending and borrowing – and its corrupting side-effects," Jubilee Research, March 2000

[7] Kofi Annan, "Development funds moving from poor countries to rich ones, Annan Says," United Nations News Centre, October 30, 2003. In this speech he said, "Funds should be moving from developed countries to developing countries, but these numbers tell us the opposite is happening.... Funds that should be promoting investment and growth in developing countries, or building schools and hospitals, or supporting other steps towards the Millennium Development Goals, are, instead, being transferred abroad."

[8] William Easterly, *The White Man's Burden: Why the West's Efforts to Aid the Rest have Done so Much Ill and so Little Good*, (Penguin Press, 2006) p. 4

[9] Dambisa Mayo, *Dead Aid: Why Aid is Not Working and How There is a Better Way for Africa*, (New York: Penguin Books, 2009)

[10] Paul Collier, *The Bottom Billion*, (New York: Oxford University Press, 2007) p.100

[11] CIDA programs can be reviewed at http://www.acdi-cida.gc.ca/index-e.htm

[12] http://siteresources.worldbank.org/DATASTATISTICS/Resources/WDI07section1-intro.pdf

[13] The disturbing exception to the gradually improving health and life expectancy of people in the developing world is parts of Africa. The HIV/AIDS epidemic has reduced life expectancy in a number of countries.

[14] Nelson Mandela, quoted in "The Oil and Gas Industry: from Rio to Johannesburg and Beyond." http://www.ipieca.org/activities/general/downloads/WSSD.pdf

[15] http://institution.ibon.org//index.php?option=com_content&task=section&id=8&Itemid=50

[16] http://laptop.org/en/laptop/

[17] International Treatment Preparedness Coalition, "Failing Women, Failing Children: HIV, Vertical Transmission and Women's Health," http://www.aidstreatmentaccess.org/mtt7_final.pdf

[18] That statement might be challenged by conservatives in the United States. They seem to believe that taxes must be cut back regardless of the harm that will do to services like education, health care and infrastructure spending.

[19] http://www.owen.org/blog/3854

[20] A system called "equalization payments" exists in Canada where less affluent provinces receive additional funds from the federal government so that all Canadians receive the same level of services from their governments. The calculations that establish the level of support are based on indicators of the wealth of each province. The system described here is quite different. It is based on a simple formula of a levy based on GDP. The advantage of a system like the one proposed is that it is objective and allows for good financial planning.

[21] I have chosen to call this the "People's Assembly" to give it a more popular title. The "United Nations Parliamentary Assembly" is easily understood by those familiar with the British parliamentary system, but it will be a mystery to many others.

[22] The United States has been the chief critic of the United Nations but criticism goes well beyond the neo-conservatives of Washington. One of the most consistent critics is Stephen Lewis, who was once the Canadian representative in the United Nations and later the U.N. Special Envoy to Africa on the HIV/AIDS epidemic. Lewis, a life long social democrat and strong critic of the neo-cons, is the one who has used the words "byzantine" and "labyinthal" to describe the U.N. bureaucracy.

[23] The preamble to the United Nations Charter outlines its roles and responsibilities.

[24] The one outstanding exception to this is the Suez Canal incident in 1956. Through the intervention of the United Nations, France Britain and Israel withdrew their troops, but in reality it was not the United Nations that made this happen. The two superpowers, United States and the Soviet Union demanded the troops be withdrawn and it was their unified action that resulted in the reversal of British and French policy and the troops being withdrawn.

[25] http://www.tomdispatch.com/post/175430/best_of_tomdispatch%3A_noam_chomsky_on_terrorizing_cuba/#more

[26] This statement, perhaps more than any other in this book, reveals the Canadian roots of its author. Canada has been a country with decades of a relatively benign government and Canadians look to government to bring about changes. In the United States and many other countries people have grown deeply suspicious of their governments. That will make it difficult to create state led movements for reform. It is up to political activists to make that happen.

www.ingramcontent.com/pod-product-compliance
Lightning Source LLC
Chambersburg PA
CBHW031501270326
41930CB00006B/185